Global Poverty and Individual Responsibility

Global Poverty and Individual Responsibility

ABIGAIL GOSSELIN

LEXINGTON BOOKS

A division of
ROWMAN & LITTLEFIELD PUBLISHERS, INC.
Lanham • Boulder • New York • Toronto • Plymouth, UK

LEXINGTON BOOKS

A division of Rowman & Littlefield Publishers, Inc.
A wholly owned subsidiary of The Rowman & Littlefield Publishing Group, Inc.
4501 Forbes Boulevard, Suite 200
Lanham, MD 20706

Estover Road
Plymouth PL6 7PY
United Kingdom

British Library Cataloguing in Publication Information Available

Library of Congress Cataloging-in-Publication Data

Gosselin, Abigail, 1977-
  Global poverty and individual responsibility / Abigail Gosselin.
    p. cm.
  Includes bibliographical references and index.
  ISBN-13: 978-0-7391-2290-7 (cloth : alk. paper)
  ISBN-13: 978-0-7391-2291-4 (pbk. : alk. paper)
  ISBN-13: 978-0-7391-3350-7 (electronic : alk. paper)
  ISBN-10: 0-7391-2290-8 (cloth : alk. paper)
  [etc.]
  1. Wealth—Moral and ethical aspects. 2. Humanitarianism. 3. Poverty. 4. Social
ethics. I. Title.
  HC79.W4G67 2009
  362.5'574—dc22   2008040439

Printed in the United States of America

♾™ The paper used in this publication meets the minimum requirements of American
National Standard for Information Sciences—Permanence of Paper for Printed Library
Materials, ANSI/NISO Z39.48–1992.

To Derrick

Contents

Acknowledgments

Regis University has been a wonderful home for me as a scholar and teacher. My colleagues and students provide invaluable intellectual engagement and moral support, for which I am grateful.

This book could not have been written without the comments and encouragement given by Alison M. Jaggar and Thomas Pogge. As my Ph.D. advisor at the University of Colorado at Boulder, Alison committed a great deal of time and energy to the early dissertation version of this project, and her support continued after I graduated. Thomas's feedback on an early draft of the manuscript helped me restructure my ideas into a more concise and focused argument. I owe so much to Alison and Thomas for their help.

My early thinking on many of the ideas that developed into this book came from discussions with various professors at the University of Colorado, including Claudia Mills, David Boonin, Jackie Colby, David Mapel, and Robert Hanna. I give special thanks to Claudia and Jackie, who in different ways were tremendous emotional supports. As fellow dissertation support group members, Theresa Weynand and Hye-Ryoung Kang helped me along every stage of the dissertation process; my ideas could not have developed to where they are without the dedicated feedback and warm support of these dear friends.

While this project began as a dissertation, the present book bears little resemblance to the dissertation that was its seed. My former colleagues at Washington State University—especially Mary Bloodsworth-Lugo, Joe Campbell, Harry Silverstein, and Mike Myers—gave me helpful feedback on parts of the manuscript and book proposal. I especially thank Mary for her advice and support on the publication process.

The refinement of my ideas benefited from discussions in my Ethical Theory seminar at Washington State University in Spring 2006, and in my Politics of Poverty class at Regis University in Fall 2007. Many students from these classes gave me unexpected insights and challenged my thinking in fresh ways. Several students from the latter class helped with the process of revisions and in researching examples for me: Neil Cheesewright, Andrew Vojslavek, and especially Bill Dong, who discussed the project with me at great length.

I thank my editors at Lexington Books for their enthusiasm with this project and their eagerness to help me through the process. In particular, Patrick Dillon, Julia Loy, Michael Wiles, and Ryan Quick were friendly and helpful in answering my numerous inquiries. I also thank the Faculty Development Committee and the Sponsored Projects Academic Research Council at Regis University for their financial support in completing the book.

The argument for identifying agent-relative duty-bearers of human rights was published as a journal article, "Global Poverty and Responsibility: Identifying the Duty-Bearers of Human Rights," in *Human Rights Review* 8, no. 1 (October-December 2006): 35-52. That argument has been revised to fit within the overall framework of this book.

Most of all, I thank my husband, Derrick Belanger, who has been supportive of me in every way possible. May our daughter grow up in a world with less poverty and more justice.

Chapter 1
Global Poverty and Responsibility

Global poverty is a severe and far-reaching problem. According to the United Nations Development Programme, 40% of the world's population, or 2600 million people, live under the poverty line of US$2 a day. Poverty causes or exacerbates a multitude of other problems, including hunger and illness. Hunger grew from 1995 to 2001 (the most recent year that data was available) by an average of 4.5 million malnourished people a year. In 2001, more than 840 million people, or 1 person for every 7 in the world, were hungry and malnourished. Each day, about 50,000 people die from poverty-related causes; this accounts for one-third of all human deaths.[1]

At the same time, there is a continuingly increasing gap between rich and poor. The income gap between the fifth richest people in the world and the fifth poorest people in the world has grown from 30 to 1 in 1960, to 60 to 1 in 1990, to 74 to 1 in 1997. Today, 16% of people living in affluent nations have 81% of all the wealth in the world, so that the 84% of people living in the poorest nations share the 19% of wealth left.[2] So while half of the world lives under the international poverty line, millions of people have enough money to live in nice houses, drive new cars, wear fashionable clothes, eat gourmet foods, take annual vacations, and keep up with the latest technology. Many of these people are not considered wealthy in their own affluent countries; compared to millionaires and billionaires they are only middle-class. Yet compared to people living in dire poverty worldwide they are extremely wealthy, in terms both absolute (i.e., wealthy by any standard) and relative (i.e., wealthy compared to others).

There is much debate about what kind of responsibility affluent individuals have toward global poverty. Philosophers frequently have addressed this issue in one of three ways. One approach is to understand poverty as a moral problem, requiring individuals to respond with some form of beneficence, or helping. A second approach is to understand poverty as a legal problem, where agents (especially governments and corporations) have duties to rectify the wrongful harms resulting in poverty which they have caused. A third approach is to understand poverty as a political problem, requiring collective action to make insti-

1

tutions more just. The problem with understanding these approaches exclusively is that each is incomplete. Moral philosophers tend to ignore the complicated structural causes of poverty, proposing that individuals make responses such as giving to charity that are woefully inadequate. Legal philosophers do not have a way to describe the responsibility corresponding to poverty caused by institutions rather than identifiable agents. In focusing on how institutions must become more just, political philosophers lack an account of the agency required to make them more just. These ways of looking at the problem should not be exclusive of each other, because individual and collective actions are inextricably tied together. This book bridges the gap between these literatures by looking at the intersection of moral, legal, and political philosophy. The aim of this project is to consider what responsibilities individuals have, *given* that global poverty is a problem with structural, political causes that generally require collective action.

Poverty

Poverty is a condition of being poor, but what exactly this amounts to is open to debate. While poverty is associated with inequality, neither of these concepts subsumes the other, for one may exist without the other. It is helpful here to refer to the common distinction between "absolute" and "relative" poverty. Absolute poverty is poverty by any standard, measured against some objective baseline of what resources are necessary for survival, or for a minimally decent life. Relative poverty, in contrast, is poverty compared to the wealth of others. An American who lives in a house and has cable television but lives paycheck-to-paycheck is poor compared to Americans who have savings accounts; but she is wealthy compared to those who are starving and homeless and who barely survive. We can also make a distinction between extreme and moderate poverty. In extreme poverty, most commonly experienced in Third World countries, people have none of their basic needs met for survival; they lack things like access to safe drinking water and sanitation, basic clothing and shelter, and access to elementary education. In moderate poverty, people have some or most of their basic needs met, but only just barely; their resources allow them to survive for now, but not necessarily to plan for the future.[3]

There is some debate about whether poverty should be understood as a lack of resources, or as lacking capabilities to act. Resources are the goods that people need to be satisfied in order to survive or thrive, including nutritious food, clean water, appropriate clothing and shelter, and access to education and healthcare; resources have economic value and can be measured empirically. As a major proponent for understanding poverty as a lack of resources, Thomas Pogge argues that how much and what kind of basic goods a person has determines her ability to survive or thrive.[4] Resource theorists tend to rely on the United Nations' list of human rights to determine which goods are necessary, and they use economic calculations to figure out how much income is needed to pay for these goods.

In contrast, capabilities are the freedoms or powers that people have to be able to do certain valued activities or to be certain kinds of people. As a chief proponent of the capabilities approach, Amartya Sen argues that poverty is not the result of insufficient resources available but rather the inability of the poor to realize a capability according to some set of valuable functionings—in other words, the inability of the poor to exercise the freedoms that are important to well-being.[5] Since what resources a person needs and is able to use differs widely across cultures, class, gender, etc., alternate sets of resources, or "commodity bundles," may be used by different individuals to meet their needs. A capability may thus also be understood as the power to use these "commodity bundles," so that poverty—as the deprivation of capabilities—is the lack of this power, or the inability to access or use resources, regardless of the presence or particular content of the commodity bundle itself. In other words, people may be poor if they lack the ability to access food, regardless of whether food is available.[6] Analogous to the list of human rights and accompanying calculations of costs to meet those rights, some proponents of capabilities make lists of the capabilities or functionings that are necessary for human survival or thriving.[7] Because they believe that the means to realizing one's capability are relative to one's situation, no capabilities theorist that I am aware of makes an economic calculation of the cost of enacting these capabilities, nor do any make specific political analyses of what enacting these capabilities requires.

Critics of the capabilities approach argue that the concept of capabilities adds nothing new to the already existing concept of human rights assumed by the resource approach; that its contextual analysis of situations of poverty is too relativistic, justifying gross neglect of the poorest of the resource-poor of the world; and that it is itself insufficiently justified.[8] Meanwhile, critics of the resource approach argue that resources are merely an end to a means and not what is *really* needed when one is poor; that the spheres of ability described by capabilities are ontologically prior to the goods and liberties guaranteed by rights; and that a resource framework invites debate about how much resources are necessary, and whether the standard should be for a minimally decent life or rather for a good life.[9]

I will not resolve this debate between the resource and capabilities approaches. Although how we define poverty has major political implications and so is a significant moral issue, it is not the main issue that I am addressing with respect to responsibility. While there are degrees of poverty and different ways of being poor, and while the significance of one's poverty often depends on its context (i.e., lacking modern technology in a region largely without it matters less than in a region where lacking modern technology can prevent one from being able to work), both analyses offer something important to our concept of poverty, namely that we need goods or resources for survival, and that we need the ability to access and use them as well. This book focuses on what the response to these needed goods and capabilities should be.

Both sides of this debate acknowledge that poverty is not merely about a lack of wealth. Poverty has many problems associated with it, including hunger and malnutrition, homelessness, disease, and low average life expectancy, not to mention lack of education, illiteracy, and general political powerlessness. Whether poverty causes them or whether they cause poverty is a complicated question that cannot be answered simply; it suffices to say that poverty and its related ills cause and exacerbate each other. Poverty makes people especially vulnerable to other problems such as hunger or disease from which affluence provides some measure of protection. Affluent people have more resources and better abilities to access resources that stave off ills such as hunger, and they also have the means to escape problems such as environmental hazards that threaten their health and well-being. For example, affluent people can afford to move away from toxic dump sites; or they can assert political clout that prevents such dump sites from being established in their neighborhoods; or they can band together to pay for the clean-up of wastes that affect their drinking water. Poor people have proportionately fewer material and political resources, making them more vulnerable and less able to escape such problems.

Poverty causes people to be more vulnerable to other problems, and it affects people who are already more vulnerable as well. In fact, poverty and hunger disproportionately affect the populations of the world already most vulnerable to oppression and injustice, particularly women and children. According to the United Nations, 70% of the world's 1.3 billion poorest people are women. There are several potential reasons for this. When there is food scarcity in the household, women and girls often sacrifice their share first for the benefit of men and boys. In addition to sacrificing more in terms of resources, women also are overworked and under-educated. If any family member has a job, it is often the woman, who will be paid less for her labor in a factory or sweatshop, while she still does household and care-taking work for no wages. Girls are the first to be removed from schooling for the purpose of saving money or putting them to work for the family, since the belief is that they will marry and not use any education. These issues make poverty a particularly feminist concern.[10]

There are different views about what makes poverty a *problem*, in other words what is the nature of poverty such that we need to justify responding to it. How we view what constitutes the problem of poverty impacts how we understand the responsibility that agents have with respect to it, for diverse understandings of poverty justify different forms of responsibility, and for distinct reasons. Here I give an overview of three main ways we can think about the problem of poverty; these serve as the basis for distinguishing the three models of responsibility examined in the next three chapters.

Poverty as Harm (A Bad State of Affairs)

One way to understand what makes poverty a problem is to view it as a harm, meaning here simply a bad state of affairs. In other words, what makes

poverty something we need to change is that it is a bad state for those who experience it. Poverty is problematic insofar as it reflects inequality of goods (such
as wealth and resources), or because it falls below a minimum threshold of these
goods that we think are necessary for survival or for a decent life. In lacking
these goods, people who are in poverty experience a bad state of affairs which
can be helped only by provision of the needed goods.

There are two primary ways to view issues such as poverty: as synchronic
(discussed here) or as diachronic (discussed in the next section).[11] When poverty
is viewed as a harm, defined here as a bad state of affairs, it is understood within
a synchronic perspective as a sort of "time-slice" that evaluates what is happening currently as if the past does not matter. This analysis frames poverty chiefly
in terms of a pattern of inequality, for example treating poverty merely as a
problem of unequal distribution or simply as an inadequate amount of relevant
goods.[12] These accounts ignore whatever role history and causation might play
and focus just on the current state of affairs.

The synchronic view of poverty as a bad state of affairs justifies responsibility in terms of benefit, aid, or assistance. These duties of beneficence are justified according to deontology, human rights, consequentialism, and virtues of
universal benevolence. In these models, the response of the affluent is regarded
as a morally required duty. These approaches justify responsibility as agent-
neutral (impartial, universal) duties that affluent individuals have toward the
poor, according to traits such as the ability of the agent and the degree of need of
the poor. In the synchronic view of poverty, those who are responsible for addressing it are those who are able to do so, regardless of its causes.

Critics object to the way the synchronic perspective views poverty as a
problem requiring moral response. For example, some people argue that poverty
is simply a natural state for which moral attention is not only unnecessary but
actually harmful. Perhaps we should see hunger as something unavoidable, so
that feeding the hungry will only prolong their inevitable suffering and encourage the propagation of more hungry.[13] On this account, it is more humane to just
let poor people die. The belief that these problems are inevitable, natural states
is common in affluent nations like the United States.

Yet global poverty is not a simple natural state to be accepted. Regardless
of whether poverty is a natural state, alleviating it is still possible and desirable.
There are many situations that we believe are natural states, yet we do not simply accept them; we often try to manipulate them for our chosen ends. The way
that water runs through rivers, for example, is a natural state, yet we manipulate
it by building dams or creating irrigation systems in order to try to improve our
quality of life. That poverty may be a natural state is no reason not to try to improve the quality of human existence. One may still object, however, that at-
tempting to alleviate poverty is futile because there are no programs that will aid
poverty effectively. For example, one may argue that since development aid has
failed in the past, we should not keep sending money overseas to be thrown
away. Just because some programs have failed, however, does not mean that all
will. Some programs do help; what is required is empirical information to evalu-

ate which programs actually work and which do not. In short, even if poverty is a state of nature, this does not imply that the affluent have no duty to respond.

Another objection to the synchronic perspective that views poverty as a bad state of affairs involves reframing what is problematic away from the state of affairs itself to how the state of affairs came about—whether the process that resulting in that condition was fair. In this view, poverty is not a problem if the conditions of the Lockean proviso are met. John Locke argued that the taking of resources and wealth is just as long as one leaves "enough, and as good" for others. This Lockean proviso can only be lifted if everyone will be better off with the lifting of this proviso than without it, and if people universally and rationally consent. While some (especially utilitarians) interpret this to mean that individuals should share goods such as food with others proportionally, libertarians like Robert Nozick believe that the Lockean proviso means that one has a duty not to *worsen* the situation of others. On this basis libertarians argue that poverty is not a problem because no one's situation has been *worsened* by the acquisition of wealth by the rich.[14]

This assertion is highly controversial, and it relies upon an over-simplistic view of what it is to *worsen* a situation. Worsening involves some idea of harming, as opposed to benefiting. Libertarians believe that as long as the wealthy do not harm, their actions are just; there is no obligation to benefit. Yet *harm* has many meanings that are relevant to poverty and responsibility. When the nature of harm is examined carefully, it might turn out that the wealthy do in fact harm the poor.

Poverty as Wrongful Harm (The Result of Faulty Action)

Another way to view poverty as a problem is as the result of a causal chain that includes faulty action. In this conception, poverty is also considered a harm, but what is meant by *harm* is not simply a bad state of affairs viewed as a time-slice independent of causal history, as above. Rather, what constitutes the badness of harm here is that it results from faulty action. In this view, poverty is still seen as lack of basic goods needed for survival, or lack of capabilities involved with accessing them, but this lack constitutes a wrongful harm, caused by specific, identifiable agents. In contrast to the synchronic perspective, this way of looking at poverty is historical, examining the causal factors that made or influenced poverty to occur as it does. While synchronic approaches evaluate the justice of states of affairs, historical or *diachronic* perspectives examine the justice of the past actions and circumstances that led to present situations.

A theory of justice that ignores the history of the just and unjust transfers that lead to present states of affairs, or that ignores the causes and consequences of specific patterns of distribution, is necessarily incomplete. What makes poverty problematic on this view is not that poverty represents a bad (e.g., unequal) pattern of distribution, but that what *caused* this distribution is unjust. Understanding poverty as merely a problem of vastly unequal distribution or merely inadequate amounts of goods ignores the factors that contributed to poverty, thereby evading evaluation of them. In contrast to this synchronic approach, the diachronic perspective evaluates the justice or fairness of the causal and structural factors that resulted in the current situation. Poverty is often caused or exacerbated by factors such as the dumping of toxic waste, the taking of land through eminent domain, taking advantage of people's ignorance to sell them goods they do not need and cannot afford, and taking advantage of people's desperation to employ them for cheap labor. These actions, which are performed by specific, identifiable agents, result in poverty that is constituted by wrongful harm and which must be addressed through redress. Structural factors resulting in poverty include colonialism, war, and practices like permissible bribery; rectifying the injustice of these requires institutional change.

A diachronic approach justifies responsibility insofar as agents have played a morally significant role in causing or contributing to currently existing poverty. The relevant kinds of responsibility involve preventing and rectifying harm. Agents have agent-neutral (impartial and universal) duties of forbearance to not engage in faulty action that leads to poverty. When agents do commit wrongful harms through their faulty actions, they have agent-relative duties of redress directed at the particular others they have harmed, to compensate for their wrongful losses. These duties of redress are a form of corrective justice, which requires that a wrong be righted or repaired, to return a situation to a state of justice. Corrective or reparative justice involves agent-relative duties to right wrongs, in contrast to the agent-neutral duties of aid involved in beneficence models of responsibility. The agent-relative responsibility to correct wrongful harm belongs to particular agents for particular justifying reasons—namely making a morally relevant causal contribution to harm—that tie the duty-bearers to particular victims of harm. While those responsible for preventing and rectifying poverty are mainly collective agents like governments and corporations, individuals have corresponding duties, especially with respect to the roles they occupy within these collectives.

Causes of poverty involve varying amounts and kinds of human agency. On one extreme is poverty that is caused by natural or mechanical forces, such as natural disasters like drought or flood; one becomes impoverished by such events through bad luck, being in the wrong place at the wrong time. At the individual level poverty may be caused by an individual's bad decisions or by bad character flaws such as laziness. At the cultural level poverty may also be caused or exacerbated by bad decisions or character flaws within one's family or community. In these situations, poverty cannot be characterized as a wrongful harm resulting from faulty action against another, and so there is no corresponding duty of redress.

On the other hand, specific agents may cause faulty action against others that result in harm. At the local or national level, poverty may be caused by local or national governments that make bad decisions, perhaps believing that they are helping the poor but in fact not doing so, for example, dismantling a welfare system with the belief that it will help the poor by encouraging them to find work. Or government officials may act corruptly intentionally, hurting the people whom they are supposed to represent, for their own gain. Corporations also contribute to poverty, usually unintentionally, when they intend to maximize profit but do so at the expense of other values, including respecting human rights. In these situations, poverty may be the result of faulty action that justifies duties of redress.

Critics argue that poverty that is caused by individual or local factors such as in the examples above may entail responsibilities of some specific agents—the poor themselves, or those who committed identifiable faulty action that resulted in poverty—but not responsibilities of wealthy people or nations in general. This is because poverty is seen as resulting from specific localized factors that are independent of the actions of most affluent people and affluent nations.[15] Even individual, local, or "bad luck" causes often must be understood within a more global context, however, particularly with respect to economic and political structures. A few examples will illustrate how global factors can be more relevant than we might initially assume. First, sometimes we blame "natural disasters" and "ethnic conflicts" for causing famines or situations of poverty, but there is also some evidence to suggest that these situations are actually man-made and contemporary, rather than "natural" or "historical," and usually global in their scope. For example, the famine of Ethiopia in the early 1980s (made famous with the Live Aid charity rock concert of 1985) did not result purely from "natural disaster" like drought, as many presumed, but actually had political and economic causes, including regional wars which drafted farm workers into the army, diminishing the labor available to produce food. These regional wars were also fueled by global political and economic influence, however; in vying for control over this area of Africa, the Soviet Union sold weapons to Ethiopia in the late 1970s, while the United States armed neighboring Somalia. International support for wars is a frequent cause of famine, especially in sub-Saharan Africa.

Similarly, the starvation in Rwanda in the 1990s was often attributed to centuries-old ethnic conflict resulting in civil war and genocide—but this ignores a coffee crisis that precipitated the war. This economic disaster caused the Rwandan government to agree to terms of structural adjustment and neo-liberal privatization or elimination of government services and subsidies, in exchange for loans from the International Monetary Fund and the World Bank. The abrupt change in the nature of the economy caused poverty to escalate, which fueled the ethnic conflict that resulted in mass genocide. As often happens in situations that we attribute to ethnic conflict, it is dire poverty that typically drives people to the radicalism or fundamentalism that results in war, genocide, and terrorism. Historical conflicts may have been brewing for centuries, but it takes extreme conditions to make them explosive.[16]

"Natural disasters" such as drought, earthquakes, tsunamis, hurricanes, or floods are also often blamed for decreased food supply, but the causes of many of these occurrences are human-made rather than "natural," and global in their reach. Western activities contribute to much of the pollution and global warm-

ing that obstruct plant growth and contribute to "natural disasters." Recent up-
surges in hurricanes and other dramatic climate events are probably caused by
the increase in global temperature and the accompanying melting of the arctic
ice. The methods of farming that are used affect food dependability as well.
Farm processes such as growing large monoculture crops, using excessive toxic
chemicals such as fertilizers and pesticides, and using genetically modified
seeds that have these chemicals already embedded within them, drain the soil of
its nutrients, turning the soil into desert, thereby decreasing food supply. These
processes are imported into Third World countries by multinational companies
that want to make a quick profit by increasing short-term yields in their crops at
the expense of long-term sustainability of the soil.[17] Many contemporary political dramas and recent natural disasters involve a complexity of contributing
causes that includes human factors with a global or international scope.

A final example for the global context of apparently local causal factors of
poverty involves political corruption. One popular argument against global responsibility for poverty points to corruption in the governments of poor, Third
World countries, criticizing these countries for not cleaning up their own act
before they are worthy of foreign aid. But there is a global context for why political elites of poor countries take money and resources intended for their country's poor for their own gain. As Thomas Pogge states, "The existing world order is itself a crucial causal factor in the prevalence of corruption and oppression
in the poor countries."[18] He points out that bribery was only made illegal inter-
nationally in developed countries in 1999, but many multinational corporations
still evade the law because it was permissible for so many years. Political elites
of poor countries must act in response to the major players in the global economic and political system, including foreign governments and multinational
corporations. This includes accepting not only unjust and now illegal bribes, but
also accepting conditions on aid such as neo-liberal, welfare-cutting practices in
order to receive loans from the World Bank or International Monetary Fund. Of
course many elites of poor countries are greedy and corrupt, but they are encouraged to be so within a greedy and corrupt global scheme. To argue that the
poor caused their own poverty, or that poverty is merely a matter of bad luck, is
often to be ignorant of the broader structures surrounding poverty and the decisions that lead to it.

Though they are not caused by specific, identifiable agents, structural factors also contribute to poverty. These include cultural practices, such as practices that treat women as second-class citizens, impoverishing them more or
differently than men,[19] as well as institutional practices, such as the practices of
bribery and corruption that Pogge describes. At the global or transnational level,
political and economic institutions of various kinds contribute to poverty; these
include governmental and corporate institutions. Formal rules made by organizations such as the World Trade Organization or the World Bank, such as those
encouraging neo-liberalism, have far-reaching effects that may cause or exacerbate poverty throughout the world. Informal corporate practices such as the out-
sourcing of labor to the cheapest manufacturing plants possible have similar

global effects, including the encouragement of sweatshops with poor working conditions. While these formal and informal institutions are not necessarily *global* in the strictest meaning of the term (i.e., with effects reaching literally across the world), they do cross national boundaries and have such wide reach that we might think of them as "global" in a loose sense; I use the term "global" in this way as synonymous with "transnational." Insofar as these practices contribute to poverty, they create institutional injustice; this grounds the responsibility of affluent individuals who benefit from these practices.

Poverty as Institutional Injustice (The Result of Systemic Vulnerability to Harm or Violation of Human Rights)

Poverty can also be viewed as a matter of institutional injustice, which has to do with the justice of how economic and political resources are distributed, rather than the correction of wrongful harm described in the previous section. An unjust distribution of political and economic goods both contributes to, and is a condition for, systemic vulnerability to harm and violation of human rights. This view of poverty is generally although not always diachronic, depending on whether its proponents believe that focusing on historical causes of injustice is required to make change. When institutional injustice is considered in a consequentialist framework, poverty is seen as systemic vulnerability to harm and is treated more as a state of affairs, where the focus is on the badness of the state of injustice itself (i.e., the lack of goods that the poor have). When institutional injustice is viewed in a human rights framework, however, poverty is seen as a violation of human rights, and its institutional causes are considered relevant in contributing to its existence and in ascribing responsibility. Insofar as poverty is a case of distributive injustice, the political and economic structures that led (and continue to lead) to poverty are relevant to its assessment and to ascribing responsibility; making this assessment and ascription involves a diachronic perspective that includes causal and historical analyses.

The conception of poverty as an injustice justifies responsibility to change the system of distribution of benefits and burdens based on the unjust benefit that some receive at the expense of others. Like the corrective justice that grounds agent-relative responsibility on an agent's particular action, distributive justice grounds agent-relative responsibility based on an agent's particular positioning within the institutions that confer benefits and burdens. While corrective justice justifies the responsibility of an agent according to her having *caused* wrongful harm, however, distributive justice justifies the responsibility of an agent according to her having *benefited* from an unjust institutional scheme of distribution. Agents that benefit unfairly from these structures have duties of institutional justice to make these institutional practices more just. Since various social, economic, and political structures condition the actions of all individual and collective agents, all have duties of institutional justice.

Each of the three main ways of understanding poverty as a problem uses terms like *benefit* and *harm* in different ways. As I explain these models of responsibility in depth, I shall clarify in more detail what these terms mean within each conception. One of the tricky issues in analyzing a concept like responsibility is that many of the terms that are used admit of many, sometimes incompatible, meanings. For this reason, those who discuss responsibility must explain what they mean by such terms.

Responsibility

The term *responsibility* is elusive and employed in a variety of ways. For example, a person can be *held responsible* by others in a blameworthy or liable sense; she can *take responsibility* for herself or her actions in a duty sense; she can *accept responsibility* for faulty or laudatory actions; she can *be responsible* in a praiseworthy way.[20] One way to categorize these different meanings of responsibility is in terms of whether responsibility for poverty should be viewed primarily as "forward-looking" or primarily as "backward-looking." Sometimes the term *responsibility* is used to designate blameworthiness, liability, and/or causation. In these contexts, responsibility is understood as generally "backward-looking," as we speak of having a responsibility *for* something that happened in the past, such as an action that we did, an outcome that we caused, or a disposition that we held. Other times, the term *responsibility* is used to designate duty. In these contexts, responsibility is understood as "forward-looking," as we speak of having a responsibility *to* something in the future, such as to perform an act, to ensure an outcome occurs, or to change a disposition. As I shall argue, these "backward-looking" and "forward-looking" characterizations of responsibility are misleading; while these meanings are often used in mutually exclusive ways, they should not be, as "forward-looking" duties often arise from "backward-looking" causation of harm or benefit from unjust practices.

I want to clarify my use of the term *responsibility* with respect to these issues. First, nowhere in this project am I using the term *responsibility* to refer to blameworthiness; as I shall explain, I do not think blameworthiness is relevant to discussions about global poverty. What is important for my inquiry about the concept of responsibility is its root word, the idea of *response*. In examining justifications for why affluent individuals have responsibilities with respect to global poverty, I am interested in the reasons why affluent individuals are obligated to *respond*, focusing on responsibility as duty. Causal responsibility and liability are also directly relevant to my project, but mainly because they justify particular kinds of duty, namely duties of redress and some duties of institutional injustice. Liability and duty are thus sometimes closely related but obviously not equivalent.

Besides the various meanings described above, there is a further confusion about the use of the terms *responsibility* and *duty* regarding scope. Philosophers

debate about whether the kind of obligation relevant to poverty should be regarded as strict "duty," with a specified, complete-able, non-discretionary scope
of action, or as looser "responsibility," with a nonspecific, non-complete-able,
discretionary scope of action.[21] In noting this distinction, I want to acknowledge
the importance of identifying the scope of a duty, but I also want to reject the
way these terms are used and applied within the context of global poverty. In
debating whether obligations should be framed as "duty" or "responsibility,"
philosophers sometimes assume there is only one kind of obligation most relevant to poverty, which must be categorized in one of these two ways. In fact,
there are several kinds of relevant obligations, which have differing degrees of
dischargeability, discretion, and specificity. In this book, I present a pluralistic
account of relevant duties, and for each duty I identify its scope, including its
dischargeability, discretion, and specificity. While I do tend to use the terms
responsibility and *duty* in slightly different ways, the difference is more intuitive
than principled. I favor the term *duty* with reference to specific *kinds* of actions
(not specific *actions*, as the philosophers above associate with *duty*) for specific
justifying reasons, while I use the term *responsibility* to describe normative,
obligatory response more generally.

I should say a word here about my method of analysis. Models of responsibility are assessed here according to how well they justify responsibility specifically with respect to global poverty. All of the models examined here have been
used to argue that affluent individuals do have responsibilities toward global
poverty of some kind, but some are more persuasive and better justified than
others. One concern in assessing justification is to what audience the argument
is made. A model that takes seriously objections made by critics fits within more
political frameworks and so is more widely persuasive to more people. This advantage speaks to a broader concern that a good model of responsibility is one
that is followable by more people, as well as action-guiding and enforceable. A
model that is too abstract and theoretical or too vague to provide standards for
action does not allow agents to take responsibility or to be held responsible, defeating the purpose of providing an account of responsibility. Moreover, since
what is at issue is responsibility specifically with respect to global poverty, any
such model should be realistic with respect to the empirical issues involved,
accounting for the political context of poverty and reflecting the nature of poverty relatively accurately. A good model of responsibility should thus be practical, persuasive, and realistic—as well as philosophically defensible, of course.

Having said all this, I do think that all three kinds of duties that are examined in this book are strongly justified. Within each model there are ways of
justifying the duty that are better than others; for example, I will argue that the
human rights and consequentialist frameworks provide more detailed justification for beneficence than Kantian or virtue approaches. Nonetheless, duties of
beneficence are not as widely justifying as duties of redress, especially to libertarians and communitarians, largely because beneficence justifications generally
provide agent-neutral reasons for action, while redress justifications provide
agent-relative reasons. I doubt that I can argue persuasively that the libertarian

or communitarianism should accept that we have duties of beneficence, especially to "distant strangers," without arguing against libertarianism or communitarianism in general. Despite this, the libertarian or communitarian still has to accept that affluent individuals have *some* duties with respect to global poverty, namely duties of redress and duties of institutional injustice. My purpose in writing this book is to show the array of duties that affluent individuals have toward global poverty and how they are justified, and to point out that—even if a person finds that some duties are unpersuasive within a particular political view, or even if some duties are overly demanding of her relative to other obligations she has, or even if some duties conflict with the expectations attached to occupational and other roles over which she has little choice—there are still *other* duties that she has with respect to poverty. In this pluralistic account of responsibility, an affluent individual has a wide variety of duties toward global poverty, so that even if she feels excused from some duties, other duties will still obtain.

Affluent Individuals

There are many agents that have duties with respect to global poverty, including governments, corporations, non-profit non-governmental organizations, and individuals. In fact, the agents that are primarily responsible for alleviating poverty are collective rather than individual, whether they are organizations with agency of their own such as governments and corporations, or whether they are groups of individual and collective agents that do not themselves have agency but whose members act in congruence with each other. There are three different kinds of collectives that have some form of responsibility toward global poverty—random collectives, conglomerates, and congregations—and this book analyzes each one as it is relevant to the form of responsibility being discussed. The fact that collective responsibility in its many varieties is necessary to alleviate global poverty does not let individuals off the hook of responsibility, however. After all, the main question the book considers is: *given* that global poverty usually has political and structural causes, generally requiring collective action for its alleviation, what responsibilities do affluent individuals have? For each form of collective responsibility, and with respect to each kind of duty that is justified, I analyze the relationship between the affluent individual and the relevant collective, in particular focusing on what aspect of the affluent individual's *affluence* is morally relevant to ground responsibility. From this analysis I describe the particular duties that the affluent individual has with respect to the three kinds of responsibility that are justified—beneficence, redress, and institutional justice—and the relevant forms of collective responsibility.

I need to clarify who I am describing with the term *affluent individual*. Just as the group of people that comprise the "poor" is an amorphous classification, so is the group of people that comprise the "affluent." As one can guess, most of the world's poor and hungry live in the region of the world referred to as the global South or the Third World, which is itself poor, while most of the world's wealthy and well-fed live in the region of the world identified as the global North or the West, which is itself affluent. However, I want to stress that poverty occurs within western nations as well as nonwestern ones, and has many of the same global, structural causes. Moreover, affluent individuals exist within nonwestern nations, and these elites generally benefit in the same unjust way from the global economic and political system as affluent individuals in western nations.

For these reasons, I do not intend to essentialize the groups of wealthy versus poor, implying that all westerners are affluent or only westerners are wealthy, or that all non-westerners are poor or only non-westerners are poor. This is just false. While I write about the agents who have duties to carry out with western affluence in mind, these duties hold for nonwestern affluent people, and in some cases poor people, whether of affluent or poor nations, as well. For example, agents that have greater means to help the poor (enacting duties of beneficence) are relatively wealthy, and most agents that have the power to causally contribute to poverty (entailing duties of redress) are also wealthy; but all agents, affluent or not, have civic duties and role responsibilities (duties of institutional justice)—to the extent that they are capable of carrying them out— to make institutions more just. Moreover, while I write about the recipients of these duties with nonwestern poverty in mind, I do so in order to draw attention to the responsibility that most western affluent individuals have with respect to *global* poverty. In some cases it may in fact be better for affluent individuals to start by addressing poverty in their own backyard, especially if this is more efficacious or if it is necessary to avoid morally pragmatic essentialism and paternalism. But being aware of poverty as a global problem also entails that our actions do not end in the backyard, that we realize the global context of the problems we are trying to address and that we make global connections with other people working on related problems elsewhere.[22]

The reason this project examines the responsibility of affluent individuals is two-fold. One reason is that I am particularly interested in what is the relevant relationship between the affluent and the poor that grounds responsibility. Each of the models of responsibility that I evaluate has a different view about what the relevant factors that ground responsibility are, and how the affluent relate to these factors. For different reasons, for example that they simply have greater means or that they benefit from unjust practices, it is crucial on each model that the affluent are *affluent* relative to the poor.

The second reason I am particularly interested in the responsibility of affluent individuals focuses on the fact that they are individuals. As stated in the introduction, different groups of philosophers have analyzed responsibility toward global poverty in different ways. Moral philosophers tend to focus on analyzing the concept of responsibility, particularly as it applies to individuals, such as what constitutes the agency and voluntariness necessary to be responsible. Legal philosophers look at the causal role that agents, whether individual or collective, played in contributing to harm. Social philosophers examine the relationships between individuals and groups in order to give an account of collective responsibility that seems relevant or necessary to address political problems like global poverty. Political philosophers focus on the political, structural nature of a problem like global poverty and argue that collectives and institutions have responsibilities to address it. All of these areas provide important parts of the answer to the question of what responsibility the affluent individual has toward global poverty, but none provides a wholly satisfactory account in isolation of the others. My interest in this question comes partly from the desire to bring these different pieces together, bridging the gaps between these different literatures by showing how each of them suggests ways to think about the relevant issues that the others lack.

In considering affluent individuals' responsibility toward global poverty, the group of people I generally have in mind are "average" middle-class Americans and similarly situated people in other affluent nations. What constitutes affluence here is its relative state, in that such people are richer than those who lack the goods necessary for survival or thriving, as well as its absolute state, for such people possess these necessary goods regardless of whether or not others do. The responsibility of these people may differ from that of the richest people in the world, the political and economic elites who control much of the world's wealth. The richest may have greater responsibilities to respond to poverty, whether on account of having greater means to do so, or of causing more harm that constitutes poverty, or of receiving greater unfair benefit from an unjust system of distribution of economic and political goods. I will point out where these different degrees or kinds of responsibility apply.

Even though the richest may have greater responsibilities, I focus on the responsibility of the "middle-class" affluent for particular reasons. More people constitute the class of "middle-class"-affluent than the richest in the world, and too often such people use the fact that they are *not* the richest of the rich, and not in positions of power whereby they can exercise significant control to change present conditions, to excuse themselves from having any relevant responsibilities. I want to examine the validity of these reasons for excusing responsibility in my analysis. Thus I do not assume from the outset that the "middle-class" affluent *do have* responsibilities, but I consider *whether* they do based on what is required to justify responsibility for global poverty, and I consider *what kinds* of responsibilities "middle-class" individuals have when other agents are better positioned to have the most responsibility. My arguments also apply to differently situated people than the group of people I have in mind, and I suggest some of these applications where relevant. In short, I use the group of "middle-class" affluent people in affluent nations as a way to focus the discussion.

Conclusion

Questions about responsibility must begin with justification. In order to determine who is responsible for what, we must first determine how responsibility is justified, in other words how is it grounded or generated. Different accounts of justification give us different answers about which agents are responsible, and what is the scope of actions that responsibility requires of them. There are at least three broad accounts that can be given to answer who has responsibility, what this responsibility consists of, and why. I devote a chapter to each of the following three models of responsibility: duties of beneficence (chapter two), duties of redress (chapter three), and duties of institutional justice (chapter four). Since so many of the relevant duties require collective agents to carry them out, I conclude with a chapter that examines the nature of role responsibility; this chapter also ends with a suggested list of the specific duties that affluent individuals have toward global poverty (chapter five).

I want to make clear at the outset that these three models of responsibility, as well as the ways they view poverty as a problem, are not meant to be exclusive of each other. Poverty often results from many different causes and usually requires a variety of responses, each for distinct reasons. Moreover, these three models of responsibility typically are conjoined with each other in various ways. My purpose in this project is to make analytic distinctions between them in order to pull apart and clarify what we mean when we talk about responsibility, and how it applies to global poverty.

This book will show that affluent individuals have a wide variety of duties with respect to global poverty, and most of them are not as simple as sending money to a charitable organization. While governments are primarily responsible for beneficent actions through foreign aid, private charities also do important work. With respect to beneficence, individuals need to elect good government officials and lobby those in power to increase appropriate foreign aid, as well as support private and civic charities through donations and volunteer work. The identifiable agents that causally contribute to poverty are mostly corporations and governments. With respect to duties of redress, individuals have role responsibilities to ensure that these groups carry out their duties to right wrongs they have committed and to prevent them from committing future harm; individuals also have duties to boycott companies that are repeat offenders and to lobby government officials to act justly. Unjust economic and political institutions confer systematic burdens to some people, impoverishing them by making them more vulnerable to harm or violating their human rights. With respect to duties of institutional justice, affluent individuals have duties to vote responsibly, get involved with politics, take on social and civic roles, and consume ethically, all with the intention of changing institutions to make them more just. Who is responsible for addressing global poverty, and why, is a complicated issue. But in all of the accounts of responsibility that can be given, affluent individuals play an important part.

Notes

1. Statistics are cited, respectively, in the United Nations Development Programme's *Human Development Report 2007-2008: Fighting Global Climate Change: Human Solidarity in a Divided World* (Basingstoke and New York: Palgrave Macmillan, 2007), available on *United Nations Development Programme*, http://hdr.undp.org/en/reports/global/hdr2007-2008/ (accessed June 30, 2008); "FoodWatch: Setback in the War Against Hunger," *United Nations Chronicle Online Edition* 2003, http://www.un.org/Pubs/chronicle/2003/issue4/ 0403p66.asp (accessed October 25, 2004); Somini Sengupta, "Global Hunger Increases: U.N. Report Blames 'Lack of Political Will' Amid Ample Food," *New York Times*, reprinted in *Denver Post*, November 26, 2003, 14(A); and Thomas W. Pogge, "Human Rights and Human Responsibilities," in *Global Justice and Transnational Politics: Essays on the Moral and Political Challenges of Globalization*, ed. Pablo De Greiff and Ciaran Cronin (Cambridge and London: MIT Press, 2002), 152.

2. Income gap statistics are from the United Nations Development Programme, *Human Development Report 1998* (New York: Oxford University Press, 1998), 3; cited in Thomas W. Pogge, "Priorities of Global Justice," in *Global Justice*, Ed. Thomas W. Pogge (Oxford: Blackwell Publishers, 2001), 13. Wealth ratios are from the World Bank, *World Development Bank Report 2003* (New York: The World Bank and Oxford University Press, 2003), 235; cited in Susan Moller Okin, "Poverty, Well-Being, and Gender: What Counts, Who's Heard?" *Philosophy and Public Affairs* 31, no. 3 (2003): 281.

3. Jeffrey D. Sachs, *The End of Poverty: Economic Possibilities for Our Time* (New York: Penguin Press, 2005), 20. See also Peter Singer, *Practical Ethics, Second Edition* (Cambridge: Cambridge University Press, 1993), 218-20.

4. Thomas W. Pogge, "Can the Capability Approach Be Justified?" *Philosophical Topics* 30, no. 2 (Fall 2002): 176-94; Thomas W. Pogge, *World Poverty and Human Rights: Cosmopolitan Responsibilities and Reforms* (Cambridge: Polity and Malden, MA: Blackwell, 2002), 37-38.

5. See various discussions in Sen's books, including Jean Dreze and Amartya Sen, *Hunger and Public Action* (Oxford: Clarendon Press, 1989), 15; Amartya Sen, *Development as Freedom* (New York: Alfred A. Knopf, 1999), 19-21, 75; Amartya Sen, *Inequality Reexamined* (New York: Russell Sage Foundation and Cambridge, MA: Harvard University Press, 1992), 107-9; and Amartya Sen, *Commodities and Capabilities* (Amsterdam and New York: Elsevier Science Publishers, 1985), 5, 9-16, 25-26.

6. In response to the myth that famine results from inadequate food supply, Amartya Sen and Jean Dreze show that food is frequently available during times of famine; for example the availability of food was at its highest when famine struck Bangladesh in 1974. Dreze and Sen, *Hunger and Public Action*, 28. In fact, poverty and hunger often flourish when there is *overproduction* of food because overproduction decreases prices, which impoverishes farmers and laborers who cannot make a living from producing food. Amartya Sen, *Poverty and Famines: An Essay on Entitlement and Deprivation* (Oxford and New York: Oxford University Press, 1981), 42.

7. For a list of capabilities, see Martha Nussbaum, *Women and Human Development: The Capabilities Approach* (Cambridge: Cambridge University Press, 2000), 78-80; for a list of functionings, see Jerome M. Segal, "Living at a High Economic Standard: A Functionings Analysis," in *Ethics of Consumption: The Good Life, Justice, and Global Stewardship*, ed. David A. Crocker and Toby Linden (Lanham, MD: Rowman and Littlefield, 1998), 356-57.

8. For the first objection, see Alison M. Jaggar, "Challenging Women's Global Inequalities: Some Priorities for Western Philosophers," *Philosophical Topics* 30, no. 2 (Fall 2002): 233-35; and Pogge, "Can the Capability Approach Be Justified?," 191. For the second and third objections, see, respectively, Thomas Pogge, "Can the Capability Approach Be Justified?," 213-217; and Alison M. Jaggar, "Reasoning about Well-Being: Nussbaum's Methods of Justifying the Capabilities," *The Journal of Political Philosophy* 14, no. 3 (2006): 301-22.

9. See, respectively, Sen, *Development as Freedom*, 19-21 and 87-89; Nussbaum, *Women and Human Development*, 100; and James W. Nickel, *Making Sense of Human Rights: Philosophical Reflections on the Universal Declaration of Human Rights* (Berkeley, CA: University of California Press, 1987), 51.

10. See Alison M. Jaggar, "Is Globalization Good for Women?" *Comparative Literature* 53, no. 4 (Fall 2001): 298-314; and Okin, "Poverty, Well-Being, and Gender," 280-316. The statistic is cited by Jaggar on page 301.

11. I owe the terms *synchronic* and *diachronic* to Alison M. Jaggar, although the distinction is made most notably by Robert Nozick, when he criticized John Rawls' *A Theory of Justice* (Cambridge, MA: Belknap Press, 1971) for ignoring the relevant history of just and unjust transfers that occurred in the past and led to present states of affairs. Robert Nozick, *Anarchy, State, and Utopia* (New York: Basic Books, 1974), 198-204. For more on the distinction between synchronic and diachronic perspectives with respect to responsibility, see also John Martin Fischer and Mark Ravizza, S. J., *Responsibility and Control: A Theory of Moral Responsibility* (Cambridge: Cambridge University Press, 1998), 170-206.

12. For example, John Rawls and Peter Singer both seem to see poverty this way. John Rawls, *The Idea of Public Reason Revisited and the Law of Nations* (Cambridge, MA: Harvard University Press, 1999), 106; Rawls, *A Theory of Justice*, 61-62; Peter Singer, *One World: The Ethics of Globalization, Second Edition* (New Haven, CT and London: Yale University Press, 2002), 79-90; and Peter Singer, "Famine, Affluence, and Morality," *Philosophy and Public Affairs* 1 (1972): 229-243.

13. For examples of this argument, see Garrett Hardin, "Lifeboat Ethics: The Case Against Helping the Poor," in *World Hunger and Morality, Second Edition*, ed. William Aiken and Hugh LaFollette (Upper Saddle River, NJ: Prentice Hall, 1996), 5-15; and Jesper Ryberg, "Population and Third World Assistance: A Comment on Hardin's Lifeboat Ethics," *Journal of Applied Philosophy* 14, no. 3 (1997): 207-19.

14. Other libertarians may argue that disproportionate resource appropriation makes everyone better off, so that therefore the proviso can be lifted, but this claim is highly debatable and it certainly has not been consented to rationally and universally. For more on Locke's proviso, see John Locke, "An Essay Concerning the True Original, Extent, and End of Civil Government," in *John Locke: Two Treatises of Government*, ed. Peter Laslett (Cambridge: Cambridge University Press, 1988), 285-302 (especially sections 27 and 33); cited in Thomas W. Pogge, "A Global Resources Dividend," in *Ethics of Consumption: The Good Life, Justice, and Global Stewardship*, ed. David A. Crocker and

Toby Linden (Lanham, MD: Rowman and Littlefield, 1998), 508. For Robert Nozick's interpretation of the Lockean proviso, see Nozick, *Anarchy, State, and Utopia*, 175-82.

15. For example, John Rawls uses Amartya Sen's studies of hunger (*Poverty and Famines* and *Hunger and Public Action)* to show that the dominant cause of hunger is the lack of distribution of food supplies. This suggests that poverty usually has local causes for which governments are themselves responsible, and that they often fail to fulfill responsibility because they are greedy and corrupt. In Rawls' view, the only duty affluent nations have is to encourage these societies to become "well-ordered" and to foster just institutions within them. See Rawls, *The Idea of Public Reason Revisited and the Law of Nations*, 107-9.

David Miller makes similar, communitarian arguments for non-intervention. Those who have the greatest obligation to help the poor are those who are members of the same (national) communities as the poor. Since these governments may not have the means to do so, however, foreign aid may be necessary to provide a minimally decent standard of living for the poorest in the world; yet it is unclear whose duty it is to provide this aid. Miller previously argued that affluent nations have a duty to respond to the suffering of others only if they engage in practices of mutual aid. This suggests that foreign aid in the absence of mutual reciprocity is at best supererogatory, not morally required. The reason for this is that Miller sees nations as collectives, so that nations are responsible for the consequences of their actions and the outcomes of their decisions, just as individuals are, based on the notion of distributive collective responsibility. In this view, nations act independently from other nations, and are seen as solely causally and therefore morally responsible for their actions; poverty is seen as resulting from these local decisions and actions, independent of the actions of affluent nations. David Miller, "National Responsibility and International Justice," in *The Ethics of Assistance: Morality and the Distant Needy*, ed. Deen K. Chatterjee (Cambridge and New York: Cambridge University Press, 2004), 123-46; David Miller, *On Nationality* (Oxford: Clarendon Press, 1995), 105, 126, and 132-40.

16. Both examples come from Francis Moore Lappe, Joseph Collins, and Peter Rosset with Luis Esparza (Food First), *World Hunger: Twelve Myths, Second Edition* (New York: Grove Press, 1998), 19-23.

17. Vandana Shiva, *Stolen Harvest: The Hijacking of the Global Food Supply* (Cambridge MA: South End Press, 2000), 11-13, chapters 5 and 6; Vandana Shiva, *The Violence of the Green Revolution: Third World Agriculture, Ecology and Politics* (London and New Jersey: Zed Books, 1991), chapter 3.

18. Thomas W. Pogge, "'Assisting' the Poor," in *The Ethics of Assistance: Morality and the Distant Needy*, ed. Deen K. Chatterjee (Cambridge and New York: Cambridge University Press, 2004), 268.

19. Making a similar argument as Pogge's argument for the global context of government corruption, Alison Jaggar cautions against blaming cultural practices for injustices, as cultural practices often have a global context. Since Western institutions often contribute to the ways that cultures treat women and other disadvantaged people, blaming cultural practices without acknowledging their global context is self-righteous and paternalistic. Alison M. Jaggar, "'Saving Amina': Global Justice for Women and Intercultural Dialogue," *Ethics and International Affairs* 19, no. 3 (2005), 55-75.

20. See also Angelo Corlett's five different uses of the word *responsibility*: causal responsibility (being responsible for causing an event to occur), praise (being responsible in a praiseworthy or laudatory sense), blame (being responsible in a blameworthy or

faulty sense), liability (being subject to punishment or rectification), and duty (having a responsibility to do something). Angelo J. Corlett, *Responsibility and Punishment* (Dordrecht: Kluwer Academic Publishers, 2001), 9-11.

21. More specifically, Larry May categorizes responsibilities as discretionary and duties as rule-bound; for Robert Goodin, the difference is that responsibilities describe outcomes while duties describe actions. The distinction between these concepts also illustrates some of the controversy over what is meant by the distinction between "perfect" and "imperfect" duty. Introduced by Kant, this distinction holds force in contemporary ethical theory, although there is much debate about what it means. Two of the most plausible candidates for distinguishing between "perfect" and "imperfect" duties are based on differences in discretion and in dischargeability. When perfect and imperfect duties are contrasted with respect to dischargeability, perfect duties are those that can be satisfied always. This implies that they must have specific, limited scope of action that can be completed so that the duty can be fully satisfied. In contrast, imperfect duties are those that can be satisfied sometimes, or that have such a wide scope their actions cannot ever be completed so they can never be fully satisfied. For discussion on the general distinctions made between duties and responsibilities, see Joel Feinberg, "Duties, Rights, and Claims," in *Rights, Justice, and the Bounds of Liberty: Essays in Social Philosophy* (Princeton, NJ: Princeton University Press, 1980), 136-38; Joel Feinberg, "Supererogation and Rules," in *Doing and Deserving* (Princeton, NJ: Princeton University Press, 1970), 3-24; Robert Goodin, *Utilitarianism as Public Philosophy* (Cambridge: Cambridge University Press, 1995), 81-87; and Larry May, *The Socially Responsible Self: Social Theory and Professional Ethics* (Chicago and London: University of Chicago Press, 1996), 88-92. For more on the distinction between "perfect" and "imperfect" duties, see Christine M. Korsgaard, *Creating the Kingdom of Ends* (Cambridge: Cambridge University Press, 1996), chapters 1, 3, and 5; and Michael J. Zimmerman, *The Concept of Moral Obligation* (Cambridge and New York: Cambridge University Press, 1996), 38-40.

22. For further discussion, see Radhika Balakrishnan and Uma Narayan, "Combining Justice with Development: Rethinking Rights and Responsibilities in the Context of World Hunger and Poverty," in *World Hunger and Morality: Second Edition*, ed. William Aiken and Hugh LaFollette (Upper Saddle River, NJ: Prentice Hall, 1996), 230-47.

Chapter 2
Duties of Beneficence

Duties of beneficence involve helping others. They are justified on several different accounts, including all three of the major ethical theories: deontology, consequentialism, and virtue ethics. Deontologists justify beneficence as an imperfect duty that agents are required to fulfill as much as possible; in human rights language, beneficence corresponds to the duties of assistance entailed by human rights to subsistence. Consequentialists justify beneficence as a requirement of the consequentialist principle to make present states of affairs better than they would be without one's action, or of the utilitarian rule to maximize happiness or welfare. For virtue ethicists, benevolence is a virtue of caring or humanitarian concern, so beneficent action is an expression of good character. These models of beneficence share the same view of what is the morally appropriate response agents should make toward poverty—helping—based on what is problematic about poverty—its harm.

Although many philosophers refer to this responsibility as "duties of *benevolence*," focusing on shared intuitions that we should respond to others' suffering with benevolence, I prefer to call it "duties of *beneficence*," in order to focus on its "helping" or "benefiting" aspect. Some accounts of beneficent duties—especially consequentialist and virtue accounts—justify these duties according to shared intuitions of benevolence that may involve intellectually or rationally justified response to other people's suffering, or emotional response based on moral feelings of sympathy (e.g., Humean sentiment) for other people's suffering. Intuitions of concern are relevant only to some of the accounts of responsibility that fit under this category, however; they are not relevant to deontological imperatives to meet people's human rights, for example. What unites all the accounts of responsibility given in this chapter is their emphasis on helping or benefiting, which in the context of global poverty corresponds to the way all these models conceptualize poverty as a "mere" harm, or as a bad state of affairs requiring active intervention in response.

Understanding poverty as a harm means seeing it as an unfortunate state of affairs in which there is too much suffering. Poverty is a condition of lacking goods important for human welfare. Since what is bad about poverty is that the condition exists, the causes of poverty or the justness of the historical or structural processes that may have led to it are considered irrelevant to moral assessment. Responsibility in these models is what some philosophers call "forward-looking," where response is to present conditions that should be changed in the *future* rather than to *past* actions that were wrong.[1]

As a result of their conceptualization of poverty as harm, beneficence models tend to understand responsibility primarily as aid or assistance, involving meeting needs or providing lacking goods. This response is generally understood as active intervention, as the verbs "helping," "benefiting," "assisting," and "aiding" all suggest. "Responding" thus means helping or benefiting the poor, which on different accounts is understood as the action that follows from care or universal benevolence, as fulfilling people's human rights, or as decreasing people's suffering and so increasing the overall good in the world.

Why Responsibility as Beneficence is Attractive: Responding to Our Common Moral Intuitions

One attraction of conceptualizing global responsibility as beneficence is that it captures many common moral intuitions about the role of the individual in response to terrible tragedies like global poverty and hunger. This is well illustrated by Peter Singer's argument for famine relief in his famous article, "Famine, Affluence, and Morality."[2] At the time it was published in 1972, this argument for beneficent duties was ground-breaking, opening the door for philosophers to reconsider the value of applying theoretical ethics to topics of everyday concern. Since then, philosophers writing on famine and poverty relief nearly always respond to this original argument, even if only indirectly.

Singer focuses on the famine involved with absolute poverty, although his argument can easily be construed to include other kinds of suffering of the poor, such as homelessness or lack of basic health care. When Singer talks about relieving poverty, he is concerned with the kind of widespread poverty that occurs mainly in Third World countries. Our ethical duties to poverty and hunger within affluent nations like the United States are less of a priority because poverty in Third World countries occurs on a much greater scale and involves more intense suffering and dying, so that aid relief will be more effective overseas.

In logical form, his argument is as follows:

1. Suffering and death from lack of food, shelter, and medical care are necessarily bad.
2. If it is in our power to prevent something very bad from happening, without sacrificing anything of comparable moral significance, we ought to do it.

3. There is some suffering and death that we can prevent without sac-
    rificing anything of comparable moral significance.
4. Therefore, we ought to prevent some suffering and death.

The premise that does all of the work in this argument is the second one,
that we ought to prevent bad things from happening when it is in our power to
do so. The first and third premises are relatively uncontroversial. Singer seems
to suggest that someone who does not agree that suffering and death from lack
of basic resources is bad must be a moral monster, or at least must have radically
different ethical and religious beliefs with which he cannot engage. That there
are actions that any agent, including average individuals, can take is also factu-
ally true; Singer and his supporters often give examples of ordinary actions,
such as sending even $1 to Oxfam that will buy about six packets of oral rehy-
dration salts and save the lives of children who would otherwise die of dehydration from diarrhea.[3] The premise that could potentially be controversial, then,
and that does all the moral work, is the second one.

Singer uses the now famous drowning-child example to illustrate the principle in the second premise. If I walk by a pond where a child is drowning, I
ought to rescue the child, even if that means my clothes will get wet. The sacrifice of getting my clothes wet is not morally comparable to the drowning that I
can prevent, nor is it even morally significant at all. Even if my rescuing the
child makes me late (and wet) for a very important job interview, this sacrifice is
unquestionably unimportant compared to the life of a child saved. This example
generates the intuitive response that Singer seeks to support his principle. When
philosophy instructors teach this article, they ask students whether they would
save the drowning child, making the sacrifice greater and greater to see at what
point the argument might break down. Only those who intend to cause a class
riot say they would not save the child. The imperative to act to prevent bad
things from happening when possible is a consequentialist principle to promote
better states of affairs than would obtain otherwise (i.e., without our action), but
it has obvious intuitive appeal to people no matter what their ethical persuasions.

Objections frequently arise regarding the demandingness of this principle,
however. The action required of us often involves some sacrifice of other interests of ours, but it is unclear how much sacrifice we ought to make. Singer's
principle may be interpreted as stronger or weaker depending on what kind and
how much sacrifice is required. A weak version of the consequentialist principle
stipulates that we must not sacrifice *anything* of moral significance. This might
be more widely appealing because it is less demanding morally, but, depending
on what counts as having moral significance, this principle might be so weak as
to require virtually no sacrifice and so have no moral force at all. A strong version of the principle, given above, stipulates that we must not sacrifice anything
of *comparable* moral significance, but what counts as a comparable sacrifice
may be controversial. Clearly, I should not kill myself in order to provide more
money and resources to someone starving, because I would be sacrificing one
life for another, but whether any other sacrifice beside my own life would be

comparable is contentious. At its most extreme, this principle would require me to give to the point of marginal utility, in which I give my resources and devote my time to alleviate others' poverty until their level of wealth and well-being is equivalent to mine—meaning that not only would theirs be significantly raised, but mine would also be significantly lowered. This strong interpretation is objectionable to anyone who is not essentially a socialist, however. In order to do any significant moral work, the argument must require that we do sacrifice some of our interests in order to create better outcomes—to prevent the most easily preventable deaths, for instance—than would exist without our actions. *Which* of our interests, and *to what extent*, are the most contentious issues in the argument for beneficent duties, as much of the discussion here tries to pin down the extent of sacrifice that should or should not be demanded of an agent.[4]

Singer's general argument is that we certainly can and ought to do more than most of us currently do. Most individuals do very little to respond to the great tragedies that befall people throughout the world, and almost all of us could do more than we do, in terms of giving time and/or money. With only a small amount of effort, many people could be tremendously better off and the world could be a significantly better place. As a utilitarian, Singer's ideal is for us all to put in a *lot* more effort and create significant change in the world, eradicating poverty completely and making it so that all people live at the same level of well-being. But he is not pushing for that. As a consequentialist, he just wants us to do *more* and to make things *better*.

The beauty of Singer's argument is that in requiring us to make the world a better place, it allows us some discretion in figuring out what action this entails. Singer's main example of what we should do is to send money to a relief organization like Oxfam, since it can use the money effectively to alleviate poverty. But if we think the cause of poverty is over-population, as many do, and we fear that relief organizations actually perpetuate poverty by prolonging the lives of poor people who will bear more poor children, then this does not let us off the hook of responsibility. In this case we then have a duty to respond to over-population, so we still have to give time and/or money to organizations that will provide birth control, promote long-term health, and educate women. If we think that the responsibility to respond to poverty does not belong chiefly to individuals, but rather to governments, this still does not let us off the hook. Then we must be involved with politics, lobbying for anti-poverty policies and working to elect officials who will carry them out—or run for government office ourselves. Even if we think that the chief responsibility to respond is the governments in which poor people reside, we still have duties: there are poor people within every country in the world, and so poverty is always *our* problem as well as "theirs." In fact, all arguments for responding to poverty, made from any philosophical persuasion, are compatible with Singer's argument in its broadest sense. If we think that poverty violates people's rights, then we need to rectify those violations; if we think that poverty results from structural injustice, then we need to change institutions to be more just.

The imperative that we must do *something* to respond to poverty is almost impossible to object to and is agreed upon by practically everyone who believes we have any kind of beneficent duty. But what this principle *means* when we spell it out is unclear. What we do know is that our first responsibility in fulfilling duties of beneficence must be to learn as much as we can about what contributes to poverty and what is effective in alleviating it, so that we can figure out how to prioritize our action. Singer's broadly consequentialist argument gives us motivation to act, but it does not give us much guidance by itself. In exploring different justifications for beneficent duties, this chapter will provide some guidance in understanding the moral intuition to help the poor.

How Poverty is Conceptualized:
As a Harm (or Bad State of Affairs)

As stated in the introduction, what makes poverty problematic and therefore justifying beneficent response is that it is a harm or a bad state of affairs. Poverty is measured against some baseline of welfare or well-being, measured by possessing adequate goods (as on the resource view, described in the introductory chapter) or abilities (as on the capabilities approach). The baseline may be an objective standard of measurement; for example, a person may be poor when she lacks sufficient resources to put her well-being above an acceptable threshold (so that she falls below some designated "poverty line"). Or the baseline may be a comparable measure, so that one is poor relative to others who are wealthy.[5]

Whatever the acceptable baseline of welfare or well-being is, falling short of it is what constitutes the harm that grounds responsibility. Whether poverty is defined according to the resource or the capabilities approach, it constitutes a lack. This lack may involve having a standard of welfare or well-being that is below adequate, such as not having enough of the goods necessary for survival or lacking the ability to access these goods. Or, more generally, this lack may consist in having less of these goods or abilities than what others have (i.e., poverty as inequality). Since what is problematic about such a condition is that it is simply a bad state of affairs, regardless of its causes, response involves "filling" the lack or providing what is missing and needed. This response is often understood as benefiting, aiding, or assisting the poor; this is what constitutes duties of beneficence. Depending on what baseline for poverty is used, the kind of benefit required is that which is necessary to meet the objective threshold of adequate resources or capabilities, or to redistribute resources to create a state of more equality. The responsibility on the part of agents who are in a position to help may be justified in several ways.

Justifying Duties of Beneficence

Duties of beneficence may be justified by all three major ethical theories: deontology, including human rights, consequentialism, and virtue ethics. This section explains how these theories justify various kinds of beneficent duties. Although the form of beneficence each theory justifies is slightly different than the others, all are duties to help or aid people in need. Furthermore, as I explain in the section that follows this one, all share the same basis for determining the appropriate agents for carrying out these duties and who are their appropriate recipients.

Kantian Imperfect Duties

In Kantian ethical theory, duties of beneficence belong to the category of duties known as *imperfect* duties. Imperfect duties are those that an agent has an obligation to do as much as she possibly can; they differ from perfect duties in that they cannot be performed at all times. For example, I can refrain from lying at all times (a perfect duty), but I cannot give money to charity at all times, for I would quickly run out of money and have none left to give nor to survive on, and conflicts with other duties would be inevitable. Yet I still have an obligation to give some money to charity—or do an equivalent action that helps others who are less fortunate—to the best of my ability within the context of my other duties (including duties of self-preservation to take care of my own well-being). Perfect duties can be performed at all times because they (at least theoretically) pose no conflict with other duties, mainly because they are duties of forbearance, in which one has a duty to *not* do something. In contrast, imperfect duties frequently conflict with other duties, both perfect and imperfect, because they are duties of action in which one has a duty to *do* something. The significance of this distinction will be discussed in much more detail throughout this book.

What justifies imperfect duties in the Kantian framework is the categorical imperative, or the overriding moral rule that is best captured by two concepts: universalization of one's maxim (or moral rule) for action, and treating people as ends always. To his example of a man who is doing well and cares nothing of others' struggles with hardships, Kant explicitly states that refusing to help others when they are in need violates the rule of universalization. We could not will that a moral rule of not helping others could hold as a law of nature for all humans, for we would be contradicted when we are ourselves in need of others' help. Humans are not capable of being purely self-sufficient; interdependence is in our nature, meaning that sometimes we need others' help and—as required by fairness, so not violating the rule of universalizing one's maxim for action—sometimes we must help others. For this reason, the duty of beneficence is sometimes understood, in the Kantian framework, as a duty of mutual aid. Moreover, refusing to help others when they are in need violates the rule to treat them as ends, or as possessing dignity and intrinsic worth. When we value people as ends, so the Kantian may argue, we respect the aims they seek because as rational beings, they can give reasons for their action that we can understand as fellow humans. When we act beneficently, we try to help them achieve at least some of their aims, especially the ones central to maintaining their functioning as human beings (such as obtaining food and shelter). Refusing to help others in need is a rejection of their aims, and so a rejection of their humanity. A moral rule not to help others treats others as means only, as objects which one may use to respond to according to one's own desire, but not according to their own humanity (as expressed here by their need). Thus on both interpretations of the categorical imperative we have an imperfect duty of beneficence.[6]

The Kantian imperfect duty of beneficence is justified entirely according to the agent's humanity, using a reasoning process that involves universalization of human need and interdependence but which occurs from the agent's (rather than the recipient's) perspective. It is unclear what view of poverty is assumed by the view and so what the outcome of beneficent duty should be (i.e., to meet a certain baseline or to redistribute resources). In some way, this is an unfair consideration, since the deontological view focuses on the action, not the outcome; but guidance in how to direct one's action is nevertheless desirable. At the very least, an agent should help those who have less than herself, who can be said to be "in need" comparatively speaking, so that they will have better well-being than they currently do.

Duties of Assistance Entailed by Human Rights

While not all deontologists are explicit Kantians, many agree with the general argumentation that justifies imperfect duties of beneficence, which is also used to justify the existence of human rights and their corresponding responsibilities. In human rights language, Kant's imperfect duties of beneficence translate into what we more commonly call duties of aid or assistance. These kinds of duties are justified in that they are entailed by human rights. Entailment describes a morally binding relationship that justifies particular responses—what we call *duties*—that agents are obligated to make as a result of their normative force. While theorists justify human rights in many different ways, the justification is generally based on some features like rationality, agency, and dignity that are shared by all humans, which is why human rights frameworks tend to be deontological.[7]

The duties that correspond to human rights involve preserving the universal human traits that ground human rights. All humans can claim these human rights by virtue of universally shared qualities such as need, interest, or requirements of agency and well-being.[8] Rights specify which goods are so important that they deserve the special protection afforded by rights. Because rights are held universally, duties corresponding to human rights are impartial in scope in that they apply to all right-claimants equally, so that one cannot choose to meet some people's needs or interests for arbitrary or partial reasons.

In the human rights framework, poverty is defined as the lack of some of the goods that are considered necessary for a minimally decent life. Poverty is viewed here, then, as a state of well-being that is below an objective standard of adequacy; this standard is described by the list of human rights. What makes poverty a problem on the human rights model is that it constitutes a condition in which people's rights are unmet or perhaps even violated.[9] Responding to poverty here means ensuring that people have sufficient means to have decent well-being and to be able to act as full moral agents. Duties of assistance (the human rights version of duties of beneficence) thus require that action be taken to ensure that individuals' well-being meets a certain standard, as specified by the relevant rights. What justify these duties are rights to specific resources that enable one to act. Philosophers sometimes call these *welfare* or *subsistence* rights, emphasizing the goods that humans need in order to survive or thrive; these correspond with what the United Nations recognizes as economic, social, and cultural rights. Examples of these rights include the right to adequate food, clothing, and shelter (Article 11), the right to physical and mental health as far as attainable (Article 12) and the right to education (Article 13).[10]

People commonly think that ensuring that subsistence rights are fulfilled means providing the resources expressed by these rights, where provision is understood as active intervention, rather than refraining from action. Subsistence rights may entail duties of several kinds, however, including duties of assistance, duties of non-interference, and duties of redress when rights are violated (such as by unwarranted interference). The latter two kinds of duties are just as important for meeting the subsistence rights relevant to poverty as duties of assistance are, but their structure—and the way they capture what is problematic about poverty—is different, and so they are addressed in the following chapter. Although duties of assistance are only one type of duty entailed by human rights claims relevant to poverty, they are the kind most commonly discussed because they involve active intervention, which intuitively seems like the most appropriate response to the unmet need expressed in a human rights claim. In expressing active intervention, duties of assistance or beneficence require that agents *do* something to provide assistance and fulfill their duties. As a result, agents may be responsible for both their actions and omissions, since they are responsible for *not* meeting people's rights as much as they are responsible for *doing* so.

Because duties of assistance require active intervention, specific agents, whether individual or collective, are responsible for fulfilling those duties. In fact, as I shall explain below, human rights theorists generally advocate collective agents like governments and non-governmental organizations to carry out duties of assistance, for two reasons: they have as at least one of their roles to meet people's basic needs, and they have greater power and more resources to carry out this duty than individuals do. Since collective agents are more appropriate duty-bearers than individuals, this situates human rights justifications for beneficence largely within political philosophy.

Consequentialist Duties of Beneficence

Duties of beneficence are also strongly justified by consequentialism. Beneficence, after all, is one of the primary actions required by the consequentialist moral rule to create better states of affairs or better consequences than would occur otherwise (i.e., without our action). Promoting the good in this way generally requires active intervention, in which we act to help or benefit others and increase their level of well-being. The duties of beneficence justified by consequentialism are thus similar to the duties of assistance justified by human rights.[11] The extreme form of consequentialism is utilitarianism, which has as its only moral rule the maximization of utility, or the duty to create the most good possible. Since maximization of utility conflicts with other moral values and commitments such as personal projects and rights,[12] more moderate versions of consequentialism also exist, which share the consequentialist goal of promoting the good or changing states of affairs for the better, mainly by reducing harm and alleviating suffering. Instead of trying to create the *best* consequences possible, the moral goal of moderate forms of consequentialism is the creation of outcomes that are *sufficiently good* or at least *better* than what would exist without the required action.[13]

Because promoting the good in any of these accounts requires weighing alternate outcomes to determine which outcome creates the *most* or at least *sufficient* utility, goods must be commensurable. That is, all goods must be comparable to each other such that they can be weighed against each other. Different *things* may be good, but what *makes* them good, or by what means their goodness is measured, is all the same kind of value. Consequentialists differ on whether this ultimate value should be understood as welfare such as pleasure or happiness, rational preference, or interest.[14] On any of these accounts of the good, poverty constitutes suffering or an objective net harm and so should be eradicated. Since poverty is generally thought of in terms of negative welfare, however, this is the interpretation of consequentialist value most relevant here.

Poverty and related issues—including famine, hunger, and wealth inequality—are favorite topics for utilitarians and other consequentialists since the eradication or at least alleviation of these conditions is a major goal to be promoted. Poverty is bad on any account, whether it is assessed according to its experience of suffering, the way it limits a person's ability to realize her desires, or the way it harms a person's ability to thrive and even to survive. Since the suffering and death caused by severe poverty is bad, relatively affluent individuals have duties to benefit the poor by alleviating their suffering and by preventing or eliminating the harms they experience. For many utilitarians, the lack that poverty consists of is having less than others, making the goal of beneficent action to redistribute resources for some end of equality; for some utilitarians the ideal would be to reach the point of marginal utility. For other consequentialists, the lack that poverty consists of is having a state of welfare that is below an objective standard of adequacy; the goal here is to create sufficient outcomes, so that people have a state of welfare that is at or above this baseline, or simply to create better outcomes that presently exist, so that the poor have comparatively more resources or better well-being than they currently do. The argument by Peter Singer discussed at the beginning of this chapter is one example of how consequentialists argue for duties of beneficence regarding poverty.

Consequentialist accounts often assume that the agents that are responsible are individuals, but this need not be the case. What consequentialism requires is that the agents with the best ability to accomplish the desired ends should do so. If collective agents like governments or corporations are better able to respond to poverty than individuals, then they are the ones that have the duty to do so. What is surprising about consequentialist discussions of global issues like poverty is that collective agents are so infrequently identified as responsible when it appears obvious that they are better equipped to deal with the tragedies that consequentialists often write about.[15] Usually consequentialists refrain from making a judgment about who, specifically, is responsible, beyond saying generically that anyone in a position to help should. The implication is that if an individual thinks that collectives are better able to respond, then her individual responsibility is to ensure that collectives do fulfill their duties. While there is an important point to be made here—about the way that individuals always have *some* responsibility with respect to poverty—it is a vastly insufficient response to the question of identifying agents responsible for carrying out beneficent duties toward global poverty. While consequentialism can have political applications, many consequentialists have disappointingly refrained from making this connection, keeping the theory largely within the realm of moral philosophy.

Virtues of Benevolence

While deontologists see beneficence as a motive for right action, and consequentialists see it as a goal for good action, virtue ethicists see it as an expression of good character. Although deontologists find moral feeling irrelevant to morality, virtue ethicists share with many consequentialists the view that feelings of benevolence are a strong motivation for morality.[16] Despite this seeming similarity, the emphasis on character as opposed to action makes virtue apply to responsibility for global poverty in a very different and somewhat more limited way than the other two ethical theories.

What all the models of beneficent duty discussed so far share is that they describe *impartial* duties involving active intervention to benefit or aid those who are in need. The virtue most analogous to these imperfect duties and most relevant to beneficent action toward the global poor is universal benevolence or humanitarian concern. This virtue is a disposition of concern directed impartially to all others who are in need. The actions that follow from this virtue are similar to those required by deontologists and consequentialists—that is, actions aimed toward people based on no distinguishing feature other than their need of our help and our ability to give it, to be prioritized on factors such as pressing-ness of need, efficacy of our aid, etc.

Like Kantian imperfect duties of beneficence, virtues of universal benevo-lence or care are justified entirely according to the agent rather than the recipi-ent, so again, it is unclear what constitutes poverty and so what constitutes an adequate or appropriate response. As in the deontological approach, these con-siderations are perhaps unfair, since virtue ethics does not care about goals. Nonetheless, guidance in how to direct one's moral attention is still necessary. What makes poverty problematic here is that the poor have fewer resources (or less ability to access those resources), perhaps falling short of some objective standard of adequacy. Moral attention should be given to increase the poor's resources and capabilities. On the virtue account, one's duties of beneficence involve having appropriate dispositions toward the poor, and making appropriate actions of helping; these express the virtues of benevolence and care.

An example of an admittedly extreme form of universal benevolence is ex-istentialist responsibility. Existentialists like Karl Jaspers argue that people have metaphysical guilt for all acts committed in the name of humanity by virtue of being human and a member of the universal, shared human moral community. Responding to the atrocities committed by Nazis in World War II, Jaspers dis-tinguishes between four kinds of guilt, describing metaphysical guilt as follows:

> There exists a solidarity among men as human beings that makes each co-responsible for every wrong and every injustice in the world, especially for crimes committed in his presence or with his knowledge. If I fail to do what-ever I can to prevent them, I too am guilty.[17]

This existential interpretation of collective guilt has been interpreted to mean that "everybody" is responsible for "everything" that occurs in the world. This is justified in the broadest sense of sharing intuitions that one should care about all the members of the universal, shared human moral community.

There is some debate about what universal benevolence, especially in the form of existential responsibility, ultimately means. Jasper's view follows from Jean-Paul Sartre's claim that existential responsibility means that we are respon-sible for everything that we do. Critics of existential responsibility have inter-preted this to mean that we are responsible for everything that occurs because we did not act to prevent it. Yet defenders of existentialist responsibility note that the relevant kind of freedom necessary for responsibility does not require that an agent must be able to control—or prevent—everything that occurs, as an initial reading of the early Sartre would suggest. Rather, freedom is situated, as the later Sartre expounded: we always have choices in how we respond, despite the fact that we are situated within specific circumstances and identities that we do not choose. For example, we largely do not choose what our race, gender, class, or nationality will be; yet being a moral agent requires that we make choices within these un-chosen contexts. An American opposed to an unjust war waged by her president does not choose to be an American, and she cannot control what the ruling powers will do. Yet she can choose how she will react and respond to events. The nature of this response—whether it is virtuous or vicious, whether it generally comes from a good or bad character—is what makes this existential responsibility a form of virtue ethics. Having existential responsibility for all the actions and events that exist thus means that we are responsible for our *reactions* to them, not that we actually *caused* them to exist or that we could have prevented their existence. This accounts for the "forward-looking" emphasis of responsibility as changing bad present conditions for a better future, making this existentialist/virtue account compatible with consequentialist and other models of beneficence.[18]

Some virtue ethicists argue for a different form of beneficence; instead of universal benevolence, they argue for a politicized, or in some cases globalized, virtue of care. For example, Robert Goodin combines the virtue of care with consequentialism to ground beneficent duties in relationships of vulnerability. In contrast to utilitarian accounts of vulnerability as need based on suffering, vulnerability in his model is a specifically relational concept, where one is vulnerable *to* someone or something. Vulnerability is susceptibility to harm that renders one a victim rather than an agent, making one have little or no ability to control the existence or effect of harm, being unable to take action that will either cause or prevent threatened harm. When other agents are in a position in which they do have such power to cause or prevent harm to the vulnerable, they have moral duties to help that are grounded on ability to help as well as sentiments of benevolent concern.[19]

Care can also be "globalized" by broadening the range of moral concern to include at the outermost circles of people with whom the affluent share global relationships, such as sweatshop workers who make their clothes or farmers who grow their food. Acknowledging the responsibilities that global relationships shows that the global poor are not as "distant" as they initially seem. The relevant global relationships are constituted mainly by individuals' roles in the processes of production and consumption in the world's economies, as well as by living under various shared political and economic institutions that distribute benefits and burdens systemically. Although these relationships are weaker than some that are "closer" (such as relationships with one's family members), these global relationships nonetheless ground some level of care.[20] Arguments for globalizing care are also consistent with Peter Singer's recent attempt to show that the world is much smaller than individuals might think, that the affluent are in fact "closer" to people they do not know as a result of the unifying force of globalization. Singer argues that all people share the same air and drinking water, and participate in the same global economy, and are subject to the same international laws and principles; while this over-simplistic understanding of the sharing of these goods ignores differences in how people are benefited and burdened by their varying access to these goods, it is a noble attempt to mobilize intuitions of moral sentiment. Combining both virtue and consequentialist justifications, "closeness" may ground duties of beneficence toward the poor insofar as the poor are needy and the affluent are in a position to help.[21]

Virtue accounts most clearly identify individuals as responsible because only individuals are capable of possessing virtues, and of moral feelings like humanitarian concern and caring. All individuals who are capable should cultivate and act upon these dispositions in order to be good people. The particular duties that individuals have depend on what actions are right for a person to do in exhibiting her virtue. In other words, they are contextual, relative to the particular individual in the particular situation. Exclusively virtue accounts are also exclusively moral, focused on individualized rather than political action, and unable to accommodate collective agents into their framework.

Factors that Differentiate Responsibility: Need, Benefit, and Ability

The duty to help those in need relies on three key concepts: need, benefit (and its contrary, harm), and ability. What gives rise to the duty to respond, according to beneficence models of responsibility, is the *need* of those who would be aided by the actions of others; if the need is great enough, and morally significant enough, someone must have a duty to respond to that need. What justifies an agent having this duty is her *ability* to *benefit* a situation. While those who have greater power to act to create help in meeting people's needs have different or greater duties than those whose power is very limited, most agents have *some* power and so have some duties of beneficence. Need, ability, and benefit are all embedded in the concept of beneficence, and so they are pertinent to all of the justifications of beneficent duties described above.

The different frameworks for justification interpret the terms slightly differently, however. Compare the human rights interpretations of *need, benefit*, and *ability* with the consequentialist interpretations. In the human rights framework, *need* is defined in terms of not having one's human rights met, therefore of being in a condition of falling below the objective threshold of what is necessary for agency and well-being. *Ability* is defined in terms of being able to provide the resources necessary for a person's human rights to be met and so to have the means to promote sufficient agency and well-being. The time-frame involved with ability should be understood as on a spectrum; an agent may be able to meet human rights at a given time through a singular action (such as providing food assistance in a famine), or continuously through regular and on-going behavior (such as adding jobs to a local economy so more people can support themselves). Whether singular action or on-going behavior is an appropriate response—and so which agents have greater responsibilities to meet human rights—depends on what is called for in the context of the particular situation. Beneficence and harm are thus objective measurements, where one's action is measured according to whether it brings a person's well-being above or below (or closer to or farther away from) some objective standard of acceptable well-being and agency. Note that meeting human rights is not necessarily a complete-able goal, as problems that impede this goal are often on-going, and may occur at any time; few or no agents have the power to ensure that all agents have sufficient well-being and agency at all times. Meeting human rights is thus an ongoing project. Agents have duties of assistance insofar as they are capable of taking the actions necessary to work toward meeting people's human rights.

In the consequentialist framework, *need* describes a lack, which constitutes a sufficiently bad state of affairs to justify moral response. Actions are justified according to their net effect on states of affairs; the ability to create better outcomes justifies the duty to do so. Beneficence and harm are comparable notions, where the states of affairs if one does act are compared to the states of affairs if one does not act. In consequentialism, "benefiting" simply means promoting the good, whether this is seen as improving welfare or increasing happiness, or alleviating suffering. While benefit involves increasing utility, "harming" someone means decreasing her well-being or diminishing her relevant state. Harm here does not refer to any notion of *wronging*, although an alternate way to understand harm that does will be discussed in the following chapter. In the consequentialist framework, benefit and harm refer only to net increases or decreases of utility in a state of affairs, or—with respect to poverty—in a person's welfare.

As measurements of change in well-being, harm and benefit compare a person's state based on whether a given action is performed or not. This is a subjunctive rather than a diachronic measurement.[22] In other words, whether I benefit or harm a person in sending her money depends on whether her well-being is increased or decreased, *not* compared to the state she was in before I sent the money to her (a diachronic measurement), but rather compared to the state she would have been in if I had not sent her the money (a subjunctive measurement). Before I sent her the money, she was destitute and depressed. Had I not sent her money, she would have lost her apartment and been homeless. Since I did send her money, she still has her apartment but also is still destitute and depressed. Her current state did not change, but it is better than it would have been had I not acted. Thus, in acting, I benefited her; had I refused her request for money, I would have harmed her by allowing her situation to worsen (at least *prima facie* on this account of harm and in this simplistic example). Harm and benefit are subjunctive measurements of changes in well-being, involving comparison to hypothetical states of affairs rather than to objective standards of well-being.

The way that well-being is measured has major implications in what the scope of duty is. When beneficence and harm are objective measurements of well-being (as in the human rights framework), the actions required for all people to have minimally decent well-being are finite in number, at least theoretically, making the duties to meet their human rights fully dischargeable or complete-able, even if requiring continuous action, and more easily specified. In contrast, when beneficence and harm are subjunctive measurements (as in consequentialist and especially utilitarian frameworks), the actions required for all people to live better than they currently do are seemingly infinite in number, making the duties to create better states of affairs only partially dischargeable because the goal is unreachable, as well as almost impossible to specify. Let me explain. In the extreme form of consequentialism, utilitarianism, all that matters morally is the overall state of affairs and how one contributes to it by harming or benefiting it. Because *all* actions and omissions have some relation to the overall state of affairs, causing net harm or benefit, all actions and omissions are morally relevant, and actions and omissions are considered to be causally morally equivalent. Shelly Kagan calls this position "extremist" because it demands that we consider the moral value of each and every action and omission based on how it contributes to the overall good, whether it increases or decreases it. If inaction causes more suffering than action, then an agent harms others by her inaction. Because omissions contribute to harm in the same way that actions do, agents are responsible for what they do *not* do as much as they are responsible for what they *do* do. Benefit and harm depend only on net change in states of affairs or well-being, not on the *kind* of action or inaction that result in this net change. This is why some strict utilitarians argue that doing evil (such as killing) and allowing evil (such as letting others die) are morally equivalent. In this extremist view, all actions carry moral weight, and all actions can be said to benefit or harm someone, so that one is always and at any time fulfilling or violating her utilitarian duty of beneficence.[23]

Such an extremist position is incompatible with options or constraints on our action. Options are moral permissions to act as we wish, such as to pursue our personal projects and goals. Constraints are limitations on our actions, such as the duties involved with respecting people's rights.[24] When we have options and constraints on our actions, then the duty to help others must be seen not as the sole project of morality, but rather as one duty in balance with other moral duties, such as duties of moral perfection or of non-interference (to be discussed in the next chapter), or even in balance with other kinds of (possibly non-moral) motives and actions. Outside of an extremist view of moral duty, then, the scope of a duty of beneficence is best understood as an imperfect duty, which a person must do as much as possible, but also in balance with other important moral demands.

For most models of beneficence, priority of response depends on who will be helped by it the most. Certainly on a consequentialist account, alleviating the worst suffering can increase *more* utility than alleviating less worse suffering or adding more happiness, when the law of diminishing returns holds. For example, giving $100 to the poorest people in the world probably will add to their well-being substantially more than giving $100 to Bill Gates, since the poorest people can now eat decent food and get some life-saving medicine with their $100 while the same amount is virtually unnoticeable to Bill Gates.[25] In the human rights framework, the people who have the greatest need are those whose human rights are most severely violated, who tend to be the poorest of the poor, justifying more urgent response. Although Kantian and virtue ethics accounts do not offer a clear way to prioritize response, responding to greatest need is a more reasoned approach than relying on contingencies like whim or personal interest. Since our obligations emerge from the moral necessity of responding to people's needs, duties of beneficence are impartial in that they do not favor any one recipient over another based on partial or arbitrary criteria. People are not all equally vulnerable, but they do all have equal potential to be vulnerable based on need, particularly those needs that arise from universal human nature and the basic requirements for human life (e.g., food, shelter, freedom from torture, etc.). Priority of response is determined by the pressingness of need, the degree of vulnerability, or the effectiveness of outcome.

Because what differentiates responsibility as beneficence is the ability that the affluent have to help, along with the need of the poor, agents (whether individuals or collective agents) have beneficent duties to address poverty based on their wealth and power. Broadly speaking, the responsibility for poverty that individuals have *qua* individuals is based on their possessing the trait of affluence. This trait is accidental or contingent; a person could just as easily be in a group of poor people as she is in a group of affluent people. This trait is also non-voluntary; people do not *choose* to be members of affluent groups, as opposed to poor groups, in any morally relevant way. (People may "choose" to be affluent, but this kind of choice is more like a desire than a reason for action aimed at intended consequences.) Yet people are responsible for what actions they perform (or fail to perform) by virtue of sharing this trait of affluence. When individuals are grouped together on account of sharing an accidental or contingent trait like affluence, their grouping is an *aggregate*, because it is the sum of all of the individuals it comprises. Because affluence is not a trait that one voluntarily chooses to possess, the kind of aggregate that groups individuals according to this trait is known as a *random collective*.[26] The responsibility of a random collective is distributive, meaning that all members of random collectives are responsible if they all act or fail to act in the same harmful way; but differentiated forms of action or different reasons for (in-)action, including factors that would count as excuses, may result in differentiated degrees of responsibility. Consistency requires that if we attribute responsibility to one member of a group by virtue of the trait that groups them (here, by virtue of being affluent), then we must logically and morally attribute responsibility to all members (here, to all who are relevantly affluent). Thus, all affluent individuals share in the collective responsibility to help the poor, based on their possessing the accidental, contingent trait of affluence.

In random collectives, concerns about responsibility generally arise when people fail to act in a way that the situation calls for, as a result of being members of their group. In other words, because there is a *group*, people often think that someone else will act, so they fail to act themselves. But because there is a group of people thinking this, often everyone fails to act, and everyone shares distributive responsibility for this failure. For example, an affluent individual may think that because there are other affluent individuals, and because many individuals are *more* affluent than she is, there is no need or less need for her to respond to poverty. But because most other affluent individuals also think this, most affluent individuals will fail to act beneficently toward the poor—and they all share distributive responsibility for this failure.

Many objections can be raised to this distributive responsibility of benefi-cence. One may object that acts and omissions are not equivalent, so that it is incorrect to suggest that affluent individuals are as responsible for "allowing" poverty as they would be if they had caused it. In the following chapter, I ac-knowledge this point, noting that different kinds of actions play distinctive roles in causally contributing to an outcome; but this only shows that different kinds or degrees of responsibility attach to each action, not that *no* responsibility at-taches. A critic may also object that sharing a contingent trait like affluence is not a strong justification for the collective responsibility of a random collective, because such a trait is not chosen and is perceived as "random." Un-chosen and even "random" traits are the basis for many kinds of responsibility, however, including the familial duties we have toward people related to us (such as par-ents, siblings, and children), the relation of which we often do not "choose." Objections that can be raised to specific models of beneficence apply as well. There is no "deontic link" between others' need and *my* particular action in re-sponse.[27] "Extremist" morality that demands we give all of our resources to the point of marginal utility and/or give up all of our personal projects for the sole pursuit of helping others is unreasonable. The need of those who are "closer" seems more pressing than the need of those more "distant." These objections cause critics, especially libertarians and communitarians, to conclude that be-neficence, while certainly not morally wrong, is at most morally praiseworthy and not morally required. In this view, beneficence should be seen as charity, not duty; as supererogatory, not obligatory. I shall consider some of these objec-tions in greater detail below.

What I want to point out here is that while critics raise important objections to individual beneficence, these objections, even if true, do not make the duty of beneficence unjustified. What these objections really aim at is not beneficence *per se*, but rather beneficence in terms of individual action. Most proponents of beneficence mistakenly situate beneficent duties in individual action, rather than in the action of collective agents. What I will argue below is that organized groups like governments and corporations are more effective and have greater ability to address poverty. Especially when they are designed expressly to ad-dress some aspect of poverty, collective agencies share relationships to the poor that are less random or contingent than those of individuals. The duty of benefi-cence is an important, well-justified duty, but it must be conceptualized not in the individualistic context in which philosophers have traditionally discussed it, but rather as a form of collective responsibility instead.

Limitations with Applying
Duties of Beneficence to Global Poverty

There are several potential problems with conceptualizing global responsibility in terms of beneficent duties. One is the problem of insufficient justification mentioned above. Critics of beneficence, especially libertarians and communitarians, argue that beneficence is insufficiently justified as a morally required duty, primarily because the link between the agent of the duty to help and its recipient is weak. While this is a good argument against the morally required duty of individuals, beneficence is still a morally required and justified response for certain collective agents that are designed for, or that have as at least one of their roles, this purpose. The second and third objections argue that models of beneficence rely on an incorrect understanding of the nature of global poverty, making beneficence an insufficient and sometimes inappropriate response. Insofar as agents are causally and structurally independent from a given case of poverty (or other global tragedy), their responsibility toward such a situation is best captured by the concept of beneficence. Yet insofar as poverty has causal and structural factors that implicate potential agents, their responsibility is of a different kind than that of beneficence: it is justified differently, and it may take a different form. This section shows that a certain form of beneficence toward global poverty is strongly justified, but that it is limited in its application.

Insufficiently Justifying Link between Agent and Recipient

One major objection to beneficent duties is that the link between the agent that has the duty to help and the recipient who would be helped is too weak to justify the action of any particular agent. In other words, there is no *necessary* reason why the particular agent that has the duty does so; the fact that she has greater means seems arbitrary and is certainly contingent. Since the ability to help does not entail duties in any logical or necessary way, it is seen as merely pragmatic and insufficiently justifying. In these moral frameworks, beneficence is seen as supererogatory: morally praiseworthy but not morally required; helping is seen as charity rather than duty. There are at least two ways to formulate the objection that there is not a sufficient link between agent and recipient, making beneficence as a morally required duty unjustified. I examine the versions of the objection made from the libertarian and communitarian points of view respectively.

Libertarians argue that there is no "deontic" or necessarily entailing link between the agent of a duty of beneficence and its recipient because the rights claim that gives rise to the duty does not specify, and so therefore does not entail, a particular duty-bearer. This is apparent when we realize that whether on a deontological or consequentialist framework, agents have a duty of beneficence based on their ability to help. This contingent, accidental trait allows these agents to be grouped as a random collective, in which each agent shares distributive collective responsibility—both a duty to help and a liability for failing to help—on account of each having sufficient means to act in the morally required way. But note that in random collectives, it does not matter which particular agent acts, so long as one does, or as long as enough do to cause the desired effect. For libertarians and other critics, this is where the problem lies: while justifications for beneficence attempt to prove that such a duty exists, they can at best show that *someone* has a duty to act, not that anyone in particular does in a necessary, entailed way. If no one in particular is responsible for carrying out beneficence, then it is hard to see how this duty is morally binding.

Another way to think about this is in terms of the seeming absurdity and logical incoherence of a certain class of rights claims that give rise to duties of beneficence. Human rights often do not specify *against whom* they are held, so it appears that they are "generic" rights "held against the world."[28] This appearance of generality results from the universality of human rights, in that all humans can claim these rights. If we assume that rights and duties correspond strictly (which libertarians do), then the duty-bearers responsible for meeting human rights are also universal or cosmopolitan in scope; in other words, all humans have duties to meet all others' rights. But this means that certain kinds of human rights, namely those that require active intervention to meet them, cannot exist. This is because not all agents *can* do something to respond to human rights involving assistance, even if they can claim rights and be beneficiaries of a duty. Certainly any one agent, whether governmental or not, cannot possibly meet all people's needs in an adequate, fair, or equal way.[29] The division of such work among agents would be absurd, as well; imagine dividing the workload equally among all relevant agents, so that all agents, individually, would have a duty to provide a proportional share of the food required to meet people's right to food.[30] Another objection to the active intervention involved with duties of assistance is that this requires using one person for the "benefit" of others—thus violating the second formulation of the Categorical Imperative, and so logically incoherent in a Kantian framework of rights.[31] Of course, this last argument assumes that any active intervention constitutes benefit, which is a highly controversial claim. Nonetheless, these libertarian objections show that a universal duty of assistance (understood in this way) is ambiguous, unenforceable, absurd, or even logically incoherent.

As long as rights claims do not identify particular agents as responsible, there is no logical entailment that any particular agent *is* responsible. But if there are generic rights "against the world," then somehow *all* agents are responsible—and this is nonsensical. For the libertarian, the only rights that are meaningful are those that identify particular agents as responsible—such as contractual rights and duties determined by the particular individuals whom the contract concerns—or those that all individuals are capable of carrying out, such as duties of forbearance (e.g., duties not to torture others). In this framework, there is no justification for the moral requirement of beneficence; it is at most supererogatory.

From the communitarian perspective, there is also no morally sufficient link between agent and recipient of the duty of beneficence, but for a different reason: the two are too "distant" to justify a particular agent having a duty to respond. Critics of universal benevolence and impartial beneficent duties agree with a common intuition that we should prioritize our moral response to those with whom we share closer relationships. In other words, helping "distant strangers" may be morally praiseworthy, but it is either not morally required of us at all—belonging to the category of the supererogatory—or it is simply not as pressing on us as duties we have toward those closer to us. What this "close-ness" means has been interpreted in many ways,[32] but the interpretation most relevant to the present discussion is the "closeness" involved in personal rela-tionships and in our memberships in communities that are constitutive of our identities, which ground benevolent response toward those with whom we share these partial and community memberships.[33]

Partialists see care and moral response as radiating outward in concentric circles, so that we have more responsibilities to those closest to us, such as fam-ily and friends, than our neighbors and various associates (such as people we know through clubs or work), and finally our compatriots. Strangers halfway around the world do not fit in this picture unless they are on the outermost boundary. On this model, the global poor, particularly those living in nonwest-ern nations, are too "distant" or far away from the affluent, particularly those living in western nations, in certain ways. Physically they are halfway around the world. Emotionally, the affluent feel no connection to the poor; they are not one's family or friends or even compatriots, all with whom one shares much closer ties. If the wealthy are not close enough to the poor in terms of partial or nationalist relationships, or even in terms of sharing physical location, then on the partial model of moral response there is not the relevant kind of connection that would ground affluent responsibilities to the poor. Individuals may want to help the poor for personal reasons, perhaps even in the virtue-oriented interest of wanting to be better people; but this makes their actions supererogatory, for there is no basis for having a duty to do so.[34]

What these libertarian and communitarian objections to beneficence share is the concern that the link between the agent who has duties to act beneficently and the recipient who would benefit from these actions is too weak to justify responsibility. Even if the recipient has sufficiently motivating need to suggest that *someone* has duties to respond, there is no basis for claiming that any *par-ticular* person has these duties; there is neither any logical entailment between the needy and the duties of any particular individual, nor a sufficiently close relationship between the poor and the affluent. Although these are strong argu-ments against ascribing duties of beneficence to individuals, these arguments do not apply to ascribing duties of beneficence to collective agents, especially gov-ernments and other non-profit agencies which have as at least one of their roles to meet people's basic needs. Many proponents of beneficence do write as if the appropriate agents for these duties are individuals, inviting these kinds of objec-tions, but there is no reason why the agents for these duties must be individuals when collective agents are in fact more suitable.[35]

If we acknowledge that the most appropriate agents to have duties of be-neficence or assistance are collective rather than individual, then we avoid the problem of insufficient justification on account of the weak link between agent and recipient. Let me start by answering the libertarian objection. Generic or vague rights are indeed empty. In order to be meaningful, human rights must be specific enough to identify agents of responsibility. But critics of duties of assistance misunderstand the nature of the duty-bearers responsible for fulfilling these duties. The fact that rights may be claimed by all humans does not imply that all humans have duties that correlate with them. Nor does this universality of need or interest imply that the appropriate duty-bearers should be *individual* humans, even if individual humans are the appropriate candidates for right-claimants, for there is nothing logically entailed by the kind of candidates eligible for *claiming* that implies anything about the kind of candidates required for *fulfilling duties*. The fact that human rights can be claimed by individuals does not entail that individuals, or even humans, are the necessary or appropriate duty-bearers, as libertarians assume. In fact, libertarian objections to beneficence can be avoided almost entirely if duty-bearers of human rights are specified as collective rather than individual agents.[36]

The appropriate agents of responsibility for certain human rights, particularly those associated with assistance, are collective agents. These collective agents include governments (public, political bodies), non-governmental organizations (non-profit associations operating in the sphere of civil society), or corporations (private economic bodies). In order to be *agents*, collectives must meet the requirements for agency, such as having the abilities to make choices, to carry out action, and to identify and communicate claims, interests, or needs. Collectives that meet these conditions are *conglomerates*, characterized by having decision-making and action-delegating procedures that allow them to choose and act as agents in the relevant way.[37]

There are two reasons for locating responsibility for meeting human rights in collectives. First, this serves a prudential purpose, in that collectives are better *able* to fill these duties. They have greater resources, more "arms" with which to act (i.e., individuals occupying roles within them and therefore able to act on their behalf), and more "heads" to share ideas in trying to acquire more knowledge and make better decisions. Second, focusing on collective agents is politically justified, since the *role* of many collectives, including governments, is to provide access and security to certain goods.[38]

Now let me address the communitarian objection. The problem with advocating partial duties in opposition to impartial duties is its absurdity. Good versions of all major ethical theories make arguments for impartial beneficence as one kind of duty, not in opposition but rather in addition to other kinds of duties. Just as impartial duties do not exhaustively describe all the kinds of duties individuals have, neither do partial duties. Although we do have partial duties to those with whom we share "close" relationships, we still have impartial duties of beneficence that are justified for different reasons than those justifying partial duties. The reason why there is this debate between partial and impartial duties really has to do with the problem of how to resolve the inevitable conflicts between them that will arise. Although I will say more in the final chapter of this book about how to balance the many different duties that individuals have, the answer that I want to give here is that many of these conflicts can be avoided (or at least described very differently) if we reconceptualize the relevant duties of beneficence as belonging to collective rather than individual agents.

As I said above, collectives like governments, United Nations agencies, non-governmental organizations, and non-profit charities have duties of beneficence because it is their role to do so, and because they have the capability to do so. The duties that collectives have may be aimed at certain groups of people who share some relationship with the collective—such as being a citizen of a specific government—but they are otherwise impartial, based entirely on need. When collectives are primarily responsible for beneficence, the nature of the duties that individuals have changes; individuals are not necessarily, or most directly, responsible for meeting other people's needs, but they are then responsible for ensuring that the relevant collectives fulfill *their* duties of beneficence. Individuals' duties are therefore usually more political in nature, making sure that government agencies carry out beneficence duties and generally act justly; their duties also require them to act responsibly in their roles within these collectives, and to create collectives for the purposes of meeting people's needs where necessary. Of course, individuals do not have these duties to *all* governments and other collectives, only those under which they are citizens, or those with which they share another morally or politically relevant relationship.

The most important duties that individuals have with respect to beneficence, then, are not the agent-neutral (impartial, universal) duties to which libertarians and communitarians object, but rather agent-relative duties (duties to particular others, at least to particular collective agents or institutional structures) to ensure that beneficence gets carried out. I shall discuss the difference between agent-neutral and agent-relative duties in greater detail in the following chapter, but here I want to point out that even in the context of beneficence agents have the agent-relative duties that libertarians and communitarians find justifiable. What provides the link between agent and recipient is the relationship that an individual has to the government (or non-governmental organization or even corporation) that itself has the duty of beneficence. Regardless of whether individuals themselves have duties of beneficence (which any ethical framework other than libertarianism or communitarianism supports), they do have other duties that are agent-relative, aimed at ensuring that collectives fulfill *their* duties of beneficence.

The next level of the communitarian objection to beneficence toward "distant strangers," of course, is to question why collective agents like governments have duties of beneficence toward the poorest in the world, particularly to those who do not live under their own laws. Why should the American government, for example, give aid to starving people in Ethiopia? The communitarian tends to take a nationalistic stance that the American government, for example, should give aid only, or at least firstly, to the American poor, i.e. to those within its own boundaries. The problem with this approach is that it oversimplifies the nature and causes of poverty, promoting a form of isolationism that assumes that poverty is caused within one's own boundaries while wealth is created in the same way. In a global world, this is absolutely false. I explain this further when I discuss the third problem with applying beneficence to global poverty; in the next section I show that beneficence, contrary to its aims, actually often causes more harm than good.

Dangers of Perpetuating Harm through Active Intervention

One concern about conceptualizing responsibility as "helping" is that those agents that are in a position to help often perpetuate the same structures that cause harm to other agents. In other words, the very act of helping may keep people in a state of vulnerability because it preserves the *status quo* and allows or even encourages the same power relationships that put some in a position of vulnerability and others in a position of power.[39] Not only does this not *reduce* harm, but it actually *promotes* it. There are at least three ways that perpetuation of harm may come about.

First, harm may arise from essentialism and paternalism regarding who makes assessments of poverty and proposes solutions to it, and why. Models of beneficent duty assume that those able to help should do so, in whatever way they see as necessary, sometimes regardless of the desires of those who would be helped, especially if one's desire is seen as conflicting with one's interest. This approach is essentialist because those who have the means to help—the wealthy and powerful—use their own knowledge about what constitutes harm, what aspects of poverty count as harm, and what actions are required in response, generalizing these answers for others who may have radically different views. This approach is paternalistic because all the decisions about what needs helping, and what is the appropriate state of affairs that should be aimed at, are made by those already in a position of power on behalf of those with less power. The powerful affluent act paternalistically by speaking for those they wish to help, as if they know what is in poor people's interests better than the poor themselves.

Paternalism is a problem for several reasons. First, it is disrespectful to the people one would help. Moral and political philosophy emphasizes the value of autonomy and self-determination so much because we think that people and groups of people have the right to choose their own ends and the means to achieve them, at least in some circumstances and at least to some extent. When the powerful act on behalf of the powerless, making essentialist assumptions about what poverty involves and what response it requires, they do not account for potential differences in perspective, and they do not respect the right to self-determination by the marginalized. Moreover, paternalistic approaches compound harm by perpetuating dependence relationships rather than encouraging self-determination, and by justifying political coercion.[40]

Paternalism is also contrary to utilitarian aims because it easily leads to harm, both through disrespect and by ignoring local knowledge. Ignoring local knowledge tends to lead to policies that are ineffective or that actually cause greater harm than the harm they are supposed to alleviate. For example, the

Green Revolution did not decrease hunger as touted, and it may have actually worsened local agricultural production as planting mass crops and spraying intensive pesticides weakens the soil for future use.[41] Even a utilitarian like John Stuart Mill supported general self-determination on such grounds, as agents know their own interests best and can pursue them better when they are allowed the liberty to do so.[42]

In an attempt to avoid paternalism, people sometimes advocate non-intervention. After all, the easiest way to avoid speaking for those with less power is to not respond to "their" issues at all. Arguments for non-intervention tend to rely on the value of being autonomous and non-dependent. Foreign aid can seem like "handouts" that promote perpetual dependency and discourage technological innovation and economic development. Critics of paternalism thus tend to advocate some form of "self-help," where wealthy nations stop giving intrusive and ineffective foreign aid and instead let the poor find their own ways into the global economy.[43]

Blanket non-intervention can be just as problematic as paternalistic intervention, however, in perpetuating harm. For one thing, non-intervention can present the same problems of disrespect and ineffectiveness as paternalism does. Self-help is only possible when agents have some resources with which to help themselves; when they do not, some form of aid may be necessary. The poorest in the world lack even the barest of resources with which to trade or innovate, making the first steps of involvement in the global economy impossible.[44] Non-intervention—even in the laudable attempt to avoid paternalism—allows grave harms to occur, often unjustifiably.

Non-intervention is not only justified as a way to avoid paternalism, but it is also often excused by simple weariness. When making beneficent responses, people often focus on the most "exciting" causes, cases that are highlighted in the media and typically that are short-term, emergency based. Problems that are long-term and chronic, such as chronic poverty and hunger, are typically ignored by affluent individuals because the problems appear inevitable, and they exist like wallpaper in the minds of the affluent, present but ignored. People may think, "Oh, they're *still* starving in Africa? They always have been and always will be." Problems that seem especially distant almost reaffirm the necessity of their tragedy.[45] To be truly helpful, therefore, beneficent actions need to be aimed at the people who need them most; these are people who are frequently not visible, whose cause may be the least exciting, and whose problems are the most chronic.[46]

The fear of acting paternalistically may make a person feel as if she has to choose between "colonial interference" and "callous indifference," neither of which is morally desirable.[47] But both paternalism and blanket non-intervention can be avoided. This middle approach can be found if the affluent engage in dialogue with the poor about their needs, a proposal that is perfectly compatible with all of the ethical models discussed here. Requests for help by those who would be aided, such as requests that Rwandans made to the United Nations and to particular European nations for help combating genocide in 1994, and similar requests by Sudanese with respect to the present genocide, are examples of situations in which beneficent action is appropriate to give without running into a danger of paternalism.

In addition to paternalistic and blanket non-intervention approaches, a third way that harm may be perpetuated is by focusing solely or primarily on short-term views of the problem and its solution. Moral philosophers tend to address poverty by focusing on small-scale, emergency relief type efforts, implying that such efforts will reduce poverty when in fact they will barely make a difference. This is *not* to say these efforts do not make *any* difference. But the difference is not nearly as significant as the goal of helping others demands. Certainly sending money to relief organizations may help in the short term; if a dollar saves a person from dying today by giving her food to get through the next couple of days, then it has some positive effect. Saving a few people from dying today in order to die tomorrow is not a long-term solution, however. The underlying causes of situations like poverty must be examined and addressed in order for their reduction or elimination to be possible. In particular, causal and structural factors—including the reasons why some agents have the means to help and others are in such a position of vulnerability—must be examined. For example, affluent countries that send foreign aid to poor countries *have* money to send in aid partly as a result of trading practices that give them an unfair advantage in the global market. Had the market been fairer, the rich countries might have less aid to give, but the poor countries might need less aid. This suggests that principles of justice that examine the distribution of burdens and benefits are just as important as, if not more so than, concerns about protecting the vulnerable and providing for the needy.

This point is also illustrated at the individual level. Peter Unger makes the absurd suggestion that a true utilitarian should try to make as much money as possible, in whatever field she can, in order to have more money to give to the needy.[48] What makes this proposal absurd is that it does not require examining the structure that underlies which jobs are well-paid, who is needy, and why the economic system is so unequal. If I work in a job that exploits people, then I participate in the structures that cause some people to be needy. For example, if I try to make a lot of money by selling diamond jewelry from Africa, I perpetuate a system that uses child labor and encourages civil wars, and I influence people to buy unnecessary goods for artificially inflated prices. Even if this job provides me with a lot of money to give to those needy, that doesn't somehow cancel out the injustice they suffer from the systems in which I participate. What is crucially missing from beneficent models of duty is a broader framework for understanding the causes of justice.

These concerns are compatible with beneficent action. After all, beneficent duties are intended truly to help, not to harm. Yet those who would fulfill these duties must be very careful that in doing so, their actions truly are beneficent and not inadvertently perpetuating harm. A good model of beneficence, then, must be combined with other models of responsibility that better account for causal and structural factors in poverty, so that people can see how they should direct their actions in order to benefit truly.

Inadequate Conceptualization of Poverty

The dangers of perpetuating harm stem at least partly from the way that models of beneficent duty conceptualize what is problematic about poverty, and consequently what the relationship is between the affluent who would help and the poor who are in a position of vulnerability. Beneficence models conceptualize poverty as a mere bad end state, denying the relevance of causal and structural factors. This suggests that poverty is a somewhat self-contained condition, in which those who would respond share no relationship to the poor other than ability to help and feelings of benevolence. Insofar as poverty results from moral (bad) luck such as natural disaster, or local factors such as civil war, any response to poverty by the non-poor does indeed require active intervention of the type described by beneficence models of responsibility. For example, the poverty that results from a natural disaster such as Hurricane Katrina, which hit the southeast of the United States in 2005, or the earthquake that shook the region of Kashmir (between Pakistan and India) in 2005, or the tsunami that hit South Asia (particularly Indonesia and Sri Lanka) in 2004, naturally invokes sympathy and benevolence. What average affluent individuals can and should do in response is best captured by the concept of beneficence, or of helping the poor, such as by sending money to relief organizations or volunteering time to repair the devastation. In the United States, many people did do such actions in response to several natural disasters, but especially Hurricane Katrina. Americans were probably more motivated to respond to Hurricane Katrina than to the Pakistani earthquake for partial reasons, for those suffering seemed "closer" insofar as they shared a national identity. The active intervention that people did in order to try to alleviate the suffering of people they did not know personally, whose suffering was caused by natural factors largely beyond human control, exemplified the appropriateness of beneficent response in certain kinds of situations.

And yet if we look deeper to the causes of the suffering ravaged by Hurricane Katrina, the analysis is not so simple. Hurricane Katrina *was* a natural disaster—but it was not *merely* a natural disaster. It was a disaster that was allowed to cause so much damage because the levees that held by hurricane waters were unprepared for a hurricane of its magnitude. This is morally significant because the levees were capable of being prepared for stronger hurricanes, but human choices in allocating infrastructure resources prevented this preparation from occurring. While humans did not *cause* Hurricane Katrina, in other words, they were able to prevent its extreme devastation and yet they failed to do so. There is also some debate about whether human activity has contributed to the extreme weather conditions that included Hurricane Katrina as well as other fearsome hurricanes, tsunamis, and earthquakes of recent years, through the process of global warming whereby human-made pollutants are warming the earth's atmosphere and thus changing the climate. While I do not want to offer a conclusive argument about the role played by causal factors such as contributing to devastation or failing to prevent its worst consequences, nor about the kinds of actions and omissions that are causally significant and so morally relevant, I do want to suggest that some such causal analysis is important to understanding what is involved with particular situations of poverty and what response is therefore appropriate. Beneficence is appropriate to the extent that poverty is somewhat self-contained and caused by bad luck, physical geography such as isolationism and/or scarce natural resources, natural disaster, and/or local political factors. But to the extent that it results from causes that implicate people beyond those suffering—such as agents that act in faulty or wrongful ways, especially when they could have done otherwise, or global economic and political structures that encourage faulty or wrongful behavior—the responsibility involved cannot be captured merely by beneficence.

The problem with both non-intervention and paternalistic beneficent action can also be understood more deeply in terms of the moral relevance of causal and structural factors. Proponents of beneficent duties often assume that issues like poverty belong primarily to those who experience them directly, i.e. those living under the conditions of poverty, suggesting that poverty has solely local or national causes such as natural disaster, inept farming techniques, corrupt government leadership, or bad cultural values. This framework ignores transnational, structural causes such as past colonialism or military interference and current economic or political policies imposed by foreign governments and transnational organizations. Providing short-term solutions like relief aid, rather than addressing underlying causes, frames poverty in the same problematic way. Those who are not themselves poor are often implicated in the causal structures that create or exacerbate poverty, as I explain in the next two chapters, and they also often feel its effects. (For example, the wealthy in the United States cannot escape increased homelessness, drug problems, and crimes that result from American poverty, as much as they try to enclave themselves from these social ills.) The paternalistic approach assumes causal independence, allowing powerful agents to evade causal responsibility for poverty while appearing to be generous benefactors. But the non-intervening approach, even when done with the good motives of not wishing to usurp power from those who already have less power, is just as problematic. By perpetuating the false belief that problems like poverty have nothing to do with them, this approach lets the affluent off the hook of responsibility unjustifiably.[49]

On any account of *badness*, poverty is bad. That something must be done in response is virtually uncontroversial, as Singer rightly points out. But what it is that *makes* poverty bad, and so what must be done in response and why, is open to debate. The main problem with beneficent models of responsibility for poverty is that they conceptualize many cases of poverty wrongly and so justify responsibility inaccurately. This is not to say that they do not justify some correct actions that individuals are required to do; but insofar as poverty is more than a mere bad state of affairs, these models justify these actions for the wrong reasons. Nor is this to say that acting out of beneficence is somehow morally wrong; if beneficence motivates one to act, and one's action truly does benefit the poor (and is not simply a misguided attempt at making the doer feel good about herself), then that is a wonderful consequence of arguments for beneficence like Singer's. But acting for the right reasons also matters in morality; good reasons provide stronger justification to those who are not persuaded by intuitions of care and moral concern, and they guide action better by specifying more clearly what it is that an agent must respond to and why. If my actions have been contributing to global poverty without my being aware of it, it is not enough for me to simply care about the global poor and send money to Oxfam; I must understand the causal relationship between my actions and others' experiences, and try to change my actions based on that understanding. Poverty *is* a bad state of affairs, but it is *also* frequently the result of causal and structural processes in which individual agents play a part, and a good model of responsibility must account for this adequately.

Applicability of Beneficence Models of Responsibility

For reasons given above, I am generally skeptical of arguments for beneficent duties. While I agree with Singer's argument that we ought to do more about poverty than we currently do, I find philosophers' debates about what the scope of duty should be, their preoccupation with the agent rather than the needy,[50] their tendency toward insufficient short-term, small-scale efforts, and their often paternalistic and moralistic tone all to be misguided and sometimes offensive. But bad arguments should not overshadow *all* arguments for beneficent duties. After all, it is true that we ought to do more than we currently do for the global poor. We just need a better way to conceptualize what it is that we ought to do.

One place where beneficent duties seem appropriate is in the arena of basic healthcare, especially vaccines or other measures to prevent diseases that have been nearly eradicated in affluent nations. Vaccines that people in developed nations take for granted, such as for polio and measles, are hard if not impossible to come by in the poorest regions of the world. People in the poorest areas of Third World countries are subject to diseases like tuberculosis, malaria, river blindness, trachoma, and intestinal worms—all of which are nearly unheard of in present-day First World countries. Because it is almost impossible to attribute the transmission of disease to any agent's actions or to any particular institutional arrangement, except in indirect and complicated ways, it is reasonable to conceptualize the problem of disease and its relationship to poverty as a bad state of affairs that requires beneficence in response.

One example of beneficent response to disease is the current attention paid to malaria, and the attempts to protect Africans from malaria-carrying mosquitoes using bed nets sprayed with insecticide. The prevention of malaria deaths became a priority in the fight against poverty in the late 1990s and early 2000s when people became aware of the relative ease and low cost of providing bed nets. United Nations Children's Fund (UNICEF) and partner organizations such as Nothing But Nets and The Global Fund to Fight AIDS, Tuberculosis, and Malaria made the distribution of bed nets a priority in African nations; in the United States, Jeffrey Sachs, Columbia University's Earth Institute, and U2 singer Bono's Red Campaign together popularized the cause. The economic value of investing in simple disease prevention measures is apparent when the cost expenditures are low compared to the benefit of saving lives, allowing for economic development that is only possible when a region's people are healthier. Since disease plays such a huge role in creating and exacerbating poverty in places such as Africa, some economists such as Jeffrey Sachs believe that some of the most pressing need for poverty relief is to combat disease, such as by providing Africans with mosquito nets and spraying DDT to combat malaria.[51]

Addressing African poverty by working on eradicating disease is an example of what Sachs calls "clinical economics," which involves making an economic diagnosis of a country or community, similar to the way a physician would. This diagnosis requires a differential analysis of the relevant economic problems, noting particularities that make one situation unique—even if in other ways similar—to another. Aid and other means of economic development should come in packages designed specifically for the economy at hand, hitting several aspects of that economy so as to combat poverty on multiple levels; in Africa, measures to prevent the transmission of disease would play a pivotal role, although certainly other means to address poverty, such as increasing access to education and building infrastructure, are also necessary. No good economist would ever claim that bed nets (or vaccines, or other disease prevention measures) alone will solve the problem of poverty; nor will education, infrastructure, good governance, the cessation of regional wars, or the elimination of trade in arms, drugs, oil, and other highly profitable goods that contribute to war and poverty. None of these *alone* will alleviate poverty, but addressing a group of such factors together will make a significant difference. Similarly, aid should never be seen as a sole solution to poverty, but it plays an important role along with other means of economic development.[52]

The responsibility that those advocating bed nets and the like is generally consequentialist, because the focus is on the *ability* that affluent nations and individuals have to give the aid that is needed. Some proponents urge individuals to make contributions through charitable donations (such as donating money to Nothing But Nets) or purchases (such as by buying "red" items like cell phones in which a portion of the proceeds benefits the Global Fund through the Red Campaign). These actions locate responsibility in the individual, suggesting a form of distributive responsibility that affluent individuals have by virtue of sharing the accidental trait of being relatively wealthy. These actions thus invite the criticism described above that is often directed at individualistic duties of beneficence. What groups like the Red Campaign try to do is show that individuals can make some difference in addressing poverty, which is important so that individuals feel that working on a global problem like poverty is worthwhile. The worry is that individuals will send their $10 or buy their red cell phone, pat themselves on the back, and feel that they have done their part to end global poverty. Individual action is important, but it is only the beginning of response, not the end. Individuals should see these actions as a good entry into global justice work, and then focus their attention more broadly toward understanding the political and structural nature of poverty, its interlocking and interdependent causes, and their roles in ensuring their governments respond properly and adequately.

A more effective way to situate beneficent duties is in collective agents such as governments, which have greater ability to meet people's needs through foreign aid. Political and economic theorists like Jeffrey Sachs recognize the value of locating this kind of responsibility in governments rather than individuals, because governments have significantly greater means to make a difference. Moreover, giving aid fulfills an important role for governments, not only in terms of being a good neighbor or engaging in mutual reciprocity, but also in terms of maintaining peace and security in foreign relations. These are all good reasons for the United States to invest in foreign aid, which it does, but at a much lower level than seems reasonable. The U.S. is one of the richest countries in the world and also one of the stingiest, contributing less money to foreign aid per GNP than any other, only 0.15% or 0.18% of GNP, depending on which investments are counted. In 2000, the U.S. (along with other wealthy nations) pledged its commitment to the Millenium Development Goals, which would halve poverty by 2015, by giving 0.7% of its GNP in direct financial aid or official development assistance. If wealthy nations such as the U.S. simply followed through on their promises they would probably be able to provide enough money to eradicate the worst cases of poverty in the world. This would also go a long way toward meeting the human rights of the poorest of the world, whose rights are often disproportionately (compared to those who are wealthy) thwarted by poverty.[53]

Critics may object to these beneficence proposals in all the ways described above, such as by arguing that ability and need do not provide sufficient justification for affluent agents to have particular duties toward the global poor, or that beneficent action is necessarily paternalistic and promotes dependency relationships; besides these ethical concerns, critics may also point out that measures such as providing bed nets to combat malaria face distribution problems that make good intentions ineffective. Affluent people feel comfortable rallying around a cause such as providing bed nets because it is an easy and inexpensive solution to lethal disease; with just $10, you, too, can feel like you are helping someone from dying by providing a tangible item like an insecticide-coated bed net. But if the solution sounds too good to be true, it probably is. Bed nets have been bought and collected, and then looted before they made it to their intended distribution sites, and sold on the black market for much higher prices than poor people can afford to pay; those who buy them often use them not to prevent malaria but for a variety of other reasons, including fishing nets and wedding veils.

In other words, bed nets frequently end up going toward wealthier people who can afford to pay the marked up prices, and the poorest people once again go without. Economists like Bill Easterly point out that high demand for a good that has low supply—or at least inconsistent distribution (partly due to the lack of infrastructure identified by Sachs)—naturally leads to black market activity. Good intentions to help the poor tend to be thwarted by the reality of the marketplace. In order to work with (rather than against) the forces of the marketplace, Easterly proposes charging all people, even poor people, for goods like bed nets. Then people will have an incentive to save their money for a good they desire, and they will have an incentive to use the good as it is intended, rather than selling it themselves on the black market, for instance, in order to make some money to be used for something else. If all bed nets are sold, rather than given away, poor people will be more invested in their distribution and use, and this will reduce black market activity and increase distribution and use by poor people. Purchasing power gives people incentives and makes them feel invested in what they buy—in what they find worthwhile to buy. Goods that must be bought have more value to people than goods that are given away.[54]

Easterly makes a good argument for why giving away bed nets can thwart the good intentions of those who wish to help, but the problem of how the poorest people in the world can afford even to buy the cheapest, most basic goods remains. People who are literally starving to death have no money and no goods to trade. Putting basic goods in the marketplace may make sense in areas where people are poor but not destitute; but where people are destitute, they may need handouts or small sums of money to buy the basic goods that are in the marketplace. Moreover, regions with this extreme poverty usually do not have the economic infrastructure to provide jobs to people who would like to work to earn the money to pay for such goods; the ability to buy even basic goods requires economic development that is beyond the capacity of those who are starving to death to implement. Easterly does seem to acknowledge that beneficence plays a role, however, as he admits that there are some cost-effective uses of foreign aid, including de-worming drugs, pesticides used to control malaria, vaccines, and dietary supplements for basic nutrients like iron, vitamin A, and iodine. However, he is also careful to note that "none of these are keys to development according to some utopian scheme," which is how he strangely characterizes Sachs' proposals; rather, these "are just modest interventions that make people's lives better."[55] What this demonstrates is that even a libertarian critic of "utopian" arguments for beneficence can agree that there is *some* role for beneficence in the form of foreign aid.

Critics may also object that providing bed nets—assuming that they do work to prevent disease transmission and death at least to some extent—is too simple and easy of a solution, something with which Sachs and other advocates would be the first to agree. Or, more broadly speaking, critics may object that whatever the target goals a proponent of aid sets, those goals are not high enough. For example, Thomas Pogge, skeptical that the Millenium Development Goals are worthy goals, would argue that Sachs' proposal for the U.S. to donate

0.7% of its GNP in aid is not strong enough. Analyzing the statistics that are used in making the goals to "halve" poverty by 2015, Pogge shows that the numbers are skewed to make very modest goals sound more significant than they are by relying on old data, considering proportions (a comparative notion) rather than actual numbers of people living in poverty, and undercounting the poor. The Millenium Development Goals to reduce poverty are so weak they are hardly worth celebrating. After all, he argues, if the United Nations created goals to reduce the rates of various genocides (whether in Nazi Germany or more recently in Rwanda or Sudan) by half over a span of fifteen years, people would not celebrate such a plan; they would be horrified at its insignificance.[56] I think that Sachs would ultimately agree with Pogge's argument, but he is making the typical beneficent appeal, following Peter Singer, that while very strong goals are ideal, even meeting modest goals would be better than the current situation. I am certain that Sachs agrees that the complete eradication of severe poverty is ideal, but if wealthy governments would *at least* fulfill the promises they made, however modest those goals are, that alone would go some way toward alleviating poverty.

Any argument for beneficence seems to encounter the same problems: it is either too strong (not proving a deontic link between agent and recipient that satisfies libertarian or communitarian justifications for response) or too weak (not doing enough to actually solve the problem). But in proposing that governments are responsible for carrying out these duties of beneficence in response to dire need, Sachs does a better job of identifying particular agents that are responsible for specific reasons. He is also more practical about how this responsibility should be carried out by suggesting actions which would help in particular cases of poverty, but noting that which actions are effective depends on the particular situation at hand. From one perspective, providing bed nets to combat malaria is an easy, inexpensive, practical, and highly effective solution to disease transmission which should be as noncontroversial as providing vaccines or salts to prevent death from diarrhea. From another, however, all beneficent actions are suspect. Even ignoring the potential ethical problems identified above of perpetuating harm by promoting paternalism and ensnaring poor people in a cycle of dependency, beneficence often does not work economically, as good intentions usually get thwarted by marketplace forces. Whether an action like providing bed nets is appropriate depends on the particular situation; as Sachs notes in proposing a "clinical economics" approach, the specific factors causing or exacerbating poverty and the particular market forces that are relevant must be accounted for. In some situations, giving away bed nets might be the best approach to reducing malaria deaths, if the problem of how to distribute them effectively—overcoming bad infrastructure and avoiding their theft and sale on the black market—can be addressed. In other situations, selling bed nets for a nominal fee might be more effective, allowing poor people to be more invested in their health, but only if they have the means to afford such basic goods. Bed nets are not a simple solution to malaria deaths. But they are one important part of the package of changes needed to alleviate poverty in Africa. Their effective use requires the differential analysis described by Sachs as "clinical economics."

So What Should Affluent Individuals Do?

One of the reasons why Sachs' argument for beneficence is more persuasive than many philosophers' is that he attributes responsibility to governments rather than to individuals. This returns us to the original concern of this book: what should the affluent individual do with respect to global poverty? The advantage of the approach taken by moral philosophers who focus on individual responsibility, as most who argue for beneficent duties do, is that they provide a clear answer to this question. More needs to be said about how those who focus on government or other collective responsibility can answer the question.

There are two ways to understand the kinds of responsibilities individuals have with respect to beneficence: the responsibilities they have *qua* individuals, and the responsibilities they have vis-à-vis governments and other agencies that have collective responsibilities. The responsibilities individuals have *qua* individuals are the moral duties they have as moral agents to act rightly. Duties of beneficence are justified as Kantian imperfect duties to aid others as much as one is able, as consequentialist duties to create better outcomes, and as virtues to be benevolent toward all of humanity and to care about all with whom one shares global relationships. In only a couple of ethical worldviews— libertarianism and communitarianism—is beneficence not justified as a duty, but even in these beneficence is usually supererogatory, still morally praiseworthy if not obligatory. There are strong reasons, then, to act beneficently as a moral agent, and even more reasons to carry out other kinds of duties with respect to beneficence, as I discuss below. The actions that beneficence and benevolence require include the typical ones of giving money to charities and volunteering time with worthy organizations that help the poor.

Since any given individual is unable to "solve" poverty, beneficent duties are only partially dischargeable—but individuals are responsible for their portion of contributing to carrying out the overall responsibility of helping the poor. Since there are too many actions that are needed for all aspects of poverty to be addressed, individuals also have discretion in choosing which beneficent actions they will perform. Individuals cannot give money or volunteer time to all worthy charities, so they must choose which ones they will support. Individuals tend to support charities that are "closest" to them in partial, emotional, or physical ways; this is unfortunate, because the people who are worst off tend to be the least glamorous, and have the least personal or physical connection to the affluent who are in a position to help. If a United Nations organization such as UNICEF could make a list of the neediest groups of people and the organizations in the best position to help them, this would provide a way for affluent individuals as well as collective agents to prioritize their beneficent actions toward those groups of people, and the organizations that could help them, more appropriately.

Beyond personal acts of charity like sending money to Oxfam, the most important acts that individuals can do with respect to beneficent duties is to ensure that governments fulfill *their* beneficent duties. This means that individuals have duties *qua* citizens to educate themselves and others on political issues particularly surrounding poverty, to be informed voters, to let their views be known to their government representatives, to run for political office themselves, and to fulfill their role responsibilities where relevant (i.e., if they are themselves governmental officials, to make decisions that help the poor). I shall discuss the nature of these political duties at greater length in following chapters as I say more about the responsibility of collective agents with respect to global poverty. Here I want to make clear that both personal acts of beneficence, and political duties to ensure that governments and other collectives carry out duties of beneficence, are important and morally required ways for individuals to carry out their responsibilities with respect to beneficence.[57] While changing institutions to be more just is a necessary response to poverty, charity or beneficence also has its place—as long as it is reconceptualized as a fundamentally collective response, requiring individual action for the sake of enabling the collective to carry out its duty.

Conclusion

Individuals have beneficent duties *qua* individuals and *qua* their institutional identity as citizens. Critics are wrong to see beneficent actions as supererogatory; they are morally required for both individual and collective agents. Collectives like governments and corporations are better able to carry out duties of beneficence more effectively, but individuals are responsible for making sure that collectives do their job, as well as for contributing their portion of the distributive responsibility that all affluent individuals share.

To avoid paternalism and universalism, it is appropriate for beneficent action to be aimed locally, as long as global connections are made as well. It is important to see the broader context of one's actions, and to understand the threads that connect the homeless people in one's own neighborhood with the starving people in a Third World country. Through this broader understanding, individuals and collective agencies can act in conjunction with others throughout the world, making connections and learning from others about how to help those in need.

As moral agents, individuals should donate money and time to global organizations such as Oxfam or UNICEF and/or their local food bank or homeless shelter. To avoid neglecting the worst off, individuals might try to respond at both local and global levels, for example volunteering time at local charities and sending money to both local and global organizations. The scope of this duty of donation is imperfect: individuals cannot do these actions constantly, and they can never complete the duty (i.e., there is always more money and time that can be given, or that is needed)—but they must nevertheless do as much as they are able, given the demands of their various other obligations and other constraints.

Individuals have an additional kind of duty with respect to beneficence. In fact, even if individual beneficence is seen as charity rather than duty—even if the justification of these actions as morally required rather than supererogatory is unpersuasive—individuals still have duties with respect to beneficence, namely duties *qua* their institutional identities as citizens. These duties involve making sure their government fulfills *its* duties of beneficence, and participating in the design of appropriate agencies to carry out these duties, especially the duties that are characterized as duties of assistance in the human rights framework. These duties shall be explained in greater detail in the final chapter. The most appropriate agents for fulfilling beneficent duties are collective agents such as governments, but this does not let individuals off the hook of responsibility; it only adds another dimension to the responsibility that affluent individuals have toward global poverty.

Notes

1. See Robert E. Goodin, *Protecting the Vulnerable: A Reanalysis of Our Social Responsibilities* (Chicago and London: University of Chicago Press, 1985), 125-34; Iris Marion Young, "Responsibility and Global Justice: A Social Connection Model," *Social Philosophy and Policy* 23, no. 1 (January 2006), 22-23; Iris Marion Young, "Responsibility and Global Labor Justice," *Journal of Political Philosophy* 12, no. 4 (December 2004), 121-22.

2. Peter Singer, "Famine, Affluence, and Morality," *Philosophy and Public Affairs* 1 (1972), 229-43.

3. For example, see Peter Unger, *Living High and Letting Die: Our Illusion of Innocence* (New York: Oxford University Press, 1996), 3-4.

4. John Arthur points out the lack of moral force of the weak version of Singer's moral principle; see John Arthur, "Rights and the Duty to Bring Aid," in *World Hunger and Morality: Second Edition*, ed. William Aiken and Hugh LaFollette (Upper Saddle River, NJ: Prentice Hall, 1996), 42. In his earliest work on the topic, Singer suggests the virtues of giving to the point of marginal utility; yet later he denies that this very demanding interpretation is necessary. Compare Peter Singer, "Famine, Affluence, and Morality," 240-42; and Peter Singer, "Reconsidering the Famine Relief Argument," in *Food Policy: The Responsibility of the United States in the Life and Death Choices*, ed. Peter G. Brown and Henry Shue (New York: The Free Press, 1977), 49. For some of the debate that ensues regarding the extent of demandingness and sacrifice required, see Richard J. Arneson, "Moral Limits on the Demands of Beneficence?" in *The Ethics of Assistance: Morality and the Distant Needy*, ed. Deen K. Chatterjee (Cambridge and New York: Cambridge University Press, 2004), 33-58; John Arthur, "Equality, Entitlements, and the Distribution of Income," in *Moral Philosophy: Selected Readings, Second Edition*, ed. George Sher (Belmont, CA: Wadsworth, 2001), 705-719; Neera K. Badhwar, "International Aid: When Giving Becomes a Vice," *Social Philosophy and Policy* (2006), 69-101;

Jonathan L. Cohen, "Who is Starving Whom?" *Theoria* 47 (1981), 65-81; Tim Mulgan, "Rule Consequentialism and Famine," *Analysis* 54, no. 3 (1994), 187-92; Liam Murphy, *Moral Demands in Nonideal Theory* (Oxford: Oxford University Press, 2000), chapters 2 and 3.

5. For more on the debate about what should constitute the baseline or threshold of adequacy, see James Griffin, *Well-Being: Its Meaning, Measurement, and Moral Importance* (Oxford: Clarendon Press, 1986), chapter 3; Murphy, *Moral Demands in Nonideal Theory*, 34-41 and 61-62; James W. Nickel, *Making Sense of Human Rights: Philosophical Reflections on the Universal Declaration of Human Rights* (Berkeley, CA: University of California Press, 1987), 51; Thomas W. Pogge, "Severe Poverty as a Violation of Negative Duties," *Ethics and International Affairs* 19, no. 1 (March 2005), 55-58; Thomas W. Pogge, "'Assisting' the Poor," in *The Ethics of Assistance: Morality and the Distant Needy*, ed. Deen K. Chatterjee (Cambridge and New York: Cambridge University Press, 2004), 273-74; Joseph Raz, *The Morality of Freedom* (Oxford: Clarendon Press, 1986), chapter 9.

6. Onora O'Neill notes that in the Kantian framework, many duties are relevant to poverty. In contrast to the imperfect duties of beneficence or mutual aid, which require us to sometimes foster others' ends, are the perfect duties of justice: these are the duties that one is required to do at all times, namely the duties that one must always refrain from violating in order never to use others as mere means. For example, duties of justice would require one not to steal from the poor, or to exploit the poor for one's own advantage. These duties will be discussed in a slightly different context as duties of institutional justice—i.e., duties to promote justice and to refrain from committing injustices—in chapter four of this book. For Kant's discussion of the duty to aid, see Immanuel Kant, *Grounding for the Metaphysics of Morals, with On a Supposed Right to Lie Because of Philanthropic Concerns, Third Edition*, trans. James W. Ellington (Indianapolis: Hackett, 1993), 32; for O'Neill's interpretation, see Onora O'Neill, "Kantian Approaches to Some Famine Problems," in *Reason and Responsibility: Readings in Some Basic Problems of Philosophy, Twelfth Edition,* ed. Joel Feinberg and Russ Shafer-Landau (Belmont, CA: Thomson Wadsworth, 2005), 641.

7. Arguments for human rights based on intuitions and assertions can be found in Jan Narveson, *The Libertarian Idea* (Philadelphia: Temple University Press, 1988), 109; and Robert Nozick, *Anarchy, State, and Utopia* (New York: Basic Books, 1974), ix. Arguments based on consequentialist reasoning include Nickel, *Making Sense of Human Rights*, 85-91; T.M. Scanlon, "Rights, Goals, and Fairness," in *Theories of Rights*, ed. Jeremy Waldron (Oxford: Oxford University Press, 1984), 137-52; and L.W. Sumner, *The Moral Foundation of Rights* (Oxford: Clarendon Press, 1987). The most popular arguments for human rights are various forms of hypothetical universalization (no doubt inspired by Kant) that regard the universal features of being human (i.e., as having the capacities of rationality and agency, and so possessing dignity) as justifying uniform treatment of other humans. One example of this argumentation is social contract theory, found in David Gauthier's book *Morals by Agreement* (Oxford: Clarendon Press, 1986) and discussed by Brian Barry in his chapter "Justice as Reciprocity," in *Democracy, Power and Justice: Essays in Political Theory* (Oxford: Clarendon Press, 1989), 463-93. Another example of hypothetical universalization is the reasoning in the original position behind the veil of ignorance described by John Rawls in his classic *A Theory of Justice* (Cambridge, MA: Belknap Press, 1971). Rawlsian overlapping consensus is used by Jack Donnelly to provide a pluralistic justification for human rights; see Jack Donnelly, *Universal Human Rights in Theory and Practice, Second Edition* (Ithaca, NY and London:

Cornell University Press, 2003). Alan Gewirth develops a reasoning process of dialectical necessity used to justify human rights; see Alan Gewirth, *Human Rights: Essays on Justification and Applications* (Chicago and London: University of Chicago Press, 1982), 20-26; Alan Gewirth, "Starvation and Human Rights," in *Ethics and Problems of the 21st Century*, ed. K.E. Goodpaster and K.M. Sayre (London: University of Notre Dame Press, 1979), 139-58; and Alan Gewirth, *Reason and Morality* (Chicago and London: University of Chicago Press, 1978), 42-47. Thomas Scanlon justifies human rights according to contractualism, which despite its name draws more from Rawls than from Hobbesian social contract theory; see T.M. Scanlon, *What We Owe to Each Other* (Cambridge, MA and London: Belknap Press, 1998). Finally, Onora O'Neill develops an explicitly Kantian reasoning process which justifies human rights that she calls constructivism or practical reasoning; see Onora O'Neill, *Towards Justice and Virtue: A Constructive Account of Practical Reasoning* (Cambridge: Cambridge University Press, 1996); Onora O'Neill, *Faces of Hunger: An Essay on Poverty, Justice, and Development* (London: Allen and Unwin, 1986).

8. For accounts of rights as responding to need, see Donnelly, *Universal Human Rights in Theory and Practice*, 13-14; Joel Feinberg, "Duties, Rights, and Claims," in *Rights, Justice, and the Bounds of Liberty: Essays in Social Philosophy* (Princeton, NJ: Princeton University Press, 1980), 139-41; Wilfried Hinsch and Markus Stepanians, "Severe Poverty as a Human Rights Violation—Weak and Strong," in *Real World Justice: Grounds, Principles, Human Rights, and Social Institutions*, ed. Andreas Follesdal and Thomas Pogge (Dordrecht: Springer, 2005), 304-7; and Raz, *The Morality of Freedom*, 166. For rights as responding to interests, see Ronald Dworkin, "Rights as Trumps," in *Theories of Rights*, ed. Jeremy Waldron (Oxford: Oxford University Press, 1984), 153; and Ronald Dworkin, *Taking Rights Seriously* (Cambridge, MA: Harvard University Press, 1977), 91. For rights as describing agency requirements, see Gewirth, *Reason and Morality*, 48-103; Gewirth, *Human Rights*, 46-59; Alan Gewirth, "Are There Any Absolute Rights?" in *Theories of Rights*, ed. Jeremy Waldron (Oxford: Oxford University Press, 1984), 91-109; H.L.A. Hart, "Are There Any Absolute Rights?" in *Theories of Rights*, ed. Jeremy Waldron (Oxford: Oxford University Press, 1984), 77; and J.L. Mackie, "Can There Be a Right-Based Moral Theory?" in *Theories of Rights*, ed. Jeremy Waldron (Oxford: Oxford University Press, 1984), 173-75.

9. Violation of human rights justifies a different kind of duty than those of assistance or beneficence, however: duties of redress, which will be addressed in the next chapter.

10. These rights are listed in the "United Nations International Covenant on Economic, Social and Cultural Rights (1966)," reprinted in *The Human Rights Reader: Major Political Writings, Essays, Speeches, and Documents from the Bible to the Present*, ed. Micheline R. Ishay (New York: Routledge, 1997), 436-38. Welfare or subsistence rights are described by Rodney Peffer in his article "World Hunger, Moral Theory, and Radical Rawlsianism," *International Journal of Politics and Ethics* 2, no. 4 (March 2003) (archived by High Beam Research at http://www.highbeam.com/doc/1G1-115035534.html; accessed October 31, 2006), 12-13; and Henry Shue, *Basic Rights: Subsistence, Affluence, and U.S. Foreign Policy, Second Edition* (Princeton, NJ: Princeton University Press, 1996), 36-37.

11. The consequentialist rule of promoting the good is justified primarily in terms of intuitions. Some philosophers make logical arguments based on shared intuitions of benevolence; see J.J.C. Smart, "An Outline of a System of Utilitarian Ethics," in *Utilitarianism: For and Against*, J.J.C. Smart and Bernard Williams (Cambridge: Cambridge University Press, 1973), 7; and Singer, "Famine, Affluence, and Morality," 229-36. Oth-

ers argue oppositely to show that our moral intuitions are often wrong by eliminating what Shelly Kagan calls "dangling distinctions" that we often use unjustifiably to limit our moral responsibilities; see Shelly Kagan, *The Limits of Morality* (Oxford: Clarendon Press, 1989), especially page 14; James Rachels, "Killing, Letting Die, and the Value of Life," in his book *Can Ethics Provide Answers? And Other Essays in Moral Philosophy* (Lanham, MD: Rowman and Littlefield, 1997), 67-80; James Rachels, "Feeding the Hungry: Killing and Starving to Death," in *Moral Issues*, ed. Jan Narveson (Toronto: Oxford University Press, 1983), 154-66; Unger, *Living High and Letting Die*. More rarely, a consequentialist may also use methods of hypothetical universalization such as universal prescriptivism; see R.M. Hare, *Freedom and Reason* (Oxford: Clarendon Press, 1963).

12. For versions of this argument, see Nozick, *Anarchy, State, and Utopia*, 28-33; Bernard Williams, "Persons, Character, and Morality," in his book *Moral Luck: Philosophical Papers 1973-1980* (Cambridge: Cambridge University Press, 1980), 1-19; Bernard Williams, "A Critique of Utilitarianism," in *Utilitarianism: For and Against*, J.J.C. Smart and Bernard Williams (Cambridge: Cambridge University Press, 1973), 108-18; and Susan Wolf, "Moral Saints," *The Journal of Philosophy* 79, no. 8 (August 1982), 419-39.

13. Negative utilitarianism is asymmetrical in requiring us to minimize suffering and evil without any corresponding duty to maximize happiness; see Karl Popper, *The Open Society and Its Enemies, Vol. 1: The Spell of Plato* (Princeton, NJ: Princeton University Press, 1966), 235 (chapter 5, note 6) and 284-85 (chapter 9, note 2); see also Jamie Mayerfeld, *Suffering and Moral Responsibility* (Oxford: Oxford University Press, 1999), 128-36. In contrast to act utilitarianism, rule utilitarianism is able to take into account side constraints or rights, recognizing that following certain rules (such as respecting certain rights) will lead to greater good than any single violation of them; see Richard B. Brandt, *Morality, Utilitarianism, and Rights* (Cambridge: Cambridge University Press, 1992), 111-36; Richard B. Brandt, *A Theory of the Good and the Right* (Oxford: Clarendon Press, 1979), chapter 15; Richard B. Brandt, *Ethical Theory: The Problems of Normative and Critical Ethics* (Englewood Cliffs, NJ: Prentice-Hall, 1959), 253-58 and 396-405. See discussion in John C. Harsanyi, "Rule Utilitarianism and Decision Theory," in *Decision Theory and Social Ethics: Issues in Social Choice*, ed. Hans W. Gottinger and Werner Leinfellner (Dordrecht, Boston, and London: D. Reidel, 1978), 3-31; and Smart, "An Outline of a System of Utilitarian Ethics," 9-12. *Satisficing* utility promotes good at least above some minimal threshold or eliminates suffering at least below a maximal acceptable level; see Russell Hardin, *Morality within the Limits of Reason* (Chicago and London: University of Chicago Press, 1998), 4; Michael Slote, *Beyond Optimizing: A Study of Rational Choice* (Cambridge, MA: Harvard University Press, 1989), 7-31; Michael Slote, *Common-Sense Morality and Consequentialism* (London and Boston: Routledge and Kegan Paul, 1985), 35-39. Hybrid accounts combine deontological and consequentialist concerns so that one's self-regarding and other-regarding duties are asymmetrical, and one has permissions but not requirements to sacrifice one's own projects for the sake of helping others; see Samuel Scheffler, *The Rejection of Consequentialism: A Philosophical Investigation of the Considerations Underlying Rival Moral Conceptions* (Oxford: Clarendon Press, 1982).

14. For welfare utilitarianism, see Jeremy Bentham, *An Introduction to the Principles of Morals and Legislation* (Oxford: Clarendon Press, 1879); Mayerfeld, *Suffering and Moral Responsibility*, 11-19; John Stuart Mill, *Utilitarianism*, ed. George Sher (Indianapolis: Hackett, 1979), 7; Henry Sidgwick, *The Methods of Ethics* (Chicago: University of Chicago Press, 1962), 436; and Smart, "An Outline of a System of Utilitarian Ethics," 12-27. For preference utilitarianism, see Harsanyi, "Rule Utilitarianism and Decision

Theory," 7-8 and John C. Harsanyi, *Essays on Ethics, Social Behavior, and Scientific Explanation* (Dordrecht and Boston: D. Reidel, 1976), 32; see also discussions in Brandt, *Morality, Utilitarianism, and Rights*, 158-75 and Brandt, *A Theory of the Good and the Right*, chapter 2. For utilitarianism that values interest, see Hare, *Freedom and Reason*, 122.

15. An exception is Robert Goodin's book *Utilitarianism as Public Philosophy* (Cambridge: Cambridge University Press, 1995).

16. For this reason, several philosophers seem to combine consequentialist and virtue theory, including Robert Goodin, Larry May, and Michael Slote. See Goodin, *Protecting the Vulnerable*; Larry May, *Sharing Responsibility* (Chicago: University of Chicago Press, 1992); Michael Slote, *Morals from Motives* (Oxford and New York: Oxford University Press, 2001); Michael Slote, *From Morality to Virtue* (Oxford and New York: Oxford University Press, 1992); Slote, *Common-Sense Morality and Consequentialism*.

17. Karl Jaspers, *The Question of German Guilt*, trans. E. B. Ashton (New York: Capricorn Books, 1961), 32.

18. For Sartre's claim that we are responsible for everything, see Jean-Paul Sartre, "The Humanism of Existentialism," trans. Bernard Frechtman, in *Essays in Existentialism* (Secaucus, NJ: Citadel Press Book, 1993), 41. H.D. Lewis criticizes this view as absurd, while Larry May defends and explains Sartre's idea of situated freedom and the responsibility it entails. H. D. Lewis, "Collective Responsibility," in *Collective Responsibility: Five Decades of Debate in Theoretical and Applied Ethics*, ed. Larry May and Stacey Hoffman (Savage, MD: Rowman and Littlefield, 1991), 17-33; May, *Sharing Responsibility*, 21-24; Larry May, "Metaphysical Guilt and Moral Taint," in *Collective Responsibility: Five Decades of Debate in Theoretical and Applied Ethics*, ed. Larry May and Stacey Hoffman (Savage, MD: Rowman and Littlefield, 1991), 240-44.

19. See Goodin, *Protecting the Vulnerable*.

20. One problem with justifying globalized care is that this form of care seems fundamentally different than the form of care directed at family members and others with whom one shares a "close" personal relationship. While the latter describes partial duties toward particular others, the former describes duties that are aimed at particular others who are nonetheless not identifiable, making these duties seem neither clearly partial nor clearly impartial. Since globalized care involves a fundamentally different form of obligation than either partial care or impartial universal benevolence, it is difficult to see how strongly or widely justifying this form of beneficence is, whether to other virtue ethicists or to those who are not virtue ethicists.

21. For arguments that globalize care, see Fiona Robinson, *Globalizing Care: Ethics, Feminist Theory, and International Relations* (Boulder, CO: Westview, 1999); Virginia Held, *The Ethics of Care: Personal, Political, and Global* (Oxford and New York: Oxford University Press, 2006), 154-68; and Marion Smiley, *Moral Responsibility and the Boundaries of Community: Power and Accountability from a Pragmatic Point of View* (Chicago and London: University of Chicago Press, 1992), 195-205; see also Peter Singer, *One World: The Ethics of Globalization, Second Edition* (New Haven, CT and London: Yale University Press, 2002).

22. This distinction comes from Thomas W. Pogge, *World Poverty and Human Rights: Cosmopolitan Responsibilities and Reforms* (Cambridge: Polity and Malden, MA: Blackwell, 2002), 15-16.

23. For more on the logic of this moral equivalency, see Kagan, *The Limits of Morality*, especially pages 53-55.

24. These terms come from Kagan, *The Limits of Morality*, 3-4.

25. Although Kagan argues that decreasing suffering and increasing happiness are morally equivalent, alleviating suffering carries greater moral weight than adding to someone's happiness because suffering is more intense, requiring more urgency in response. The worst suffering is more intense and more urgent, so response to worst kinds of suffering alleviates more need and therefore is more effective. Jamie Mayerfeld, *Moral Responsibility and Suffering*, 131-36.

26. For more on aggregates, see Peter A. French, "Types of Collectivities," in *Individual and Collective Responsibility, Second Edition*, ed. Peter A. French (Rochester, VT: Schenkman Books, 1998), 42-44. For more on random collectives, see Virginia Held, "Can a Random Collection of Individuals Be Morally Responsible?" in *Collective Responsibility: Five Decades of Debate in Theoretical and Applied Ethics*, ed. Larry May and Stacey Hoffman (Savage, MD: Rowman and Littlefield, 1991), 89-90. Spatio-temporal location is the most common example given by philosophers of an accidental, contingent trait that groups individuals into a random collective. For example, see Joel Feinberg's discussion about people who happen to be in the "right" place at the "right" time to witness a child drowning but then fail to do anything to prevent this from happening. Joel Feinberg, "Collective Responsibility," in *Collective Responsibility: Five Decades of Debate in Theoretical and Applied Ethics*, ed. Larry May and Stacey Hoffman (Savage, MD: Rowman and Littlefield, 1991), 73. Peter Singer also uses this example as an analogy to argue for beneficent action toward famine and poverty in "Famine, Affluence, and Morality," 231.

27. This concept comes from O'Neill, *Towards Justice and Virtue*, 127.

28. This is described by Carl Wellman in *A Theory of Rights: Persons Under Laws, Institutions, and Morals* (Totowa, NJ: Rowman and Allanheld, 1985), 57-59.

29. This point is made by Joel Feinberg in *Harm to Others: The Moral Limits of the Criminal Law, Volume One* (New York: Oxford University Press, 1984), 134; and by Marilyn Friedman in "The Practice of Partiality," *Ethics* 101, no. 4 (July 1991), 831.

30. Narveson, *The Libertarian Idea*, 47.

31. Nozick, *Anarchy, State, and Utopia*, 32-33.

32. For discussion, see Rudiger Bittner, "Morality and World Hunger," in *Global Justice*, ed. Thomas W. Pogge (Oxford: Blackwell Publishers, 2001), 24-31; F. M. Kamm, "The New Problem of Distance in Morality," in *The Ethics of Assistance: Morality and the Distant Needy*, ed. Deen K. Chatterjee (Cambridge and New York: Cambridge University Press, 2004), 59-74; F.M. Kamm, "Faminine Ethics: The Problem of Distance in Morality and Singer's Ethical Theory," in *Singer and His Critics*, ed. Dale Jamieson (Malden, MA: Blackwell Publishers, 1999), 162-208; Samuel Scheffler, "The Conflict between Justice and Responsibility," in *Global Justice (Nomos XLI)*, eds. Ian Shapiro and Lea Brilmayer (New York and London: New York University Press, 1999), 86-106; and Singer, *One World*, 150-95.

33. Some virtue theorists see universal benevolence as one important virtue to be balanced with other, more personal expressions of caring; for example, see Slote, *Morals from Motives*, 70-73. Others, however, view universal benevolence as less morally significant than particular care. These virtue ethicists argue that we should prioritize our responsibility to those "closest" to us in a partial sense, referring to personal relationships or our relationships to those individuals and communities that constitute our personal identities. See John Cottingham, "Partiality, Favouritism, and Morality," *The Philosophical Quarterly* 36, no. 144 (July 1986), 357-73; John Kekes, "Morality and Impartiality," *American Philosophical Quarterly* 18, no. 4 (October 1981), 295-303. Some partialists identify themselves as care ethicists, reclaiming the value of care in opposition to tradi-

tional "masculine" ethical theories that purportedly dismiss it in favor of impartiality. See Annette C. Baier, "The Need for More than Justice," in *Justice and Care: Essential Readings in Feminist Ethics*, ed. Virginia Held (Boulder, CO: Westview Press, 1995), 47-58; Friedman, "The Practice of Partiality," 818-25; Carol Gilligan, *In a Different Voice: Psychological Theory and Women's Development* (Cambridge, MA: Harvard University Press, 1982); Held, *The Ethics of Care*; Nel Noddings, "Caring," in *Justice and Care: Essential Readings in Feminist Ethics*, ed. Virginia Held (Boulder, CO: Westview Press, 1995), 7-30; Slote, *Morals from Motives*; and various discussions in the anthology edited by Eva Feder Kittay and Diana T. Meyers, *Women and Moral Theory* (Savage, MD: Rowman and Littlefield, 1987). Other partialists identify themselves as communitarians, embracing the value of communities and traditions as constitutive of personal identity and agency, and hence of moral concern. See Alasdair MacIntyre, *After Virtue: A Study in Moral Theory, Second Edition* (Notre Dame, IN: Notre Dame Press, 1984); David Miller, "National Responsibility and International Justice," in *The Ethics of Assistance: Morality and the Distant Needy*, ed. Deen K. Chatterjee (Cambridge and New York: Cambridge University Press, 2004), 123-46; David Miller, *On Nationality* (Oxford: Clarendon Press, 1995); Richard W. Miller, "Moral Closeness and World Community," in *The Ethics of Assistance: Morality and the Distant Needy*, ed. Deen K. Chatterjee (Cambridge and New York: Cambridge University Press, 2004), 101-22; Michael J. Sandel, *Liberalism and the Limits of Justice, Second Edition* (Cambridge: Cambridge University Press, 1998); Charles Taylor, *Sources of the Self: The Making of the Modern Identity* (Cambridge, MA: Harvard University Press, 1989); Michael Walzer, *Thick and Thin: Moral Argument at Home and Abroad* (Notre Dame, IN: University of Notre Dame Press, 1994). "Closeness" here refers to physical location and emotional bond.

34. As explained above, virtue ethicists who argue that care should be globalized, based on global relationships that the affluent and poor share, try to answer the partial objection that the global poor are too "distant" from the affluent to be recipients of their care. I am not convinced that this approach addresses the issue adequately, as it runs into the same problem that partial approaches do: the framework of care assumes, falsely, that the appropriate agents for responding to those in need are individuals (who are the only agents capable of caring).

35. The exception is virtue or care approaches, for only individuals are capable of virtue and have the appropriate moral feeling to respond with care or benevolence. Sometimes we speak of corporations or other collective agents as wanting to appear "caring" by marketing themselves as socially compassionate and giving back to the community, but this kind of language is misleading. Corporations and other collective agents have sufficient agency to make decisions and act (see below), but since they lack the experiential aspect of personhood, it is a mistake to ascribe moral feeling and virtue to them.

36. The real problem here has to do with specification, as human rights claims only invite these sorts of objections on account of being vague and not specifying their appropriate duty-bearers. If collective agents are specified as appropriate duty-bearers, libertarians may still object to the idea that the role of certain collectives (such as governments) is to help meet basic needs, but this objection would require significant argumentation about what the roles of collectives such as governments, United Nations agencies, or non-governmental organizations should be, probably requiring reconceptualizing the nature of collective agents entirely.

37. French, "Types of Collectivities," 44-45.

38. Agreeing that there is a strong need to identify the agents responsible for meeting human rights claims, Wilfried Hinsch and Markus Stepanians also argue that respon-

sibility is best assigned to states for these two reasons: governments are better capable of meeting people's human rights, and it is their *role* to do so. Rather than arguing for this role based on Kantian universalization of obligations, however, they argue that, "given the need for coordinated social action," states are the "natural addresses of human rights claims," noting that many political theorists, including John Rawls, support this view. In addition, they argue that while states are necessary agents to allocate responsibility for meeting human rights, they are not sufficient, as not all states have the ability or interest to fulfill this function. Hinsch and Stepanians, "Severe Poverty as a Human Rights Violation—Weak and Strong," 309-12.

39. Robert Goodin calls this the "circularity" objection because helping the vulnerable merely keeps all players in the same position so that the same vulnerable agents must be helped by the same powerful agents again. Goodin, *Protecting the Vulnerable*, 124.

40. Versions of this argument can be found in Peffer, "World Hunger, Moral Theory, and Radical Rawlsianism," 24; and Miller, "Moral Closeness and World Community," 110. Poor people do make their needs and desires known, however, when affluent people listen to them. See the *Voices of the Poor* series, in which World Bank researchers compile interviews with more than 20,000 poor people from around the world about how they understand their situation and what changes they would like made. Deepa Narayan, et al., *Voices of the Poor: Can Anyone Hear Us?* (New York and Oxford: Oxford University Press, 2000); and Deepa Narayan, et al., *Voices of the Poor: Crying Out for Change* (New York and Oxford: Oxford University Press, 2000).

41. Food First, 2000, "Lessons from the Green Revolution," on-line at: http://www.foodfirst.org/media/opeds/2000/4.greenrev.html (accessed January 15, 2004); Vandana Shiva, *The Violence of the Green Revolution: Third World Agriculture, Ecology and Politics* (London and New Jersey: Zed Books, 1991), chapters 3 and 4.

42. John Stuart Mill, *On Liberty*, ed. Currin V. Shields (New York: Liberal Arts Press, 1956), 93.

43. For examples of these arguments, see William Easterly, *The White Man's Burden: Why the West's Efforts to Aid the Rest Have Done So Much Ill and So Little Good* (New York: Penguin Press, 2006); Thomas Friedman, *The World is Flat: A Brief History of the Twenty-first Century* (New York: Farrar, Straus, and Giroux, 2005), especially pages 262-63 on the value of motivation for technological innovation; and James W. Nickel, "A Human Rights Approach to World Hunger," in *World Hunger and Morality: Second Edition*, ed. William Aiken and Hugh LaFollette (Upper Saddle River, NJ: Prentice Hall, 1996), 171-85. Easterly in fact argues that the poor should pay for basic services like health care in order to make providers more accountable.

44. Thomas Friedman partly acknowledges this in his explanation of the way illness traps people in poverty and prevents them from having the hopefulness necessary for technological innovation. Friedman, *The World is Flat*, 375-82.

45. Susan Sontag says in *Regarding the Pain of Others* (New York: Farrar, Straus, and Giroux, 2003), 70-71:

> The more remote or exotic the place, the more likely we are to have full frontal views of the dead and dying....[These images] show a suffering that is outrageous, unjust, and should be repaired. They confirm that this is the sort of thing which happens in that place. The ubiquity of those photographs, and those horrors, cannot help but nourish belief in the inevitability of tragedy in the benighted or backward—that is, poor—parts of the world.

Judith N. Shklar notes in *The Faces of Injustice* (New Haven, CT and London: Yale University Press, 1990), 112:

Americans do react quickly to individual cases of injustice but put up with social unfairness. How could it be otherwise? Social information just dribbles in, bit by bit, and we simply get used to it. A single story about a person really hits home at once, but the grinding injustices of daily life are endured. It is easy to ignore them and we do.

Jeffrey Sachs also discusses this wariness and the false myths that it supports, especially regarding poverty in Africa; see Jeffrey D. Sachs, *The End of Poverty: Economic Possibilities for Our Time* (New York: Penguin Press, 2005), chapter 16.

46. Part of the problem is that beneficence is often a response to emotional inclination and desire. To deal with this emotional aspect of beneficence (perhaps another dimension of what is meant by the value of "closeness" in prioritizing one's beneficent action), rhetoricians such as Dr. Frank Beer and Dr. Jerry Hauser, both at the University of Colorado in Boulder, have suggested to me that causes such as global poverty and hunger, sweatshops, and the like need better marketing and advertising to attract supporters and advocates of responsibility. This is a creative response to the problem of how to change the way affluent individuals ignore their responsibility toward global poverty. I am not wholly convinced of its merits, however, largely because it uses rather than challenges the neo-liberal, consumer-oriented framework, which itself exacerbates the existence of poverty, in that it understands political response as voluntary charity based solely on consumer choice.

47. Alison M. Jaggar, "Western Feminism and Global Responsibility," in *Feminist Interventions in Ethics and Politics*, ed. Barbara S. Andrew, Jean Keller, and Lisa H. Schwartzman (Lanham, MD: Rowman and Littlefield, 2004), 186.

48. Unger, *Living High and Letting Die*, 151.

49. See Linda Martin Alcoff, "The Problem of Speaking for Others," *Cultural Critique* (Winter 1991/1992), 17-20.

50. Many of the debates regarding beneficent duty—particularly debates about what the scope of beneficent duty is, or whether universal benevolence is morally necessary or efficacious, or whether agents really have duties to others in an impartial or universal way—show that the concern of philosophers is often more about the agent who would help than about the needy who would benefit from help. Despite earlier nationalistic arguments that suggested otherwise, David Miller's argument for a pluralistic account of responsibilities that is aimed at making sure the needs of the poorest are met is an exception. See David Miller, "Distributing Responsibilities," in *Global Responsibilities: Who Must Deliver on Human Rights?* ed. Andrew Kuper (New York and London: Routledge, 2005), 95-117.

51. Sachs, *The End of Poverty*. He discusses mosquito nets and DDT on pages 196-200 and 259-65, especially 262. For more on the value of bed nets and the money raised to distribute them, see The Global Fund, "The Global Fund," *Product RED* 2008, http://www.joinred.com/globalfund/ (accessed on May 13, 2008); Nothing But Nets, "Nets Save Lives," *Nothing But Nets* 2007, http://www/nothingbutnets.net/nets-save-lives/ (accessed on May 12, 2008); and UNICEF, "UNICEF Ethiopia Malaria" *UNICEF* 2008, http://www.unicef.org/ethiopia/malaria.html (accessed on May 12, 2008).

52. Sachs, *The End of Poverty*, 74-89, 255-57, and 292-93.

53. The statistics are from Sachs, *The End of Poverty*, 303 and 213, respectively. Sachs' human rights arguments are on pages 253-54.

54. Easterly, *The White Man's Burden*, 13-14.

55. Easterly, *The White Man's Burden*, 375.

56. Thomas W. Pogge, "The First UN Millenium Development Goal: A Cause for Celebration?" in *Real World Justice: Grounds, Principles, Human Rights, and Social Institutions*, ed. Andreas Follesdal and Thomas Pogge (Dordrecht: Springer, 2005), 318-29.

57. Debating about which response is prior to or more essential than the other is misguided. Even though I agree with Andrew Kuper that Peter Singer's exhortation to do more and better than we currently are doing is too vague and needs specification, he overstates his case in his debate with Singer when he says that giving money to Oxfam is morally wrong. Andrew, Kuper, "Global Poverty Relief: More than Charity," in *Global Responsibilities: Who Must Deliver on Human Rights?* ed. Andrew Kuper (New York and London: Routledge, 2005), 155-72.

Chapter 3
Duties of Redress

Responsibility for global poverty may be justified according to its causes, for poverty that is caused by wrongful or faulty action entails redress. On this model, an agent is responsible when she makes a morally relevant causal contribution to harm through her actions. The idea of attributing moral responsibility based on causal connection to harm comes mainly from legal philosophy.

Sometimes this causal approach to responsibility is called a "liability" model because of its emphasis on attributing responsibility as liability, particularly as it applies to reparations, blame, or punishment. Because I prefer to focus on what kinds of duties these are—involving rectification, or righting wrongs within a framework of corrective justice—I call the responsibility described by this model "duties of redress." Redress, rectification, and reparation are all terms that refer to righting wrongs as a way to correct injustices. This model justifies responsibility according to what actions have been performed, what harm has been caused, and what actions and harm need rectification as a result.

On the redress model, poverty is viewed as a harm, but its meaning here differs from the way beneficence advocates use the term. Harm is a bad state of affairs resulting from a causal chain in which one of the causes is faulty action. The kind of harm that is morally relevant is not merely an unfortunate state of affairs, as on the benevolence model, but rather it is an outcome of particular causal process. In particular, the kind of harm that justifies duties of redress is *wrongful* harm. I explain the meaning of this harm below.

Affluent individuals are responsible to the global poor by virtue of actions—and, sometimes, omissions—of theirs that cause harm to the poor. In this model, agents are responsible primarily for what they *have done* to others, for example by taking away land that would allow poor people to obtain sustenance through farming. They may also be responsible for what they have *not* done, particularly when they fail to meet expectations for how they should act, for example by failing to inform people, who gave consent to the selling of land near where they live, that the land would then be used to build a toxic waste dump. Responsibility for omissions, especially involving a failure of meeting

65

expectations for appropriate action, is responsibility for negligence. Actions and omissions thus may be equal in their moral relevance, depending on the contexts of expectation in which each occurs. Note that primarily what agents are responsible for is what some philosophers call "backward-looking," meaning that the emphasis here is on looking at what happened in the past in order to see how past actions created the present state of affairs. Responsibility here is not solely "backward-looking," however, since causes may also continue or maintain present conditions and so might not necessarily remain in the past as something with which one is "done." Responding to poverty here means redressing or rectifying the harms of poverty to which one has causally contributed.

Duties of redress are justified within the framework of corrective justice, particularly in the legal concept of strict liability. Liability can be understood as the allocation of risks and losses between injurers (the legal term for those who play a role in causing loss or injury) and "victims" (the legal term for those who suffer loss or injury).[1] Losses and harms must be absorbed by someone. When a victim suffers a loss or harm, either she must absorb those costs herself, or she must prove that the injurer is liable for them. If the injurer is found liable, then he is legally obligated to compensate for the losses; this legal obligation constitutes what I am calling duties of redress. Liability is easily determined in cases in which harms are intentionally inflicted, but loss often occurs without intention, and sometimes has confusing causal factors. In some of these cases it is unclear who should absorb the losses incurred, for it seems unfair for the victim to suffer needlessly, but it also seems unfair to require the alleged injurer to compensate for unintended and perhaps unclearly caused harms. Assessments of liability, particularly strict liability, ultimately come down to a question of which party—the victim or the injurer—is the one to which it is more just—or, more likely, is less unjust—to ascribe responsibility for absorbing the loss.

Within this liability framework, we can understand poverty as a harm that is suffered by the global poor and that has many causal factors that can be traced to the actions of multiple specific agents. Agents have duties of redress with respect to poverty insofar as it is more appropriate—less unjust—to ascribe to them the responsibility for absorbing the losses that constitute poverty. The justice of ascribing responsibility is determined by the nature of the harm experienced and the nature of the wrongdoing that played a causal role in contributing to it.

Why Responsibility as Redress is Attractive: How Redress Provides Agent-Relative Justification of Responsibility

In the models of responsibility considered in this chapter, what is problematic about poverty is that it is a condition of wrongful harm, meaning that it results from a rights violation. Responsibility for addressing poverty is thus understood in terms of rectifying that violation when it occurs, and so entailing duties of redress when poverty does exist; and simply not violating relevant rights in the first place, and so entailing duties of forbearance to prevent the existence of poverty. Not all cases of poverty, and not all aspects of any given case of poverty, result from a violation of rights, of course. The responsibility discussed in this chapter deals only with the aspects of poverty that do result from a violation of rights. While this limits how applicable redress is to global poverty, it is still an important form of responsibility that is more widely justifying within more ethical and political frameworks than is beneficence.

Redress is more widely justifying because it can avoid the problems raised by the beneficence model's two main groups of critics, partialists and libertarians. Both share the same complaint that beneficent duties are problematic in requiring impartial or agent-neutral active intervention. In the previous chapter, I discussed one interpretation of this objection in terms of the value of "closeness," as espoused by various partialists; here, I focus on a different interpretation of this objection in terms of freedom of action. This objection can be made in two ways, both leading to a need for duties to be agent-relative. The first form of this objection argues for the priority of being able to pursue one's personal projects and life plans, independently of the demands of impartial morality.[2] When responsibility is understood impartially, as in the beneficence models, one's personal projects will often conflict. While utilitarians frequently argue that impartial morality should trump personal projects, this response does not take seriously the concerns that critics of impartial morality raise. The best way to resolve this conflict is to re-conceptualize the relevant responsibility as agent-relative, so that it is necessarily *part of* rather than in contrast with one's projects, for example as a contractual duty that one has chosen to take on, or as a duty arising from one's un-chosen commitments (such as the duties an individual has toward her family members).

The second form of the objection to agent-neutral active intervention that I want to discuss here arises from valuing freedom of action in libertarian terms. Although the personal project view is compatible with libertarianism, it is not equivalent to it, for one can prioritize personal projects over impartial duties without being a libertarian regarding freedom and action. What both views share is a need for agent-relative reasons for action regarding responsibilities of wide scope, such as toward global poverty. For while communitarians and care ethicists place primary value on the personal relationships and community memberships that constitute one's identity, libertarians place primary value on individual freedom.[3] Libertarians interpret freedom in a "negative" way as meaning non-interference, so that a person is free if no one coerces or manipulates her to act otherwise than as she chooses. This is in contrast to the view of "positive" freedom assumed by those rights theories that support duties of beneficence, as having the resources and ability to do as one chooses. While "positive" freedom focuses on having the sufficient means to act, "negative" freedom focuses on avoiding coercion.

The difference between the "negative" freedom espoused by libertarians and the "positive" freedom supported by beneficence advocates involves a distinction between active intervention and non-interference. Duties of beneficence, including the duties of assistance entailed by rights to subsistence, are understood as involving active intervention, as requiring agents to *do* something in response to poverty, and as holding agents responsible for what they do *not* do as much as for what they *do* do. Critics of these duties object that active intervention is insufficiently justified as morally obligatory. A person is responsible for what she *does* do when it is wrong, such as stealing from the poor, but she is not responsible for what she does *not* do, such as not giving to the poor. Because of the priority of liberty, a person has the right to do what she wishes as long as she does not commit wrongdoing, which would infringe upon others' liberty. The rights to be able to act as one desires, within some limits (namely, not infringing on others' same rights), are often called rights of non-interference. Philosophers also sometimes call these *liberty* or *security* rights, in that their purpose is to protect people's interests and liberty; these correspond with what the United Nations recognizes as civil and political rights. Examples of these rights include freedom of movement (Article 12), freedom of thought, conscience, and religion (Article 18), and freedom of opinion and expression (Article 19). These rights imply that duty-bearers have duties to let others act as they wish given the bounds expressed by the rights.[4]

As discussed in the last chapter, rights are a special protection afforded to those interests that are so important that they deserve this special protection. The existence of rights justifies duties in that they share a relationship of entailment, for a right is meaningful only if it is respected by others. This obligation of respect is what we call the *duty* that a right entails. Rights of non-interference justify two kinds of duties worth mentioning here.

First, agents have duties of forbearance to prevent wrongful harm from occurring by refraining from violating people's rights of non-interference. These are duties that people can fulfill simply by not acting, by omission or refraining from action. Since people have rights of non-interference universally—in other words, all people have the grounds to claim freedom from the intervention of others—and since meeting these rights is the kind of thing that can be done at all times (i.e., is a perfect duty, in Kant's terminology), people have duties to respect these rights universally and impartially. Duties of forbearace are thus agent-neutral, meaning they apply to all relevant agents and recipients impartially, or without features that distinguish between particular individuals. Agent-neutral duties of forbearance are universal in scope, held by all agents and directed at everyone.

Second, agents have duties of redress to rectify wrongful harm that they have caused by infringing on people's rights. Since infringement occurs in particular cases, duties to redress infringement are agent-relative, that is, an agent's duty is relative to the specific harm that she caused. Duties are agent-relative when they apply to particular agents for specific justifying reasons.[5] These duties are local and specific in scope, not necessarily *partial*—in other words, based on the relationships of "closeness" discussed in the previous chapter—but they are at least *particular*—based on some specific, morally relevant relationships, such as those that form when one enters into contract agreements. It is important to note that it is not only rights of non-interference that entail duties of forbearance and of redress; rights to subsistence may entail these duties too. For example, the right to subsistence can generate a duty of forbearance to not block one's access to food, such as through theft; when this duty is not fulfilled, the right may be said to be violated, and so a duty of redress may result. What is special about these duties, however, is that they fit the libertarian valuation of "negative" freedom.[6]

As a result of their valuation of this kind of freedom, libertarians support agent-neutral duties of forbearance (duties to respect *everyone's* liberties), which involve refraining from acting in a way that could restrain a person's freedom to do as she chooses; and agent-relative duties involving active intervention (such as duties to aid those with whom I enter into contracts, or those with whom I have otherwise special relationships, such as my children), which involve action that one has freely and voluntarily chosen to undertake. What libertarians object to are the agent-neutral duties requiring active intervention involved in beneficence. In order for duties that require active intervention to be acceptable to libertarians, particular duty-bearers must be identifiable for specific justifying reasons. Responsibility as redress provides these reasons, because particular duty-bearers are identified as responsible based on agent-relative reasons of having caused harm to others that they now must rectify.

While many philosophers argue that libertarian reasons for requiring agent-relative reasons for active intervention are misguided, these concerns are nevertheless worth taking seriously. Although I do not wish to defend libertarianism, I do think that the strongest models of responsibility are those that are acceptable within the widest variety of political frameworks.[7] In order for duties regarding global poverty to be more strongly justified, or at least more compatible with more political systems, they must account for libertarian values of "negative" freedom and the need for agent-relative reasons for duties involving active intervention.

Libertarians value the duties that are entailed by rights of non-interference because duties that allow others to do as they wish encourage the propagation of more liberty. While non-libertarians may argue that duties regarding subsistence also promote freedom, libertarians are not easily convinced that the freedom gained by receiving assistance is worth the cost of freedom to provide it. Many philosophers have attacked libertarians on this very issue, providing arguments to try to disprove these convictions.[8] Rather than arguing in this way, I think it is more productive to figure out how responsibility regarding global poverty can fit within the libertarian framework. Global responsibility that is acceptable to libertarians—as well as to communitarians, care ethicists, and similar critics—involves agent-relative duties that specify particular duty-bearers for particular justifying (i.e., non-arbitrary) reasons.

Models of responsibility as redress solve the problem that beneficence poses for libertarians and other critics because they provide a way to specify particular duty-bearers for particular justifying reasons. While beneficence models conceptualize poverty as a bad state of affairs independent of causal or structural factors, redress models see poverty as a rights infringement that must be rectified. In conceptualizing poverty as a wrongful harm, these models provide justification for the responsibility of particular duty-bearers based on their contribution to *causing* the harm. While their conceptualization of poverty leads beneficence models to understand the resulting responsibility as impartial or agent-neutral, therefore, redress models conceptualize poverty in such a way as to understand the resulting responsibility as agent-relative based on causal contribution. This provides a more satisfactory justification of responsibility to critics of beneficence.[9]

How Poverty is Conceptualized: As Wrongful Harm

In considering poverty a harm, redress models of duty nonetheless view poverty very differently than beneficence models, for *harm* has a different meaning in the context of redress than it does in beneficence. A harm is not simply a negative state of affairs (such as a lack of food), or a net negative change in outcome (such as losing one's source of food); rather, it is something that is *caused*. This is not to say that poverty describes any harm (or wrongful harm) that is caused by identifiable agents, of course. In redress models, poverty is still understood generally as a *lack*—whether of resources or of capabilities—but it is not merely a lack; it is a lack that is caused by identifiable agents, wrongfully. In conceptualizing the harmfulness of poverty as a bad state of affairs, beneficence models disregard the moral importance of the reasons for how this state came about. In contrast, redress models consider how harm is caused to be of crucial moral significance for justifying response and identifying what forms of response are appropriate.

My understanding of harm in this context comes from Joel Feinberg, who defines *harm* in a wide sense as a "thwarting, setting back, or defeating" of an interest. An *interest* is something in which a person has a stake. Regarding poverty, one's interests include whatever goods are considered necessary for human survival or thriving, i.e., the goods that poverty and affluence measure. Interest is also a "risk"; a *stake* is "the amount risked by a party to a wager, or match, or gamble, a thing whose existence, or safety, or ownership depends on some issue."[10] In other words, a person has a stake in something when she stands to lose or gain depending on the condition or nature of the thing. That loss is what constitutes *harm*. A person is harmed by virtue of her poverty when she stands to lose by the conditions that constitute her impoverishment.

Interests have varying significance, which we acknowledge with differing degrees of legal protection. While any interest can be injured, a harm is an injury only of legitimate interests. The most important of legitimate interests are protected by rights, and when these legitimate interests are injured, so that a rights violation occurs, this constitutes a wrongful harm. While thwarting of legitimate interests *may* justify claims of reparation, only the thwarting of the most important legitimate interests—the ones afforded protection by the existence of rights—constitutes a wronging and therefore *entails* duties of redress.[11] The kind of harm that grounds duties of redress, therefore, is *wrongful* harm, which can be understood as rights violation.

As in all understandings of harm, the wrongful harm that constitutes loss and that justifies compensation is measured according to some baseline. For the corrective justice required by liability assessments, this baseline is historical. Harm measures the net loss that a person experiences when we compare her present situation to her situation at some specified time in the past, before the action that harmed her occurred (for example, comparing the health of a person before a car crash with her health afterward). Ideal compensation for this harm involves returning present states of affairs to the *status quo ante* that existed before the wrongful harm; real compensation for harm usually involves some substitution that is deemed to be of comparable worth (such as an amount of money that is somehow comparable to the loss of health that the car crash incurred).

Justifying Duties of Redress
Based on Wrongful Harm

The idea of righting a wrong, central to the concept of corrective justice, means that agents that have played a morally significant causal contribution to bringing about this wrongful harm have duties to redress it. People may be wronged without being harmed, of course, when the wrongful action actually furthers or keeps stable their interests. Duties of redress may be justified not only according to the *loss* that is suffered but according to the *wronging* itself.[12] In this conception, wrongings must be righted regardless of whether the victim suffers a loss (i.e., a harm or setback of interest). In other words, even if a victim actually *gains* from the wrongful action done to her, she is still owed some compensation on account of being wronged (i.e., having her rights infringed upon).[13] For example, if a woman working in a sweatshop is denied the right to use the bathroom regularly (a denial of the right to bodily integrity), this may allow her to produce more widgets in a given time frame, allowing her to make more money if she is paid by the number of widgets produced—but it also is a serious wronging that demands to be righted. On the other hand, if people are harmed without being wronged, i.e. when their interests are set back but no rights violation occurs—for example, if they make less money because they are less productive as a result of labor standards being enforced—they are not owed reparation. When morally significant human rights are violated (as is the case when poverty results from rights violation), however, this itself generally constitutes a setback of interests.

A rights violation is simply a state of affairs that justifies duties of compensation; it is not by itself a moral evaluation of action. Invasions of rights may be justifiable or excusable, depending on the circumstances. Any action contrary to a right, whether or not it is justifiable or excusable, constitutes a *wrong*; this term is used synonymously with *wrongful harm*. The scope of a *wrongdoing* is much narrower, however, involving unjustifiable harming. An agent may wrong others without committing a wrongdoing; in other words, she may invade another's right but do so justifiably. For example, theft is sometimes justifiable—even though it violates rights to property—when the alternative is death, for example stealing food to save a starving child or stealing medicine to prevent life-threatening illness.

In a strong model of redress that admits only liability with fault, only wrongdoings (those wrongs that are unjustifiable) entail duties of compensation or redress. In a weak model of redress, however, even justifiable wronging may be owed compensation for the invasion of rights, depending on the circumstances; this weak model of redress constitutes strict liability. Since liability is an evaluation only of actions, not of agents, agents may be blameless even if their actions are faulty, where their wrongdoing involves a failure to meet standards of acceptable behavior. Under strict liability, in contrast, an action may result in wrongful harm that is justifiable or excusable, yet which nonetheless requires rectification, for it is the nature of the action as wrongful harm—as violating another's right—that grounds claims of compensation or duties of redress.

In order to understand how these concepts apply to global poverty, let us consider a couple of examples, first summarizing the meanings of the terms that we are using. A *harm* occurs when a person's interests are set back. An action is *faulty* when an agent acts to produce certain harmful consequences or the risk thereof, regardless of whether such consequences or risks are intended. An action is a *wrongdoing* if it is morally indefensible, neither excusable nor justifiable. Finally, an action *wrongs* a person when it violates her rights.[14]

In the first situation, we will assess whether a corporation harms and/or wrongs employees when it out-sources American jobs to Third World countries. Since the out-sourcing generally sets back the interests of the First World workers, then it does constitute a harm. If the corporation acted with the intention to produce harmful consequences, or to produce the risk of such consequences, then its action would be faulty. In general, corporations do not *intend* to set back the interests of their workers. They are, however, generally aware of the risks that interests will be set back; the fact that American workers will lose their jobs as a result of out-sourcing is a foreseen if not intended consequence, seen by the company as an externality. Whether such risks can be explained as part of the corporation's *intentions* involves the difficult act of describing the agent's intentions, the problems with which are discussed below. Even trickier to answer is the question of whether the out-sourcing is a morally indefensible (inexcusable and unjustifiable) act. Out-sourcing is at least justifiable in the global economic context of needing to make or increase profits in order to stay in business. Whether the generalized, institutional practice of out-sourcing, or more generally of increasing profits regardless of (non-monetary) costs, is *just* is another issue. But insofar as such practices are not unjust, one particular corporation's involvement in the practice is morally defensible. Easiest to answer is whether out-sourcing violates the rights of the American workers who lose their jobs, for there is no right to hold or keep any particular job.[15] A corporation thus harms its American workers by out-sourcing jobs to Third World countries, but it does not wrong them. Despite its harm, then, out-sourcing entails no duties of redress.[16]

The second situation regards whether sweatshop conditions harm or wrong those working under them. Whether sweatshop conditions set back the interests of those who work under them, and so constitute a harm, varies depending on what conditions actually obtain, and so answering it involves some empirical assessment. To the extent that any particular sweatshop involves the horrific conditions that the term "sweatshop conditions" conjures up, such as working twelve or more hours per day, and/or having no breaks during the workday even to use the lavatory, at least some of the interests of the workers will be set back. The reasons workers have for consenting to work under these conditions (assuming consent is given) may involve a furthering of some of the workers' other interests, however, such as to make an income or to exercise independence.[17] So this will be a very difficult question to answer, and it will involve a cost-benefit analysis of looking at how interests are set back or furthered on the balance. Regarding fault, owners, managers, and corporations probably do not *intend* to set back the interests of their workers, or to produce the risk of such harmful consequences. They are, however, generally aware of the risks that interests will be set back; again, the conditions that workers must work under in order to produce goods at the rate they are expected to is a foreseen if not intended consequence. While descriptions of agents' intentions are just as tricky in this example, the risks here are clearer, especially as they involve violations of human rights, and the awareness of such risks might be easier to incorporate into a description of agents' actions.

Whether sweatshop conditions are morally indefensible (inexcusable and unjustifiable) is also tricky. Like out-sourcing, sweatshop conditions are at least justifiable in the global economic context of needing to make or increase profits in order to stay in business. The justice of the global practice of sweatshop conditions is again a separate but here more closely related issue, particularly when rights violations are involved. The *reasons* for violating rights, in order to make or increase profit, are generally not excusable or justifiable. Often, indeed, sweatshop conditions do violate the rights of those who work under them, and so constitute a wrong. If rights are not violated, of course, there may be no wronging or injustice involved. Note that this question can be applied either to legal or moral rights. In many Third World countries workers do not have relevant legal rights that would be violated by sweatshop conditions, and so there would be no (regional or national) legal basis for corrective justice. Yet moral rights may exist where legal rights do not, and if working conditions violate human rights then there is a moral basis for duties of redress, and there may be a legal basis for international corrective justice as well. Thus, sweatshop conditions may or may not harm those who work under them, depending on the particular case. Insofar as these conditions violate human rights, however, they do constitute a wrong and therefore ground duties of redress, or duties to correct the injustice and right the wrong. Sweatshop conditions have in fact been found in legal cases to violate human rights, such as when Saipan garment workers brought cases against 27 American retailers and 23 Saipan factories; the retailers and factories were found liable, and their duties of redress consisted of an award of US$20 million.[18]

Some aspects of global poverty clearly constitute wrongful harm. What is wrong about poverty in this framework is that it involves a rights violation; in these cases, justice demands that wrongs are righted. Agents thus have responsibilities toward the poor insofar as they are liable for the wrongs that constitute (certain aspects of) poverty. More must be said about how agents cause these wrongful harms, however. Rather than analyzing causation in the abstract, the following section discusses the ways in which we can say that poverty is caused. This analysis of how poverty results from causal factors helps explain the relevance of the criticism that beneficence does not account for causal factors and so show the importance of redress models for conceptualizing poverty in this way.

In What Ways Poverty Is Caused

Duties of redress are most strongly justified according to the causal relationships an agent has to a harmful outcome, when an agent has made a morally relevant causal contribution to harm.[19] This section gives an account of causation that is applicable to global poverty with all of its complexities. Complicated causal explanations can account for the multiple and sometimes over-determining factors involved with global poverty, making sense of how responsibility can be attributed in a liability model of redress. For responsibility to be ascribed, causes must be sufficiently distinguishable that agents can be identified. While this is a difficult project for a complicated political problem like global poverty, this section shows that it is not impossible.

Causal explanations describe the conditions that contribute to producing a particular outcome. The conditions that lead to poverty necessarily vary from case to case, even when we include only structural (not individual or bad luck) factors. For example, one list of conditions might include: a lack of investment in healthcare (making it unavailable except in cities), a commitment to exporting food grown (such as a condition for obtaining a World Bank loan), and a removal of land from common use (requiring people to rely on industry for jobs rather than growing their own food). In another place, the list might include: a corporate monopoly on health insurance (making it too expensive for most to afford), a shift of decent-paying jobs overseas for cheaper labor (resulting in lack of jobs with a livable wage), and a dismantling of social welfare services (so there are fewer resources for people to fall back on in a time of need). In any given case of poverty, some list can be given of conditions that are present and that somehow play a causally relevant role in leading to or comprising poverty.[20]

The relationships between such varying factors may be intricate and complicated, but good causal explanations can account for their complexity. What causes an effect is a conjunction of conditions, one of which is what we generally think of as "the cause," and the others of which are additional conditions—both positive conditions of things that are present, and negative conditions of things that are absent—necessary to bring about the effect. We *select* which of the conditions we think is the most relevant one to count as "the cause," while the other conditions are necessary but accepted as "normal" and therefore in the background. For example, the causal conditions of a fire might include a lit match, the presence of flammable wood (a positive condition), and a lack of wind to blow out the lit match (a negative condition). We would consider the lit match to be the cause of the fire, not the flammable wood or lack of wind, yet the flammable wood and lack of wind are nonetheless conditions that must necessarily be present—at least in conjunction with each other—in order for the fire to occur. This is because a lit match is insufficient to cause fire by itself, even though it is necessary in this circumstance. It is the *conjunction* of these conditions that allows the fire to occur.[21]

Many background conditions are present in any causal field from which relevant causal factors are selected.[22] What is included in the set of background conditions versus the set of relevant causal factors depends on what appears to be "normal" or "abnormal." For example, because environmental catastrophes, or what we call "natural disasters," strike us (*qua* humans) as abnormal, we often pinpoint natural disasters as the "cause" of human problems. Thus we are likely to attribute famine to the drought from which it seems to result, if for no other reason than because the drought seems abnormal. This may result in ignoring other conditions that appear normal but that nonetheless play a causal role in bringing about certain outcomes, such as economic and political conditions that prevent trade or make agricultural prices plummet. Because these economic and political conditions often at least *seem* normal, they may not be looked at in the causal evaluation.

This suggests that the causal and moral relevancy of present conditions is not a closed matter, that what counts as a "background" or "foreground" condition is open to debate as we revise the way we describe causes and actions. Causal inquiries use action descriptions, which are explanations of how different events seem to relate to each other logically. These action descriptions are made by humans, based on our observation, understood with our limited reasoning skills, and explained within the confines of our language. If our understanding of causation is essentially a description of logical relationships between occurring events, then there is no objective fact—at least to which humans have access—

about how events relate to each other. Action descriptions arise from the way that we see the world; as our observations and understandings of events in the world change over time; the kinds of descriptions about how things happen also change. Action descriptions and responsibility ascriptions are made inter-subjectively, as a collective human endeavor within particular social contexts, and they are subject to revision based on the acquisition of new knowledge.[23]

While the causal theorists who apply action descriptions or causal explanations to the moral sphere are themselves anti-realist about metaphysics and morality,[24] we need not commit ourselves to philosophical anti-realism in order to take seriously the role of action descriptions in understanding causal events and human interactions. The process of figuring out causes of a situation is an epistemological inquiry of trying to acquire as much knowledge about this situation as possible in order to understand it better. Whether this tells us an "objective" fact (i.e., independent of human observation and explanation) about what constitutes causes is irrelevant. What is important is that causal and moral inquiry as action description allows room for revising our moral understandings, including what we understand our moral and political responsibilities to be, based on acquiring new and better knowledge about what occurs.

In many cases of poverty, multiple conditions may be causally relevant that not only exacerbate each other (worsening the state of poverty), but that actually over-determine the existence of poverty. Over-determination occurs when there are multiple sets of causally relevant conditions present, any of which alone would be sufficient to create a particular outcome, but all of which occur together. Causal explanations account for over-determination by describing causation as a set of conditions that as a whole is unnecessary but sufficient to produce the effect. Any number of sets of conditions may be sufficient—though none necessary—to cause poverty. For example, a person may be poor as a result of poor decisions her family made about how to invest their resources, *and* as a result of political actions by her government resulting in war, *and* as a result of recent droughts that made farming unprofitable. Any one of these sets of conditions would have been enough to have made her poor; none is by itself necessary to produce the effect.[25]

Independent over-determination occurs quite frequently in relation to structural injustices like global poverty. Here, two (or more) events occur independently of each other and not necessarily at the same time, either of which would be sufficient to produce a certain outcome, but only one of which *actually* produces the outcome and just because it occurs earlier. Commonly, several factors co-exist, each of which would be sufficient to create some condition of poverty, but instead all of which contribute to the condition. Often, these multiple factors actually exacerbate each other to make an outcome like poverty even worse than it would have been had only one such factor existed.[26]

For example, several factors may co-exist that successfully eliminate the ability for indigenous people to be small-scale subsistence farmers. If the nation accepts a World Bank loan that requires it to grow food for export, mainly Western foods like wheat and sugar, farming will have to turn away from the variety of small-scale, local crops to massive monoculture crops. If a government leader sells land previously used in common by indigenous people to a multinational corporation for profits and the hope of future taxes, indigenous people will have less land available for them to farm on. The more that multinational agricultural corporations patent particular varieties of seeds, and develop protections against people using them without paying for them (such as the ability to sue farmers when their crops include the genetic mutation, even if the crop acquired it through accidental cross-pollination by natural spread of seeds), the more expensive it is to farm and the less that individuals can do it without working for a major agricultural company. Any of these conditions would be sufficient to drive out small-scale farmers, but all of these conditions together contribute to the outcome and in fact probably worsen its severity by closing more and more options.

Note that in this example, *how* the case is described is of particular significance. If we describe this case as agents acting on helpless victims, then the harmfulness and wrongfulness of the case is more apparent. On the other hand, if we describe this case as a complex interaction between various agents, some of whom *consent* to practices that in different circumstances might seem unjust or harmful, it is harder to see how this is an example of a *wrongful* harm justifying redress. The fact that these different descriptions significantly impact our moral evaluation of the case shows the importance of what action descriptions we make in explaining causal processes and using them for moral evaluation.[27]

In contrast to independent over-determination, linked over-determination is the phenomenon of two (or more) events occurring *in relation* to the other in order to produce the same outcome. In other words, if one event fails to happen, there is a back-up action that will guarantee the same outcome that would have happened had the first event occurred.[28] A strict example of linked over-determination is a foreign government that plans to install a puppet government of its own if a rebel *coup d'etat* does not occur as planned. Linked over-determination can also be understood more loosely as a model of causal relationship that explains a lot of corporate and government activity. Examples include exclusive partnerships that allow a particular corporation to have naming rights, "official sponsorships," and other monopolizing practices where one corporation plans to accept these deals when they become available, if another company does not. Similarly, a powerful company may be ready to take over a smaller company in a corporate takeover, if another powerful company does not do so. Cases in which the two corporate agents do not act in accordance with each other are not strict examples of linked over-determination; nonetheless, the model still provides a useful way to conceptualize the relationship between the relevant causal factors.

In particular, it offers a way to understand the context of social or institutional expectation, making an agent feel compelled to act a certain way since another agent will do the same if the first agent does not. This kind of thinking occurs when a company decides it needs to be the first to introduce an innovative practice that is economically profitable to the company even if it exacerbates the poverty of others, in order to reap the profits it gains by beating the competition. One example of this involves the decision of technology companies to use deceptive accounting practices in the late 1990s to boost their stock. Their motive might have been to not be left out; they might have thought, "If we don't do it, someone else will—and beat us economically, so potentially putting us out of business." But this practice ultimately bilked these companies' shareholders out of millions of dollars as stocks later crashed. Similarly, energy companies like Enron deceived people into believing there was an energy crisis around the same time period; this allowed the companies to save money with electricity blackouts, to negotiate favorable policies from state governments, and to steal money from citizens who had inflated energy bills. Linked over-determination provides a way to understand the motivation for such practices, though it certainly does not justify them, as these practices clearly play a causal role in contributing to faulty action.

Linked over-determination also explains the social expectation for behavior associated with roles. If a person does not act as she is required by her role, then she can be replaced by someone else acting in the same role who will do what she should have done. This is often used as an excuse by individuals who are "just following orders" in acting immorally, such as those who acted in roles that required them to send Jews to concentration camps under Nazi Germany, or those who obey the orders they are given as soldiers to massacre villages.[29] Linked over-determination shows the diminished causal importance of the actions of any particular agent, since another agent presumably would have acted in her place. This makes ascribing agency and responsibility with respect to roles very difficult.

Assessing causal responsibility in complicated cases like these, when there are multiple necessary causal conditions and even multiple sufficient sets of conditions, can be very difficult. Making these judgments is like doing detective work. It involves human judgment about "what counts," what is relevant, and it requires learning as much about a situation as possible in order to make decisions based on the most complete relevant knowledge available. Yet the fact that untangling a causal network of events is very difficult does not imply that it is impossible; even if it is impossible, this does not imply the endeavor is irrelevant. We may in fact *never* know all the relevant information, so that our understanding of the relevant causal web is always incomplete. Yet we can and should make decisions about what to do based on whatever knowledge we do have about relevant causal relationships.

Factors that Differentiate Responsibility

The agents that are responsible for righting wrongs they have caused may be individual or collective. The collective agents that are responsible in this way are collectives only of a certain kind, however, for they must have relevant and sufficient agency to be said to act, to cause specific outcomes, and to be accountable to them and capable of rectification. The kind of collective that has this agency is a *conglomerate*. In contrast to collectives that are aggregates, such as the random collectives described in the previous chapter, conglomerates group people together in a non-accidental or non-contingent way. Three features distinguish conglomerates from aggregates: they have an internal organization that includes decision-making and action-delegating procedures; they hold their members to standards of conduct to which they do not hold non-members; and their members have differing defined roles, some of which grant them power over other members. While the aggregate's unit of agency is ultimately the individual, the unit of agency in a conglomerate is the group itself. One implication of this is that no particular individuals are required to fix a conglomerate's identity, for the whole is greater than the sum of its parts. Since its identity cannot be reduced to its individual members, a conglomerate can exist even with varying membership. What gives a conglomerate this independent status of agency is that it has decision-making and action-distributing procedures independent of the individual members that comprise the group.[30]

Common examples of conglomerates include governments, corporations, and non-profit non-governmental organizations (NGOs), all of which have the requisite decision-making and action-distributing procedures to make them agents in their own right, independent of the particular individuals who occupy roles within them. Some philosophers object to the concept of a "conglomerate" or a collective that has agency of its own, arguing that only individual human beings have the relevant kind of agency that justifies and enables responsibility. Although there may be some debate about whether corporate acts have enough intentionality for responsibility to be ascribed to them, if we understand intentions in a broad way as reasons for acting, then conglomerates like corporations certainly have intentions.[31] After all, corporations, governments, and NGOs all have goals and mission statements which describe their intentions, and they often have charters which describe their procedures for making decisions and carrying out actions. As we consider factors that mitigate responsibility, then, let us keep in mind that the agents whose responsibility we are discussing are those agents capable of committing wrongs that need to be redressed, including both individuals and collectives, especially governments and corporations.

Responsibility as redress admits of degrees, depending on the agent's morally relevant causal contribution to harm. As suggested by the above discussion, there are many factors that go into making such a contribution, which can be classified as two primary concerns. One is the deontological focus on how much control or voluntariness an agent had in acting and how her[32] intentions, desires, and related mental states helped "cause" her actions. The other is the consequential focus on how harmful the outcome is, and what kind of action the agent performed that contributed to it. In what follows in this section I give an overview of these and related factors that may strengthen or diminish one's responsibility.

Ignorance

Since moral responsibility is something that belongs only to agents, intentions and mental states are important in assessing degrees of responsibility insofar as they are related to control and voluntariness in action. Conditions that reduce the control an agent has over her behavior tend to mitigate the responsibility she has for it.[33] While these conditions are sometimes called "excuses," particularly in philosophy of law, this terminology should not mislead one into thinking that these factors absolve responsibility, especially in the context of the present discussion. As factors that reduce an agent's control all admit of degrees, so does the responsibility that may be diminished or enhanced by their presence or lack.

Ignorance is one of the oldest factors thought to diminish responsibility in certain circumstances.[34] When it is not reasonable to expect a person to have the relevant knowledge to be aware of the effects of her actions, their moral relevance, and possible alternate actions, ignorance may be a justified excuse.[35] Not knowing the speed limit does not excuse an individual from having to pay a fine for speeding, because we expect that a person should be alert enough (paying attention to signs) to find out what the speed limit is, or at least err on the side of caution; a person who was incapable of doing either of these things is incapable of driving safely. In some cases, however, our expectations for obtaining relevant knowledge are much lower because of the seeming difficulty in acquiring it, and so we would be more willing to accept ignorance as an excuse.

Ignorance of how one's actions affect others is a primary excuse used to try to mitigate responsibility for global poverty. If the causal factors that lead to poverty are complicated, it may not be reasonable to expect affluent individuals to discern them and to change their actions based on them. Similarly, affluent individuals may not understand why their actions are morally objectionable (and not just part of an unfortunate system) or what alternatives they may have to act differently. Whether it is reasonable to expect affluent agents to have this knowledge, or to what extent they should have this knowledge, is often difficult to determine.

Ignorance is less easily an excuse for collective agents, however, particularly those that are larger and more powerful. Even if causal factors that lead to poverty are complicated, we do—or at least *should*, morally speaking—expect governments to take the time to sort them out in order to make good policy regarding poverty; we also should expect corporations to consider whether their economic practices—such as using sweatshop labor in manufacturing, or using scarce natural resources as material for their goods—contribute to poverty. Claiming they have "no alternative," or that practices that happen to contribute to poverty are just how politics and economics operate today, is not a good excuse. We hold conglomerates to different standards than individuals because they have more resources and more power to obtain relevant knowledge about the causal relations between actions and outcomes, and to consider alternate courses of action. Individuals' ability to acquire relevant knowledge is more limited, but it is not impossible, which is why individuals still have some important responsibility to learn about the effects of their actions; having greater ability, conglomerates have even greater responsibility in this regard.

There is also much debate about what the morally relevant difference is between intentions and foreseen consequences, sometimes known as the doctrine of double effect.[36] If an agent knows that a particular risk, which is not the purpose or intention of her action, is a likely outcome of her action, does she have just as much responsibility for its occurrence as if it were her intention? Think back to the examples assessed above. The purpose of a corporation's outsourcing jobs for cheaper labor or turning a blind eye to sweatshop working conditions is to increase profits as much as possible. Yet the harm done to First World workers who lose their jobs or to Third World workers who work in sweatshop conditions is a risk with high probability that it seems the corporate decision-makers should be aware of and take into account. While at least *some* such knowledge about risks is necessary, *how much* knowledge decision-makers are expected to know and account for regarding such potential harms, and the probability that such harms will occur, is an open question. Furthermore, the extent to which such risks are morally relevant even if they are not intentions for action is debatable. Without going into depth on the issue of intentions versus foreseen consequences, I want to suggest that the greater the harm and the greater the likelihood that it will be experienced, and especially the easier it is for agents to acquire this knowledge, the more that it matters morally in making decisions about how to act. Agents that choose to act in spite of easily knowing about grave harms that will result from their actions have greater liability for the harm they cause.

Kinds of Intentions

Evaluating an agent's mental states, especially her intentions, is one important aspect of determining whether an agent has the requisite control or voluntariness that can make her morally responsible for her action. An intention is an agent's reason for acting, sometimes considered a "cause" of her action.[37] Because an intention is an intensional state (i.e., a state internal to the agent rather than extensional, or external), it is tricky to determine; it is not the kind of thing that can be observed by others. Determining an agent's intentions is a controversial aspect involved in attributing responsibility because others do not have first-hand knowledge of one's intention, and one's own self-report is easily false or misleading.

Besides the difficulty in describing what an agent's intentions are, there is some debate about what it means to act intentionally, and what kind of intentional action grounds responsibility. For example, intentionality may refer to any of the following: *that* one acts, or that one acts in a certain way, or that one's action brings about a certain outcome. That one acts (that one intended to do some action) is the most broad category of intention, including the most actions; that one brings about a certain outcome (that one intended to cause a certain result) is the most narrow category of intention, including the fewest actions.[38] Different forms of intention seem to imply different kinds or at least degrees of responsibility for action, as an agent may have some responsibility for inadvertent or accidental action or for unintended consequence (particularly in the strict liability model), but have greater responsibility for bringing about a specific harmful outcome as an intended consequence of one's action.[39]

Intentions must be described relative to circumstances. For example, an action description that says an agent intentionally makes a choice for something is not specific enough; the action description must describe the choice contextually, as choosing one thing over a different option, or choosing one thing from a specific range of options. Agents have degrees of intentionality depending on the degrees of control or voluntariness they have, given the conditions in which they choose, in other words *given the options from which they are able to choose.*[40] An action done in very limiting circumstances may be less wrong than the same action done under a greater range of options. For example, I may intend to avoid supporting Wal-Mart's unjust practices regarding its treatment of employees, the sweatshop workers who make its products, and the communities hurt by its presence, and so instead I shop at Target. Yet in so doing, I inadvertently continue to support some of the same practices, including unjust treatment of sweatshop workers who make Target's products. Even though I don't intend the latter, I act intentionally, and on a broad account of intentionality, I am fully responsible for this action. On a narrower, contextual account of intentionality, however, my responsibility is at least contextualized, if not diminished.

Depending on my reasons, and on what other options are also available (especially if there are no other department stores offering goods I can afford and in reasonable driving distance, as is the case in many rural areas), supporting Target rather than Wal-Mart may be less wrong than supporting Target *simpliciter.*

Degrees and Avoidability of Harm

While the beneficence model grounds responsibility according to the badness of the state of affairs itself, the redress model justifies responsibility according to an agent's contribution to the bad states of affairs. Yet consequentialist concerns still matter. The degree of harm caused can impact the degree of one's responsibility for it, so that the greater the harm, the greater one's responsibility for it if one played a causally relevant role. Or, when the cause of harm is irrelevant, we may turn to consequentialist considerations of who could have prevented the harm; if harm could have been prevented, sometimes the agent that is considered liable for that harm is the one that was in the best position to have prevented it, and we would consider an agent responsible for her omissions if she failed to perform the action that was expected of her. In some liability assessments, when harm is so great, it is irrelevant whether the outcome was an avoidable consequence of one's action or not, or whether the harm was in any way preventable, or whether one had any choice in participating in the actions that led to it; if an agent made some relevant causal contribution, then she is considered liable.[41]

For many people, ascribing responsibility this way goes against intuitions. If changing one's action does not prevent a harm from occurring, it seems that's responsibility for it should be excused or at least diminished. We generally ascribe moral responsibility to agents, who have some control over their actions. If they are unable to change the course of events at all at will, then it is hard to see how they can have this control and therefore be responsible.[42] When an outcome is bad enough, however, the fact that the harm was unavoidable does not necessarily or completely undermine responsibility. For example, a company may be unable to avoid contracting with a sweatshop, given what factories are available with which to contract—but the company still has some responsibility to compensate for human rights violations and to work with the sweatshop to create better working conditions. In the framework of liability, when a substantial loss has occurred, that loss must be either absorbed by the victim or compensated for by the agent that is said to have caused it. It may be unfair to require an agent that could not have avoided causing that loss or could not have prevented that loss to repair it—but it may be even more unfair to require the victim to absorb that loss, especially when that loss is a violation of human rights. While unavoidability of causing harm rarely excuses responsibility completely, it does at least sometimes diminish it.

How we describe an agent's actions and causal effects is relevant to determining whether harm was avoidable or preventable, of course, just as it is regarding most excusing factors. Agents, both individuals and conglomerates, often use the unavoidability of causing harm as an excuse for their actions with the hope that it will absolve all responsibility. But whether their actions were indeed necessary to do in the circumstances, and whether the harm they caused was unavoidable, depends a lot on interpretation of the act and its effects. In terms of government actions, a government may justify its intervention as necessary for the sake of helping people. For example, President Bush claimed that one of the motivations of the United States government in bombing Afghanistan in 2002 was to help the Afghani women who were disempowered under Taliban rule; the intention of helping people who were oppressed under Saddam Hussein's dictatorship was also used as a reason for intervening in Iraq at the beginning of the 21st century.[43] But while governments justify some of their actions by helping those in need, they willfully ignore situations in other countries where the need is arguably greater, and where help is explicitly asked for. This willful non-intervention occurs especially when there is no profit to be gained from intervention, such as the genocide in Rwanda in 1994 and the genocide currently taking place in the Darfur region of Sudan. The harm of allowing genocide to occur even while engaging in military occupations of regions that do not want the intervention is clearly avoidable. While intervention is often justified according to helping those in need, it is generally practiced according to what is in the greatest interest of those who would help.

Necessity and harm are contextual with respect to corporate actions as well. A corporation may claim that it had to do a certain action (such as outsourcing its manufacturing labor to sweatshops) because of economic conditions and expectations it had no control over (for example, that it would have gone out of business if it had not outsourced to sweatshops) and that the effects of this action (such as violating human rights by having a physically unsafe working environment through sexual harassment or working on dangerous equipment without safety features) were unavoidable by the corporation. Only on one interpretation of the intentions, actions, and consequences involved is this true. A different action description can be given that would describe this act and its consequences as going along with dominant economic practices for the sake of increasing profits without regard to moral decency. If the corporation were creative in considering how to stay profitable in a cutthroat business environment, it might have imagined different options that would promote profitability and corporate survival, for example selling more expensive specialized products made with fair labor, and/or promoting its use of fair labor as opposed to the competitors' sweatshop labor. After all, there is a market for ethically made products, and businesses that promote their ethical practices can reap the economic rewards of moral action.[44] So unavoidability of harm is an excuse that must be taken with a grain of salt, so to speak, and the relevant action descriptions must be examined closely to determine how well this excuse holds in mitigating responsibility.

Kinds of Action

Another factor that is commonly thought to affect the degree of responsibility an agent has is what *kind* of causal contribution she makes to harm, what kind of action or omission she makes, and what the action's relation is to the relevant causal processes. Because what counts as an action is contextual, however, depending on what action description seems most appropriate for the given circumstances, the responsibility that follows from particular kinds of action must be understood contextually as well.

Some moral philosophers have a narrow view of what causal contribution is necessary for responsibility, as initiating a causal chain.[45] In this view, an agent has sufficient causal involvement to be held morally responsible when she is the "starting point" of a course of action that ends in harm. Being an initiator means that one is only responsible for one's actions and not for one's omissions. What counts as "initiating" a causal chain is highly debatable and sometimes impossible to determine, however, so few philosophers take this position seriously. Causal chains can stretch so far back in history that no initiator can be found. In fact, often it does not make sense conceptually to seek out a starting point for a causal process, especially since understanding causation involves making action descriptions about what *appears* to be the case. Triggering events already set to occur may be more morally relevant than initiating events; making a decision to act may be more morally relevant than actually doing the action.[46] Causation may also be thought of as an intervention in the existing or expected state of the world, but what is an "intervention" and what states of affairs would be expected is equally controversial.[47] A lot hinges on how we describe our actions and their relations to the events that lead to particular outcomes, and we can always re-describe those if we have reason to select different causal factors as morally relevant.

What makes distinctions between the moral relevance of different kinds of actions very tricky is that they assume a separation between the events that can be described as human action and the rest of causal processes, almost as if there could be a pure "course of events" that would occur separate from human action, and that occurs differently with the right kind of human intervention. For example, consider Samuel Scheffler's argument that the main problem with the various metaphysical distinctions about action is a question about how we see ourselves as moral agents. He argues that a person's views of herself involve a strong tension. On one hand she sees herself as an agent with special responsibilities for the "primary manifestations" of her own agency, or what we might think of as "doings" or "actions" (versus "allowings" or "omissions"). On the other hand, she sees how her actions belong to the causal order of nature, and how causal processes occur with or without her intervention. The result of this tension is that we tend to think we have greater responsibilities for what we "do" and lesser but still significant responsibilities for what we do *not* "do."[48]

The problem with a view like Scheffler's is that what is morally relevant is not only how we see ourselves as agents, but also how we describe our relationship to other causal processes. It is not that some reified "causal processes" occur out there, and our actions occur somehow independently, as some form of intervention to what is already there, separated from us. Rather, our actions are a form of causal activity, and there are other causal activities that occur, and the conjunction of all these activities creates some complicated, interdependent causal process. Which outcome we can attribute to which of our particular actions is very difficult to determine, because of the necessarily interrelated way that our actions conjoin with other causal activities. This does not make causation and kinds of action irrelevant factors to assigning or taking responsibility. But it does suggest a different, more complicated way of understanding how individual actions relate to various other causal processes. Metaphysical distinctions between "doing" and "allowing," etc. suggest an overly simplistic notion of "intervention" that human agents make relative to other causal processes.

For example, on Feinberg's understanding of wrongful harm, an agent harms another by setting her interests back wrongfully. This thwarting is indeed a form of intervention into the state of affairs that might otherwise occur without such action. Yet what counts as a causally and morally relevant interaction such as to affect states of affairs is an open-ended question, and Feinberg argues that omissions may count as much as actions, depending on the circumstances and expectations that we hold for what people should do in such circumstances. This

view is largely argued within a regularity account of causation, in which causation is a logical sequence of regularity based on human observation and description. Realists of causation, who argue that causation is a metaphysically real fact
independent of human observation or description, may object that views about
what counts as acts or omissions are misguided.[49] Regardless of the metaphysical fact about causation, however, and regardless of metaphysical distinctions
about kinds of actions, what is relevant to morality and assessments of responsibility is what actions or omissions are *expected* of agents to do given particular
circumstances.

How we describe our actions and their effects, and how they relate to other
events, depends on the contexts in which we make these action descriptions,
which clearly invites debate. To the extent that we agree that ascribing moral
responsibility involves making human judgments rather than discerning absolute
or "objective" judgments made from a "God's eye view," social expectations for
what agents ought to do are crucial to assessing the moral relevance of different
kinds of actions, and so to assessing responsibility. What kinds of actions are
associated with what kind or degree of responsibility depends on these social
expectations.

Social Expectations

Social expectations provide a context for describing the metaphysical and
moral nature of the kinds of actions agents perform, and how this enhances or
diminishes responsibility. To explain the role of social expectations in determining responsibility, let us start with a discussion of the moral relevance of omissions. While utilitarians equivocate acts and omissions, and libertarians deny
that omissions are ever as morally relevant as acts, many moral and legal philosophers see their moral relevance as somewhere in the middle of these positions. One way to account for omissions is to treat them as morally relevant
when they constitute failures to meet expectations for what people should or
should not do, in others words when a person's act or failure to act falls below
some standard; these standards may consist of the responsibilities that attach to
agents' social roles. While locating the moral relevance of omissions in the expectations attached to social roles is promising, we need to be wary of accepting
social expectations as given, rather than evaluating them morally.[50]

Social expectations or standards are a norm, but they are not necessarily
normative. Morally speaking, we ought not to accept them as given without
evaluating them; there may be good reasons why we should change them. We
can rely on these social expectations for evaluating the moral relevance of omissions only if the standards are themselves justified—but then what grounds the
significance of omissions is not the expectations themselves but rather what
grounds *them*. While roles help ground social expectations to some extent, they
cannot do all the work themselves. Role expectations involve action descriptions, which are themselves objects of moral assessment; role responsibility de-

pends on what description we make of a person's action. As long as roles are themselves not subject to moral scrutiny, however, they provide norms that are not necessarily normative, just as the social expectations for which they provide a context for justification do.

To address the problems of normativity, we need to understand the context for social expectations more broadly. Social expectations are organized around the ends of particular communities and are thus inter-subjectively determined by the members of these communities. What constitutes these expectations depends on what power relations are present, of course, as those who have more power socially, politically, and economically tend to have more power defining what these expectations consist of. The relationship between social expectations and action descriptions is a dynamic one, however, for describing an action is not really a descriptive process of relating neutral "fact" about causes and effects, but is rather a prescriptive process that shapes how we should think about different actions and responsibility for consequences. As a result, these expectations, despite being a result of existing power relations, have a normative function and are thus always subject to community revision. When we re-describe actions, therefore, we change our normative views.[51]

The action descriptions and resulting responsibility ascriptions occur within the public sphere and may either maintain or challenge existing power relations as the case may be. All community members have some power in describing an action and in determining what causes of an outcome are morally relevant, and so in constructing normative morality, including responsibility ascription. Of course, the ability for ordinary individuals to have some power here depends at least partly on there being a thriving public sphere with open communication, where both political figures and the media are seen as accountable to citizens. This thriving public sphere is admittedly idealistic. While some openness and accountability must be present for action descriptions and responsibility ascriptions to be able to challenge existing power relations, to what degree they are required is a bit unclear.

To understand how social expectations for what agents should or should not do affect how we describe actions and ascribe responsibility, and to see how changing social contexts can in turn change how we understand the causes of and responsibility for outcomes, let us turn to an example. Consider the argument that when young women in Caribbean countries work as prostitutes, or when parents in East Asian countries like Thailand sell their young, underage daughters to brokers who employ them in the sex industry, they do so out of pure choice. Even though their options may be limited, this view regards their actions nevertheless as resulting from choice, so that the young women and/or their parents are ultimately the only ones responsible for their actions. Only in an extremely individualistic framework of choice and control over one's actions could this make sense. In contrast, we might understand such a decision as arising out of socio-economic coercion, when the only other option for a young woman and/or her family besides her sex work is starvation. If we understand the causal factors that influence a person's choice more broadly, we see the social context that conditions what options are available, and we broaden our understanding of who shares responsibility. For example, the businesses that take advantage of lax laws and of the desperation of young women and their families to earn money are responsible for making this an available and attractive option. The men who are complicit in sex work by supporting and participating in it are also blameworthy for taking advantage of the opportunity to do so; rather than judging the situation as bad by refusing to support it, they implicitly judge it as good, or at least morally acceptable, by participating in it. They thus share some responsibility for the maintenance and growth of the global sex industry and its consequences, including trafficking in women, especially youths. The governments that allow the sex trade by not creating laws against it or by not enforcing existing laws also share responsibility. As long as we view sex work very narrowly as arising out of an individual's choice, then we do not need to blame those who create its conditions or who allow and support it. When we understand the causal factors more broadly, however, and acknowledge the causal roles that governments, sex businesses, and men who frequent them play, then we see that they also share in responsibility. As our social expectations for what these players should do change, we will describe the causal relations involved with sex work and the sex trade differently, and we will ascribe responsibility to different players. It is not merely the individual's actions that matter causally and morally, but also the omissions of other agents that play relevant roles in contributing to the outcome. Our understanding of what those roles should be, and what we should expect of such agents, affects how we ascribe responsibility and is changeable as we change our social understandings and expectations for appropriate moral action.

One of the most important ways that our social expectations affect responsibility ascriptions concerns the tension between economic and ethical value. When we think that a company's primary role is to maximize profit, we do not hold it responsible for bad social effects of its activities. A sex business is just trying to make money like any other business, after all. On the other hand, when we think that a company also has a social role to fulfill of being a good citizen, and promoting good social effects or at least not promoting bad ones (having duties of forbearance if not those of beneficence), then we do hold it responsible for bad effects that arise from maximizing profit. Changes in the past several decades regarding safety, health, environmental, and labor regulations in the U.S. reflect a shift in our expectations for a company's actions. Sometimes we demand corporate accountability for unethical behavior, as happened in the wake of the Enron scandal, but we still make excuses for companies that try to profit regardless of the ethical costs. We do not have a clear resolution for this tension, though I believe economic value should never trump ethical value, at least not absolutely. The concept of human rights would be empty if it did.[52]

Proportionality of Causal Contribution

Proportionality of causal contribution relative to others is also relevant to assessing duties of redress. Since here the grounding for any particular agent's responsibility is the agent's relevant contribution to harm, and not simply her ability to alleviate the harm, it seems that her particular responsibility should correspond with the degree of harm to which she contributes. Those who contribute more in causing harm are generally more responsible than those who contribute less.

Proportionality is especially relevant when responsibility is distributive. Distributive responsibility is that which is shared among various agents. This concept refers to the kind of responsibility that groups may have, so that a group has distributive responsibility if its members share in its liability or its duties of redress. Individuals within the group may have different duties regarding redress depending on their different actions and how they led to harm, or on their differentiated roles within the group. For example, group leaders have more responsibility if they coordinated or suggested the actions that led to harm; those who carried out harmful actions have more responsibility than those who did not but retained their group membership nonetheless. Those who were group members and did not know about the actions occurring, or did not know their harmful nature, or were not able to prevent their occurrence, or perhaps were not even able to renege their group membership (such as national or ethnic identity) have diminished responsibility because their causal and intentional relationship to the harm is much weaker.

How these various factors may undermine responsibility will be shown near the end of this chapter, when I illustrate how duties of redress are justified, what they involve, and what mitigates or differentiates them, with a detailed example. Before explaining how duties of redress apply to global poverty, I discuss limitations of these models.

Limitations with Applying
Duties of Redress to Global Poverty

Several objections can be raised to the attempt to apply the concept of redress to the responsibility for global poverty. First, relying on causal explanations that depend on human interpretation and social expectations for appropriate behavior raises worries about normativity. Second, the "backward-looking" emphasis of relying on causation for a model of moral responsibility seems inappropriate to complicated issues like global poverty in which the causal mechanisms involved are unclear. Finally, these models of responsibility raise worries about conservativism, for action descriptions and causal explanations can overlook important power relations by treating them as background conditions that are accepted as part of the *status quo,* rather than questioned and morally evaluated.

Lack of Normativity

A great concern is that this approach is descriptive rather than normative. One reason for this worry is that the model relies on action descriptions that operate within a framework of causation as regularity rather than realism. Regardless of whether there is any objective fact about the nature of morality or causation, our moral *understanding* is constructivist, meaning that it involves a process of trying to attain better knowledge and make better moral judgments based upon what we are able to know. After all, humans do not have a "God's eye" view of how the world works and what role human action plays within it. Causal facts may in fact exist, as realists claim, but to what extent we are able to know them is a separate question; it is this latter question that is relevant to assessing the moral understandings that ground judgments about responsibility.

The other reason for worrying about normativity is that an anti-realist justification for responsibility as redress depends at least partly on social expectations and roles that may seem pre-moral. The responsibility that attaches to roles, and the expectations we hold for people acting within roles and under social institutions, must be subject to moral evaluation as well, however. The extent to which people have duties within these capacities depends on what choice they have in taking them and what power they have within them. Roles and social expectations are not simply givens, but they may be transformed as we find reasons to judge their present states as morally unacceptable.

Related to concerns about normativity is the objection that the redress model might describe some form of responsibility, but not *moral* responsibility. Commonly we think of moral responsibility in terms of blame, where responsibility consists of the reactive attitudes that we hold toward a person based on whether her actions are socially approvable or not.[53] Responsibility as reactive attitudes focuses on the blameworthiness of an agent, where factors such as a person's intentions and her ability to control her faulty actions are relevant to making moral judgments and holding corresponding moral attitudes toward people. In contrast, the strict liability approach assesses only fault of the action, not of the agent. In denying the relevance of blame, the strict liability approach might be seen as making an assessment of fault that is strictly non-moral.

Critics may worry that focusing on strict liability rejects *moral* responsibility because moral responsibility is predicated only of agents. If what is important is the action, and not so much the agent, then it seems that the kind of responsibility we are concerned with here is simply the causal responsibility involved with event-causation, rather than the moral responsibility involved with agent-causation.[54] Yet these critics would be wrong to assume that the alternative to reactive attitudes toward agents simply reduces to event-causation and causal responsibility. What makes an agent an *agent* is not only some element of voluntariness or control—but also certain mental states, especially those involved with rationality. The capacity for rationality (or its analog regarding collective agents) is necessary in order to discern harm, to acknowledge one's participation in it or contribution to it, to rectify harms that have occurred, and to change behavior in the future where possible. Causal mechanisms that do not involve agents, i.e. that are involved in event-causation only and can be "responsible" only in the causal sense, do not have these capacities. Focusing on the action rather than the agent both in assessing responsibility and in redressing harm does not necessarily reduce to event-causation when the rational states of agents are necessary to action and response.

Inapplicability of "Backward-Looking" Approaches

The causal model of responsibility links an agent's intentions, her actions, and consequences. In doing so, it provides a historical account of responsibility because it determines what action an agent *should* take in the future based on what her intention and action *were* in the past, and how they causally contributed to harm. Political philosophers who put forth a view of poverty as structural injustice (examined in the next chapter) argue that responsibility for global poverty should be understood in a "forward-looking" way rather than as a historical "linked chain" account.[55] In their view, causal and legal responsibility focuses attention on the wrong thing, what already happened in the past, rather than on what should happen in the future, i.e. how structural conditions should be changed. Yet *taking* responsibility to change conditions for the *future* requires understanding the causal circumstances from the *past* that lead to the structures that create presently existing conditions of poverty.[56] The distinction between "forward-looking" and "backward-looking" approaches to responsibility therefore presents a false dichotomy.

Many causal factors that create present harms are on-going, rather than merely in the past. Tracing these causal factors does not involve simply looking at the past but also looking at the present, especially when the relevant causal factors continue or maintain wrongful harms perpetually. In fact, present structural conditions are largely the result of these on-going factors, rather than of finite events with specifiable beginnings and endings.[57] Regardless of whether we understand causal factors to have occurred in the past or to occur presently, the denial of the relevancy of "backward-looking" approaches seems to result from conflating causal inquiry with seeking liability and blame. But causal inquiries can examine causation—even agent-causation—without assigning culpability, such as to figure out the structural forces, involving individual and collective human action, that lead to poverty, so that we can have control over them and change them in the future.[58]

I want to re-emphasize here that I think it is misguided to focus on the *blame* aspect of the liability model to the exclusion of its causal components. Although causal considerations are often used for the purposes of assigning fault or blame, they do not reduce to culpability. Causal explanations describe how we understand causal relationships between the factors that lead to specific outcomes. We may use this understanding to assign blame—but we may not. We may also use our causal understandings simply to understand what occurs so that we can change it for the better.

Consequentialists will agree that it is important to look at what happened in the past to see how harm can be prevented in the future. There is little controversy about this weak use of "backward-looking" inquiries. But even a stronger use of such inquiries, one with which consequentialists will not agree, is important. It matters *who* is liable. What is morally relevant is not only what caused a bad state of affairs such that it can be avoided in the future, but also *who* caused it and how that agent can prevent future harm as well as rectify already caused harm. This stronger sense of understanding what happened ties a particular agent to a particular wrongful harm, providing the agent-relative reasons for action that libertarians require. Certainly not all of global poverty can be understood as wrongful harms in this way. But at least some of global poverty is indeed caused wrongfully, more so than some political philosophers acknowledge.

Conservativism

Another objection to applying responsibility as redress to global poverty is that causal explanations are too limited in their scope, that they necessarily exclude certain relevant information because they accept politically dominant norms unquestioningly. This makes the redress model conservative, perpetuating the *status quo* in terms of how poverty is understood as a problem, what agents have causally contributed to it, and what duties are entailed as a result.

This objection concerns the way causal explanations are made, as failing to account for the power relations and social structures that condition how we understand reality. Power relationships necessarily enter how we make decisions, including whose voices are listened to and taken seriously, so moral understandings are necessarily arbitrary and biased. Moreover, causal inquiries typically accept certain facts as background conditions, allowing them to be basically ignored on account of their being "normal" or typical. Yet what is normal and typical is often exactly what causes problems—particularly when the problem is structural in nature. Action descriptions and responsibility ascriptions are typically false or at least incomplete to the degree that they ignore, accepting as "normal," the very background conditions that constitute unjust circumstances.[59]

Given that many causal conditions exist, it can be difficult to select *which* factors are the most causally and morally relevant contribution that led to the outcome. What we select as "the" cause depends largely on what we are seeking in our causal inquiry. Often we select for conditions that seem to be "abnormal," as opposed to the background conditions that are taken to be "normal." What we consider "normal" or "abnormal," therefore, affects whether we treat a causal factor as a background condition or as a morally relevant condition requiring response from us. Environmental catastrophes, natural disasters, or what matters of seeming bad luck strike us as abnormal, so we frequently treat these as "the" causes of human problems. Our assumptions about normality easily result in ignoring other causal conditions, however. Other conditions that contribute to situations like global poverty—including economic and political factors but also factors such as diseases like AIDS and malaria—are most likely ignored because they frequently seem "normal" relative to other factors like natural disasters that seem more "abnormal." As critics of liability approaches to responsibility point out, however, those conditions that *seem* normal must be questioned as well. What appears to be "normal," or common, is not necessarily what is normative, or justifiable.

Economic and political conditions may seem normal relative to the context of time or to the context of other places in the world. When these changes occur too gradually and subtly for people to notice, we do not acknowledge their "abnormality." For example, the shift in the 1980s in the United States from the "Made in the U.S.A." campaign (encouraging people to buy goods made in the U.S. with union labor) to the large-scale outsourcing of manufacturing jobs (largely to factories that do not enforce labor, safety, or environmental laws, thus tending to constitute sweatshops) in the 1990s occurred so subtly that most people did not seem to notice this shift until it had already happened. In addition, when economic changes occur throughout the world, they do not seem abnormal because they occur so broadly. Outsourcing of manufacturing jobs seems normal because it is so common at this point in the globalization of the world's economies,[60] but this normality does not justify it as an ethical *norm*. Nor is this to say that outsourcing is necessarily unethical; my point is that its ethical status must be assessed, and must not be taken for granted just because it is common.

Since the objection here concerns how we make judgments, not about the fact that we make them at all, the correct response is to make our understandings better. Critics make an important point about the need to account for the way power relations necessarily enter the way we make causal explanations. Yet they have no essential disagreements with regularity theorists of causation who argue that moral judgments are simply descriptions that humans make as best as they can, but necessarily fallibly and incompletely. In fact, the causal model of responsibility actually supports this political concern. If background conditions are relevant to understanding the causal relationships in a situation better, they must enter the foreground for what counts, causally and morally speaking. In other words, if the *status quo* is what is causing harm or injustice, it can no longer be treated as background conditions to be accepted and ignored. Action descriptions and responsibility ascriptions occur within social contexts, and their intersubjective nature points to a need for just discourse about what counts in our moral understandings. The more that we learn about a situation, the more knowledge we can account for in understanding what is going on, selecting what is relevant, and making judgments based on these considerations.

The objection that the redress model is conservative is thus not defeating. Within the regularity view of causation and the constructivist framework of moral understanding and judgments of responsibility, causal explanations and action descriptions are open to interpretation and revision. The worry is that this allows them to be used to perpetuate unjust power relations, making the model a conservative one, and to be abused to assign causal fault wrongfully or to evade responsibility. Yet these are problems that any model of moral understanding would encounter, and this merely points to the need to create the most just conditions for such understandings to occur.

Applicability of Redress Models of Responsibility

Redress models of responsibility can avoid the above problems. Judgments about liability and role responsibility need not be pre-moral; act and role descriptions, as well as responsibility ascriptions, can be made which appropriately challenge the *status quo*. "Backward-looking" liability is the most appropriate form of responsibility that can be ascribed in certain contexts, when wrongful harm contributing to poverty has been caused by an identifiable agent.

Duties of redress hold an important place in our understanding of global responsibility, as they are a form of duty that agents have as a result of causing wrongful harm. The redress framework gives us a way to hold corporations, governments, and individuals responsible for particular actions they have done and a way to require them to make up for wrongful harms through reparations, punishment, and/or blame. While critics are right to show some limitations of the way these models apply to global justice issues like poverty, they are wrong to suggest that duties of redress are irrelevant to global poverty. A good example of the relevance of redress involves the liability of and sanctions against companies like Nestle that make infant formula and push their product on new mothers in Third World countries with problematic marketing such as by providing free samples.

The practice of giving free infant formula samples is controversial enough in affluent nations, but in the poorest regions of the world it is especially problematic. When a mother stops breastfeeding and starts using formula to feed her baby instead, her body quickly stops producing milk, so she is unable to breastfeed even if she wants to do so. Infant formula costs money, while breastfeeding basically involves no costs. Not only do the poorest women in the world lack money to pay for infant formula once their free samples are used up, but they also are much more likely to lack access to safe drinking water to use in mixing the formula. While relatively affluent women can usually afford to buy formula and usually have access to clean water to mix it with, and therefore have the options to make a reasonable choice about whether to breastfeed or use formula, the poorest women in the world lack these resources and so lack the options to make a meaningful choice. In addition to lacking the necessary resources to be able to feed babies formula in a healthy way, women also might lack knowledge about the consequences of their formula use, i.e., that their bodies will stop producing milk and that they will lack the means to use formula safely. Without an understanding of the consequences, these women are unable to make a meaningful choice about using formula. When very poor women have used infant formula samples, allowed their bodies to stop producing milk, and then lacked hygienic water or money to buy more formula, their babies have starved to the point of sickness or even death.

Nestle and other infant formula companies heavily marketed their infant formula to new mothers in both First and Third World countries in the 1960s and 1970s as a convenient replacement for breastmilk. As marketing got more intense in the 1970s, several organizations throughout the world opposed it, and by 1979, the World Health Organization (WHO) and the United Nations Children's Fund (UNICEF) proposed an international code of marketing for infant formula, which in 1980 the World Health Assembly adopted and with which the major infant formula companies refused to comply.[61] In 1981 an international boycott of Nestle began and lasted, on and off, for decades into the present. The boycott was suspended when Nestle would promise to comply with the marketing code, but resumed again when the company failed to follow through on its promise. The ridiculous length to which Nestle refused to comply with the code is demonstrated by its attempt to sue other infant formula companies in the U.S. in 1993 for *following* a ban on advertising infant formula. Nestle lost the court case in 1995, but the voluntary ban collapsed anyway (as one can tell when perusing any parenting magazine). While infant formula companies including Nestle continue to push their formula onto new mothers, the WHO continues to work on finding ways to implement the code against such marketing. This is especially important in the Third World where the danger of resulting starvation is so much greater; the WHO estimates that at least 1.5 million babies die each year (mostly in the poorest countries of the world) as a result of dehydration and starvation resulting from bottle-feeding.[62]

The liability involved in this situation is liability for a particular aspect of poverty, namely the dehydration and starvation, and often death, of babies. While there are many potential causal factors leading to these conditions, one in particular stands out: not feeding babies adequately. The most common reason for not feeding babies adequately is replacing breastfeeding, which provides safe and adequate nutrition, with formula feeding, which—without access to safe drinking water and/or without sufficient means to buy adequate amounts of formula—results in inadequate and unsanitary nutrition. The reason that mothers replace breastmilk with infant formula is that they are *urged* to do so. This occurs for a variety of reasons as well, including ignorance about the quality of breastmilk and ease of bottle-feeding compared to learning how to breastfeed. But the most important, morally significant causal factor that leads to a mother choosing not to breastfeed is that she is *encouraged* not to do so by infant formula companies. This encouragement takes a variety of forms involving several aspects of marketing, including giving free samples of formula as well as gifts like diaper or bottle bags to women upon the birth of their baby (especially in hospital settings), promoting bottle-feeding to health care workers who pass on misinformation about breastfeeding vs. bottle-feeding to new mothers, advertising the convenience of bottle-feeding but not the costs involved (including both the expense of formula and the need for safe drinking water), and playing on uneducated women's ignorance about their bodily functions by colluding in misinformation about the way their bodies make milk or about the quality of breastmilk. While there are multiple causal factors resulting in infant mortality, a major, morally significant, easily identifiable cause is the marketing of infant formula to replace breastmilk.

Encouraging women to feed their babies formula instead of breastmilk is clearly a harm when women do not have the means to use formula safely, because it sets back the important health and well-being interests of the baby. It is also a *wrong* because it violates human rights to sustenance.[63] This marketing involves faulty actions because they result in harmful consequences that are easily foreseen and easily avoidable. Since there is no excuse or justification that makes these actions morally defensible, they also constitute a wrongdoing. Thus the companies that produce and market infant formula are justifiably *liable* for their actions. Note that responsibility here is agent-relative: relative to the agents that cause the wrongful harm through faulty, morally indefensible actions. The responsible agent here is only, or mainly, the companies that produce and market infant formula, and those that market it in the most objectionable ways— such as Nestle—are the most liable for their actions.[64]

The responsibility of infant formula companies here is significant, and no factors are present that would diminish the responsibility these companies have. Clearly the companies' primary intention is to profit from selling their product. Although they may claim the intention to help provide mothers with nutrition for their babies, this goal is obviously thwarted when the result is malnourishment from inadequate feeding with formula. Moreover, in not acknowledging the costs involved with formula feeding, their advertisement of its convenience amounts to misinformation, especially for very poor women. And while it is true that some women are incapable of breastfeeding, so that infant formulas are necessary to save babies' lives, the vast majority of women are capable of breastfeeding, especially with help in getting started, and so formula is unnecessary for them. Since there is overwhelming evidence of this causal relation between replacing breastmilk with infant formula and infant mortality from trustworthy sources such as the World Health Organization, there is no way that companies like Nestle can claim ignorance. In fact, in addition to playing a clear and morally significant role in causally contributing to infant mortality, infant formula companies also exploit poor women and babies through their actions. Insofar as poor women make a choice to feed their babies infant formula, it is not a meaningful choice when they do not fully understand the options involved and their consequences, particularly when they do not have the means to make good use of those options. Infant formula companies that collude in providing misinformation take advantage of women's ignorance for their own profit.

The harms of replacing breastmilk with formula are completely avoidable— by not encouraging the use of infant formula, and by providing it only to women who are unable to breastfeed or who at least have enough money to pay for it and who have reliable access to safe drinking water. The kind of action that infant formula companies perform is utterly straightforward and uncontroversial: they perform "positive" actions of advertising their product and providing free samples in ways designed to encourage women to use their product. Their actions are a major factor in explaining why women use formula instead of breastfeed; in a morally significant way, women's actions regarding feeding their babies do "originate" in the infant formula company's actions. The proportionality of causal contribution by the actions of infant formula companies, in relation to other causal factors of infant mortality, is huge, and hugely significant, especially as their actions cause an easily preventable harm.

The responsibility that infant formula companies have involves various duties involved in the liability framework, and they are subject to various sanctions that will be effective in enforcing these duties. First of all, the companies have a duty of forbearance to simply *stop* marketing their infant formulas and encouraging women to replace breastmilk with formula, especially in the poorest regions of the world where women do not have the means to use formula safely. This does not mean formula should not be made available; it can save the lives of babies unable to breastfeed, and for women who have the means to use formula safely it provides a welcome choice and convenience. What the duty of forbearance does require is that formula should not be promoted in the ways described above.

Secondly, the companies that continue to market their infant formula to poor women have duties of redress, and they should receive sanctions until they have fulfilled some obligation of reparation. The form of redress that seems most appropriate here is for the offending companies to give funds to agencies that promote infant health and well-being, such as the World Health Organization and UNICEF. These funds would serve both as a punishment to companies like Nestle and as a form of reparation. No amount of money can compensate for the loss of 1.5 million lives a year, but money aimed at saving some of those lives can help. Paying a hefty fine that is donated to a relevant non-profit organization serves as a sanction against the companies where it hurts the most— the bottom line—with the hope that it will serve as a deterrent aimed at preventing future wrongdoing.

Unfortunately, we do not have an international court that can enforce international codes of conduct, so reparations such as this are difficult to require of companies. We must use other methods of sanction instead, or until we find a way to enforce international duties of redress. Some of these methods include public education about the problem, public boycott of the offending companies, attempts to legislate in various nations the standards determined by the international code, and legal sanctions in particular countries that have laws that match the international code.

A third duty that companies like Nestle have is one that will be described in more detail in the following chapter, but which is worth mentioning here: the duty to promote institutional justice by committing to engage in just corporate practices. This goes beyond the duty of the agent to not commit harm, as it is a political duty requiring agents to change their practices according to the de-

mands of justice. For corporations, this means engaging in corporate social responsibility. A good start for a corporation like Nestle is to abide by voluntary
codes like the international code of marketing for infant formula, and to commit
to the Global Compact, a set of principles promoting corporate social responsibility managed by five United Nations agencies. Critics object to the voluntary
nature of such codes of conduct for a variety of reasons, including the fact that
their compliance is not enforceable, that pledging to them can make companies
look good without requiring any particular action from them, and that they tend
to attract less powerful corporations rather than those that would have greater
influence on changing institutional practices as a whole.[65] Nonetheless, the voluntary nature of these codes allows companies to act as the moral agents they
are: to choose how they will act, and why (based upon what reasons), and to be
accountable to these actions. If voluntary codes are insufficient, and other agents
(individuals, governments, NGOs, and other corporations) are not able to hold
these companies accountable for not changing their immoral, human-rights-
violating actions to be more just, then these other agents must change the politics and policies that govern such codes to make them required by law—even if
this means setting up a system of international law and enforcement.

Companies' marketing of infant formula to poor mothers who are unable to
use the formula in a healthy way is only one example of how identifiable agents
can cause or exacerbate poverty. Agents can cause or worsen poverty by engaging in other practices as well, such as when corporations dump their toxic waste
in poor neighborhoods, and sicken or kill residents, or when governments take
property from people through eminent domain for development. Analyses of the
wrongful harm and resulting liability of these situations can be made, similar to
the above analysis of Nestle's practice of pushing infant formula on poor mothers. When identifiable agents cause wrongful harm, they are liable for their actions, and they have duties of redress to right their wrongs.

So What Should Affluent Individuals Do?

So far what I have sketched out is the responsibility that conglomerates
such as corporations like Nestle have regarding wrongful harms they have
caused. But the question remains: what should an individual do? What is the
individual's role with respect to the responsibility of groups like corporations?

Remember that conglomerates are those groups that have decision-making
and action-guiding procedures that allow them to have agency and to be treated
as agents. This is because agency of the conglomerate does not reduce to agency
of the individuals. The roles that members occupy within conglomerates are
such that a change in which individuals occupy these roles does not change the
identity of a conglomerate collective. Individual members occupy various roles
within a conglomerate; using the metaphor of an algebraic equation, we can
think of these roles as placeholders, and the individuals that occupy them as
variables.[66] Since the whole of the conglomerate is greater than the sum of its

parts, its liability is non-distributive, meaning that the action of the group was necessary to cause harm but no individual action was sufficient, so that no individual is at fault. Individuals may nonetheless be blameworthy or have responsibilities to redress harm that the group caused, but this blame or responsibility stems from the individual's relationship to the group in terms of her role, not in terms of personal contribution to harm or identification with the group. In other words, the kind of agency an individual has with respect to conglomerates is different than the kind of agency she has as an individual in her own right. Whatever responsibility an individual has here is responsibility *qua* her role, not *qua* her individual identity.

Individuals thus have two kinds of responsibilities with respect to conglomerate liability for wrongdoing. First, individuals who have roles within offending conglomerates have duties to ensure that the conglomerate fulfills its duties insofar as their roles allow them power to do so. The greater power that an individual has within a collective, the greater is her responsibility in this regard. Individuals who hold positions in governments and corporations have duties not merely to carry out the actions required by their roles—but also to ensure that the collective makes just decisions and acts justly, and, when it does not, to ensure that it fulfills its relevant duties of forbearance and duties of redress. Individuals who hold the highest positions, of course, such as elected government officials, corporate executive and financial officers, and executive board members, have the greatest responsibility on behalf of the collective, while individuals who hold less powerful positions, such as government or corporate office workers have a much smaller, more limited degree of responsibility.

The responsibility individuals have *qua* role is highly differentiated, and appropriate actions depend on the nature of the role. For example, the executives at Nestle who allowed the marketing of infant formula to poor women share the bulk of responsibility for now getting Nestle to stop such practices and to redress them. The individuals who came up with plans on how to market the formula, as well as those who implemented the plans, share some responsibility for their particular contributions; however, since occupants of roles can change, the individuals who have done these actions in the past may be different from those who are capable of doing such actions in the future. And so, those who have duties of forbearance and redress are those who are now in a position to change or otherwise influence policy at Nestle and to enact reparations of regret.

A second kind of responsibility individuals have with respect to conglomerate liability is to respond, independently of whether or not they inhabit roles within the collective. This responsibility is neither *qua* individual identity nor *qua* role, but rather *qua* institutional identity. In other words, individuals have responsibilities to react to conglomerate liability insofar as they share a relationship of living under the same institutional structures—i.e., the same government rules and/or economic structures. Individuals' duties here arise from their identities as citizens and consumers. Individuals responding to corporate liability have political duties to express their concern to their elected representatives and to increase public awareness of this issue, and they have economic duties to participate in boycotts against companies that participate in especially objectionable practices or at least to voice their concerns to these companies as consumers whose loyalty depends on ethical corporate behavior. So, for example, individuals responding to Nestle's wrongdoing in marketing infant formula are right to participate in a boycott of Nestle's infant formula; they should also make this information available to other mothers who can participate in the boycott; and they should voice their concerns both to Nestle and to their national leaders. The more public attention that can be brought to conglomerates' wrongdoing, the more power that individuals have—collectively—to change and repair it.

Conclusion

Insofar as poverty is a harm, and is caused wrongfully, agents that contributed to this wrongful harm in a morally significant way have duties of redress to right this wrong. Agents cause or exacerbate poverty in a variety of ways, especially by reducing or destroying the resources that poor people have access to for their survival. By setting back people's interests to create or exacerbate a lack of basic goods for survival, in a way that is not justifiable or excusable, and especially when this set back constitutes a violation of human rights, agents contribute to other people's poverty in the morally relevant way. The resulting responsibility consists in agent-relative duties to right the wrongs committed.

Duties of redress are narrower in scope than duties of beneficence, applying to specific agents for specific reasons, and often involving specific actions rather than broad outcomes or general requirements of agency. The actions that agents must perform to fulfill their duties of redress are those that will approximate a "return" to the victim's interests before they were set back. These actions are more likely to be fully dischargeable by a given agent than the actions required by beneficence, and agents have no discretion in which actions to perform unless a judge offers a specific choice.

While corporations and governments are the agents that have the most power to cause this wrongful harm, individuals have duties with respect to redress according to what roles they occupy within these collectives, as well as according to their institutional identities as citizens and consumers in which they interact with these collective agents under the same over-arching political and economic institutions. Redress thus describes a specific category of duties toward global poverty that collective and individual agents have according to what causal role they play in contributing to poverty.

Notes

1. Jules Coleman, *Risks and Wrongs* (Cambridge: Cambridge University Press, 1992), 382.

2. Bernard Williams, "A Critique of Utilitarianism," in *Utilitarianism: For and Against*, J.J.C. Smart and Bernard Williams (Cambridge: Cambridge University Press, 1973), 108-18.

3. It is strange but intriguing that although they understand the self very differently—as necessarily relational for the partialists and as strictly autonomous for the libertarians—the two views agree in their main objection to agent-neutral duties of active intervention.

4. These civil and political rights are listed in the "United Nations International Covenant on Civil and Political Rights (1966)," reprinted in *The Human Rights Reader: Major Political Writings, Essays, Speeches, and Documents from the Bible to the Present*, ed. Micheline R. Ishay (New York: Routledge, 1997), 428-31. Liberty or security rights are described by Rodney Peffer in his article "World Hunger, Moral Theory, and Radical Rawlsianism," *International Journal of Politics and Ethics* 2, no. 4 (March 2003), which is archived by High Beam Research at http://www.highbeam.com/doc/1G1-115035534.html (accessed October 31, 2006), 12-13; and Henry Shue, *Basic Rights: Subsistence, Affluence, and U.S. Foreign Policy, Second Edition* (Princeton, NJ: Princeton University Press, 1996), 36-37.

5. The distinction between agent-neutral and agent-relative duties—or reasons for action—can be described in different ways, though I think these definitions preserve the same basic meaning. Derek Parfit describes an agent-neutral approach to ethics as one in which common moral aims are shared by all agents, in contrast to an agent-relative approach in which different aims are held by different agents. According to Thomas Nagel, an agent-neutral reason can be given generically, without essential reference to the person whose reason it is, whereas an agent-relative reason necessarily includes this essential reference to the person whose reason it is. And in defending agent-centered morality, George Harris describes agent-relative reasons for action as those regarding what is good for a specific agent, in contrast to agent-neutral reasons for action that regard what is good to anyone or everyone in general. All of these definitions ultimately align agent-neutral reasons for action (and duties) with impartiality and universality, and agent-relative reasons for action (and duties) with partiality and particularity. See George W. Harris, *Agent-Centered Morality: An Aristotelian Alternative to Kantian Internalism* (Berkeley, CA: University of California Press, 1999), 6; Thomas Nagel, *The View from Nowhere* (New York and Oxford: Oxford University Press, 1986), 152-53; and Derek Parfit, *Reasons and Persons* (Oxford: Clarendon Press, 1984), 27.

6. Rights of non-interference also may entail "positive" obligations for their fulfillment, for example active intervention that involves stopping at a red light when driving, in order to not interfere with others' safety, or, more dramatically, speaking out against torture (such as in disobedience to one's commanding officers) in order to refrain from torturing. Libertarians most likely would not object to most actions that involve "positive" action or active intervention, when they are undertaken for the sake of universal, agent-neutral respect for people's liberties or rights of non-interference. See Rowan Cruft, "Human Rights and Positive Duties," *Ethics and International Affairs* 19, no. 1 (March 2005), 30-32; Thomas W. Pogge, "Severe Poverty as a Violation of Negative Duties," *Ethics and International Affairs* 19, no. 1 (March 2005), 68.

7. This follows what seems to be Thomas Pogge's motivation in showing how his theory of institutional justice is compatible with libertarianism. Thomas W. Pogge, *World Poverty and Human Rights: Cosmopolitan Responsibilities and Reforms* (Cambridge: Polity and Malden, MA: Blackwell, 2002), 64-67.

8. For examples, see Jack Donnelly, *Universal Human Rights in Theory and Practice, Second Edition* (Ithaca, NY and London: Cornell University Press, 2003), 27-31; Alan Gewirth, *The Community of Rights* (Chicago: University of Chicago Press, 1996), 31-70; and Shue, *Basic Rights*, 22-34.

9. While I do not wish duties of redress to be seen as a *replacement* or *alternative* to duties of beneficence, they do provide a model of responsibility that answers critics' objections to beneficence—and does so in a way better than partialist models do—by accounting for the nature of poverty differently. Although "negative" freedom does not exhaust the nature of our liberties and responsibilities, duties of redress are supported by any account of rights, not only a libertarian account, and so are justifiable to everyone who accepts the concept of rights.

10. Joel Feinberg, *Harm to Others: The Moral Limits of the Criminal Law, Volume One* (New York: Oxford University Press, 1984), 33.

11. See Coleman, *Risks and Wrongs*, 330-31; Feinberg, *Harm to Others*, 105-6.

12. Compare Jules Coleman's justification of redress based on wronging with Sandra Marshall's justification based on the loss suffered. Coleman, *Risks and Wrongs*, chapters 16 and 17; Sandra Marshall, "Noncompensatable Wrongs, or Having to Say You're Sorry," in *Rights, Wrongs and Responsibilities*, ed. Matthew H. Kramer (Basingstoke and New York: Palgrave, 2001), 209-24.

13. I will explain the relevance of this distinction in more detail in the next chapter when I discuss the concept of exploitation.

14. In addition to Jules Coleman's explanation of these terms, I am also using Joel Feinberg's criteria for establishing harm, fault, wrongdoing, and wronging in *Harm to Others*, 105-6. To be clear, fault does not entail wronging, though wronging does entail fault (of *action*, note, not necessarily of the agent). A faulty action may violate a person's right, such as when I steal your wallet and violate your right to personal property, but it also may not, such as when I loan your jacket to a friend with your permission, but I forget to remove your wallet which she finds and takes. In the latter example, I risk you harm by my negligence but I did not *wrong* you since I did not violate your rights (although my friend may have). Since rights describe the most important of a person's interests, any rights violation is necessarily faulty, for it produces at least the risk of harm. While any rights violation sets back some of a person's interests, it may also put forward other interests. As I explain in the following chapter when discussing exploitation, a rights violation (or wrongful harm) may actually produce more benefit than harm on the whole—yet, as a rights violation, the action is still wrong regardless of the net benefit.

15. The United Nations does declare a right to safe employment ("the right of everyone to the enjoyment of just and favorable conditions of work"), but this does not imply a right to any particular job. See Article 7 in the "United Nations International Covenant on Economic, Social and Cultural Rights (1966)," reprinted in *The Human Rights Reader: Major Political Writings, Essays, Speeches, and Documents from the Bible to the Present*, ed. Micheline R. Ishay (New York: Routledge, 1997), 436-38.

16. This is not to say that corporations have *no* responsibilities with respect to outsourcing, for they may have duties of structural justice, as the next chapter discusses; but they at least have no duties of redress.

17. For descriptions of sweatshop conditions, see Naomi Klein, *No Logo: Taking Aim at the Brand Bullies* (New York: Picador, 1999), chapter 9; Jeffrey D. Sachs, *The End of Poverty: Economic Possibilities for Our Time* (New York: Penguin Press, 2005), 11; and David Vogel, *The Market for Virtue: The Potential and Limits of Corporate So-*

cial Responsibility (Washington, DC: Brookings Institute Press, 2005), 99; for reasons why some consent, see Sachs, *The End of Poverty*, 12.

18. Nikki F. Bas, Medea Benjamin, and Joannie C. Chang, "Saipan Sweatshop Lawsuit Ends with Important Gains for Workers and Lessons for Activists," *Clean Clothes Campaign*, January 8, 2004, http://cleanclothes.org/legal/04-01-08.htm (accessed December 4, 2006).

19. Joel Feinberg describes this morally relevant causal connection as a contributory fault condition (CFC). The CFC establishes the liability of an agent that grounds duties to rectify the harm one has caused. Three conditions must be satisfied for a CFC to exist. First, it must be true that a person did the action in question, or at least that she made a substantial causal contribution to it. Second, the causally contributory action must somehow be *faulty*. Third, there must be a necessary, relevant, and direct causal connection between the faulty action and its consequence (the harm that occurs as a result). If these three conditions can be satisfied, then the relevant causal connection between an agent's action and harm holds, justifying the liability of the agent. Joel Feinberg, "Collective Responsibility," in *Collective Responsibility: Five Decades of Debate in Theoretical and Applied Ethics*, ed. Larry May and Stacey Hoffman (Savage, MD: Rowman and Littlefield, 1991), 53.

20. Each list will be some combination of factors that is particular to the situation. Jeffrey Sachs gives the following list of potential causal factors of poverty: lack of capital, physical geography, government debt, lack of money for infrastructure, government corruption, cultural barriers, geopolitics (i.e., barriers to trade coming from the potential trading partners), lack of technology, and demographics (e.g., increased fertility). Sachs, *The End of Poverty*, 56-66.

21. Here I rely on John Mackie's description of causation as an INUS condition, which is an Insufficient but Necessary part of a conjunction of conditions, which as a whole is Unnecessary but Sufficient to produce a particular effect. In logical notation, the conjunction of conditions that constitutes an INUS condition can be written as CA~B, where C stands for what we generally think of as the cause (either a single condition or a set of conditions), and A and ~B are two other sets of conditions that are necessary to produce the effect. A is a set of positive conditions of things that are present, while ~B is a set of negative conditions of things that are not present. John L. Mackie, *The Cement of the Universe: A Study of Causation* (Oxford: Clarendon Press, 1974), 62; John L. Mackie, "Causes and Conditions," in *Causation*, ed. Ernest Sosa and Michael Tooley (Oxford: Oxford University Press, 1993), 34.

22. For discussion, see Joel Feinberg, "Causing Voluntary Actions," in *Doing and Deserving: Essays in the Theory of Responsibility* (Princeton, NJ: Princeton University Press, 1970), 162; H.L.A. Hart and Tony Honore, *Causation in the Law, Second Edition* (Oxford: Clarendon Press, 1985), 11-13 and 34-41; and Mackie, *The Cement of the Universe*, 34-36.

23. For an account of causation as action descriptions, see Joel Feinberg, "Problematic Responsibility in Law and Morals," in *Doing and Deserving: Essays in the Theory of Responsibility* (Princeton, NJ: Princeton University Press, 1970), 25-27. For an account of the social and inter-subjective nature of these descriptions, see Marion Smiley, *Moral Responsibility and the Boundaries of Community: Power and Accountability from a Pragmatic Point of View* (Chicago and London: University of Chicago Press, 1992), 115 and 179-85.

24. For Joel Feinberg's and John Mackie's own accounts of their anti-realism, see Feinberg, "Problematic Responsibility in Law and Morals," 25-37; Feinberg, "Causing

Voluntary Actions," 158-67; J.L. Mackie, *Ethics: Inventing Right and Wrong* (New York: Penguin Books, 1977), 15-49; and Mackie, *The Cement of the Universe*, 29-58.

25. A simpler example may also help. A fire may be caused by other factors besides the ones given above (lit match & flammable wood & lack of wind). A fire can also be caused by a hot oven burner (C'), along with an oven mitt that fell on top of the burner (A') and the absence of a person to turn the burner off and pour water over the oven mitt (~B'). Or a fire can be caused by a lit candle (C"), along with wind blowing papers on top of it (A"), and a lack of sprinklers to put it out (~B"). A sufficient cause of fire may be CA~B, C'A'~B', or C"A"~B" (not to mention various, potentially indefinite, other combinations of factors). Any of these conjunctions of conditions is sufficient, but none of them is necessary.

26. Hart and Honore, *Causation in the Law*, 235-49; and Michael Scriven, "Defects of the Necessary Condition Analysis of Causation," in *Causation*, ed. Ernest Sosa and Michael Tooley (Oxford: Oxford University Press, 1993), 57.

27. Although I do not have space to develop this line of thought in any detail in this book, there are good reasons to assume that those who consent to harmful practices are sufficiently rational agents whose self-determination should be supported. On the other hand, such consent always occurs within particular contexts that limit and enable various options, and that make some options seem more or less attractive than they actually are. Consent and choice should always be understood within given contexts, within which they should always be assessed, and which are themselves open to moral evaluation. It should also be kept in mind that consent and choice admit of degrees just as harm, wronging, liability, fault, responsibility, and related concepts all do.

28. Hart and Honore, *Causation in the Law*, 249-53; and Scriven, "Defects of the Necessary Condition Analysis of Causation," 58.

29. For discussion of the Nazi example, see Hannah Arendt, *Eichmann in Jerusalem: A Report on the Banality of Evil* (New York: Penguin, 1964), 15-17; and Stanley Milgram, "Obedience to Authority," in *Delight in Thinking: An Introduction to Philosophy Reader*, ed. Steven D. Hales and Scott C. Lowe (Boston: McGraw-Hill, 2007), 26-34. For discussion of the military example, see various essays in *Individual and Collective Responsibility, Second Edition*, ed. Peter A. French (Rochester, VT: Schenkman Books, 1998), especially the following: Kurt Baier, "Guilt and Responsibility," 94-99; Haskell Fain, "Some Moral Infirmities of Justice," 81-85; and Peter French, "The Responsibility of Monsters and Their Makers," 9-12.

30. Peter A. French, "Types of Collectivities," in *Individual and Collective Responsibility, Second Edition*, ed. Peter A. French (Rochester, VT: Schenkman Books, 1998), 44-45. Note that in the previous chapter I argued that conglomerates, though they have some agency, are not *Kantian* agents. Conglomerates can be—and generally are—treated primarily as means; corporations, for example, are used for the sake of pursuing profits. Just because they have decision-making and action-delegating features does not mean they therefore ought to be treated as ends in themselves. The fact that conglomerates do not have sufficient rationality and autonomy to have *dignity*, in Kant's sense, is what allows us to design them specifically for specific purposes, such as to meet human rights (as on O'Neill's account, discussed in the previous chapter). We should understand conglomerates, therefore, as having some degree and some kind of agency, though not quite the same kind and degree as humans have.

31. See Manuel Velasquez's criticisms of ascribing intentionality to corporations and Peter French's response: Manuel G. Velasquez, "Why Corporations Are Not Morally Responsible for Anything They Do," in *Collective Responsibility: Five Decades of De-*

bate in Theoretical and Applied Ethics, ed. Larry May and Stacey Hoffman (Savage, MD: Rowman and Littlefield, 1991), 122; Peter French, *Collective and Corporate Responsibility* (New York: Columbia University Press, 1984), 39-41.

32. I use the pronouns *she* and *her* to refer to the generic agent, whether individual or collective, and if individual, whether male or female. Most of the present discussion refers to collective agents, who are more likely to have duties of redress, but using the pronoun *it* consistently is awkward. Since we view conglomerates like corporations as pseudo-persons, it is just as well to use a personal pronoun to refer to them.

33. John Fischer and Mark Ravizza call the factors that may diminish an agent's responsibility "responsibility-undermining factors." John Martin Fischer and Mark Ravizza, S. J., 1998, *Responsibility and Control: A Theory of Moral Responsibility* (Cambridge: Cambridge University Press, 1998), 30.

34. Contemporary philosophers frequently draw upon Aristotle's discussion of excuses to develop their own accounts. The two primary excuses Aristotle identifies are compulsion and ignorance. Compulsion includes both physical force and mental, emotional, or psychological duress. In developing a conception of compulsion, Jonathan Glover includes in this category excuses in which one acts intentionally but under force or duress, such as threats, torture, and extreme need. While compulsion sometimes may be relevant to assessing responsibility for acts undertaken by the poor (i.e., under conditions of extreme need), it is not particularly relevant for assessing responsibility for global poverty. Ignorance, however, is. See Aristotle, "Nicomachean Ethics," in *A New Aristotle Reader*, ed. J. L. Ackrill (Princeton, NJ: Princeton University Press, 1987), 387-90 (Book III, Chapter 1, 1109b30-111b); Mackie, *Ethics*, 204-5; Jonathan Glover, *Responsibility* (New York: Humanities Press, 1970), 4-13 and 61; Gary Watson, "Excusing Addiction," *Law and Philosophy* 18 (1999), 603-6.

35. Many philosophers argue that only a general capacity for acquiring relevant knowledge about the moral significance and potential consequences of one's action is necessary, that actually having this knowledge or actually having the capacity for it in a given instance is not necessary for moral responsibility. For reasons I cannot develop here, I disagree with this common view. See Tony Honore, "Responsibility and Luck: The Moral Basis of Strict Liability," in *Responsibility and Fault* (Oxford and Portland, OR: Hart Publishing, 1999), 29; and R. Jay Wallace, *Responsibility and the Moral Sentiments* (Cambridge, MA: Harvard University Press, 1994), 190.

36. See various discussions in *Killing and Letting Die: Second Edition*, ed. Bonnie Steinbock and Alastair Norcross (New York: Fordham University Press, 1994), including N. Ann Davis, "The Priority of Avoiding Harm," 298-354; and Philippa Foot, "Killing and Letting Die," 280-89. See also Thomas Nagel, "War and Massacre," reprinted in *Moral Philosophy: Selected Readings, Second Edition*, ed. George Sher (Belmont CA: Wadsworth, 2001), 749-65.

37. French, *Collective and Corporate Responsibility*, 40.

38. The distinction between these three categories of intention comes from Lawrence H. Davis, "Wayward Causal Chains," in *Action and Responsibility: Bowling Green Studies in Applied Philosophy, Volume II-1980*, ed. Michael Bradie and Myles Brand (Bowling Green, OH: Applied Philosophy Program, Bowling Green State University, 1980), 56-58. Peter French argues for ascribing responsibility based on a broad understanding of intentionality: that a person intends to do *something*, even if she does not even do the act she desired, never mind if the desired outcome does not occur. Peter A. French, *Responsibility Matters* (Lawrence, KA: University Press of Kansas, 1992), chapter 1. While it may be that a person never *intends* to cause wrongful harm or injustice, so

that it is impossible to make responsibility ascriptions based on the narrowest category of intentionality (as intending a certain outcome), the broadest category nonetheless describes causal relations inaccurately, so that it is unfair to make responsibility ascriptions that are based on it.

39. Further analysis of intention and its moral relevance requires examining related mental states like desire, which I will not do here. I refer readers to the relevant literature on free will and philosophy of mind and action.

40. John Mackie says, "A plea of duress or 'necessity,' therefore, should not be seen as canceling an agent's responsibility, but only as modifying the description of the action for which he is responsible, and so claiming either justification or mitigation. In evaluating any such plea, we must take account of the relative badness (of whatever sort) of the alternatives X and Y." Mackie, *Ethics*, 205.

41. For more on how consequentialist considerations can be viewed as causal factors, see Smiley, *Moral Responsibility and the Boundaries of Community*, 186-87. Remember that assessments of liability and blame are distinguishable, and that an agent can be liable, i.e. have duties to rectify harm caused, without fault.

42. Moreover, it is difficult to see how any action undertaken by agents is truly *unavoidable*; agents always make choices and have alternative options, except under conditions of force or coercion, in which case responsibility is usually absolved entirely. Unavoidability should thus not be seen as metaphysical necessity, but as severe social constraint. For example, companies may have few options but to act in ways that harm workers if they are going to stay competitive and remain in business. We may argue that they should refuse to engage in these actions, but it is not a reasonable expectation that they should do so when the future of their existence is at stake—assuming that their existence has some arguable public good. (The continued existence of a company is not inherently good; its value depends on the value of the company. A company engaged in the sex trade does not have enough value to justify harmful actions that enable it to stay in business; a company that distributes food to grocery stores may.)

43. For some discussion, particularly on "helping" Afghani women, see Alison M. Jaggar, "'Saving Amina': Global Justice for Women and Intercultural Dialogue," *Ethics and International Affairs* 19, no. 3 (2005), 55-75.

44. David Vogel argues that businesses that engage in corporate social responsibility are neither more profitable nor less profitable than those that do not. With the current trend toward "green" products and lifestyles, however, it may be becoming more profitable to be ethical than it used to be. Vogel, *The Market for Virtue*.

45. This involves being what Philippa Foot calls the "origin" of evil, or what R. Jay Wallace calls the "uncaused initiator" of an action. Foot, "Killing and Letting Die," 284-87; Wallace, *Responsibility and the Moral Sentiments*, 87.

46. For more on triggering events, see Feinberg, "Causing Voluntary Actions," 167-72; for more on the moral priority of decision-making versus action, see Arendt, *Eichmann in Jerusalem*, 247.

47. Tony Honore describes causation as intervention; see Honore, *Responsibility and Fault*, 2. Some philosophers try to explain acts that are causally and morally relevant "interventions" by making distinctions between different kinds of actions. Some of these distinctions include acts versus omissions or inactions, doings and allowings, and killing versus letting die; see the various discussions in Steinbock and Norcross, *Killing and Letting Die*. The purpose of making these distinctions is to show different ways that human behavior interacts with other causal processes, to show what kind of agency and control humans have relative to events.

48. Samuel Scheffler, "Doing and Allowing," *Ethics* 114 (January 2004), 215-39. While Scheffler analyzes this tension in terms of the individual agent, I believe it applies to the collective agent as well.

49. See the argument by Michael Moore in his book *Placing Blame: A General Theory of the Criminal Law* (Oxford: Clarendon Press, 1997), 251-332.

50. For utilitarians that equivocate acts and omissions, see Shelly Kagan, *The Limits of Morality* (Oxford: Clarendon Press, 1989), chapter 3; James Rachels, "Killing, Letting Die, and the Value of Life," in his book *Can Ethics Provide Answers? And Other Essays in Moral Philosophy* (Lanham, MD: Rowman and Littlefield, 1997), 67-80; and James Rachels, "Feeding the Hungry: Killing and Starving to Death," in *Moral Issues*, ed. Jan Narveson (Toronto: Oxford University Press, 1983), 154-66. For libertarians that deny that omissions are ever as morally obligatory as acts, see Jan Narveson, *The Libertarian Idea* (Philadelphia: Temple University Press, 1988), 57-59; and Robert Nozick, *Anarchy, State, and Utopia* (New York: Basic Books, 1974), 30-35. John Harris explains the moral relevance of omissions as failures to meet social expectations; while John Casey explains these relevant standards in terms of the responsibilities that attach to people's roles. John Harris, "The Marxist Conception of Violence," *Philosophy and Public Affairs* 3, no. 2 (Winter 1974), 192-220; John Casey, "Actions and Consequences," in *Morality and Moral Reasoning: Five Essays in Ethics*, ed. John Casey (London: Methuen, 1971), 155-205.

51. Smiley, *Moral Responsibility and the Boundaries of Community*, 190-95 and 206-11.

52. For more criticism of profit maximization as a sole value, see Lawrence E. Mitchell, *Corporate Irresponsibility: America's Newest Export* (New Haven, CT and London: Yale University Press, 2001).

53. For the original account of reactive attitudes, see Peter Strawson, "Freedom and Resentment," *Proceedings of the British Academy* 48 (1962), 1-25. For more recent discussions, see various articles in *Perspectives on Moral Responsibility*, ed. John Martin Fischer and Mark Ravizza, S.J. (Ithaca, NY: Cornell University Press, 1993).

54. For further discussions about this difference, see Tony Honore, "Are Omissions Less Culpable?" in his book *Responsibility and Fault* (Oxford and Portland, OR: Hart Publishing, 1999), 41-93; Judith Lichtenberg, "The Moral Equivalence of Action and Omission," in *Killing and Letting Die, Second Edition*, ed. Bonnie Steinbock and Alastair Norcross (New York: Fordham University Press, 1994), 210-29; and Hillel Steiner, "Choice and Circumstance," in *Rights, Wrongs and Responsibilities*, ed. Matthew H. Kramer (Basingstoke and New York: Palgrave, 2001), 225-41.

55. Robert E. Goodin, *Protecting the Vulnerable: A Reanalysis of Our Social Responsibilities* (Chicago and London: University of Chicago Press, 1985), 125-34; Peg O'Connor, *Oppression and Responsibility: A Wittgensteinian Approach to Social Practices and Moral Theory* (University Park, PA: Pennsylvania State University Press, 2002), 52-58 and 111-34; Iris Marion Young, "Responsibility and Global Justice: A Social Connection Model," *Social Philosophy and Policy* 23, no. 1 (January 2006), 121-22; Iris Marion Young, "Responsibility and Global Labor Justice," *Journal of Political Philosophy* 12, no. 4 (December 2004), 378-79. O'Connor calls the causal model a "linked chain" account; see O'Connor, *Oppression and Responsibility*, 113.

56. Young does acknowledge this. Young, "Responsibility and Global Labor Justice," 379; Young, "Responsibility and Global Justice," 121.

57. Although philosophers like Young may use this present, on-going causation of structural conditions to deny the importance of liability or causal approaches to global

responsibility, causal theorists sometimes explicitly acknowledge that most causal factors do not have specifiable beginnings or endings; this is not a feature special to the creation of present structural conditions. See Feinberg, "Causing Voluntary Actions," 158-67.

58. Joel Feinberg's distinction between three different criteria we can use to select a cause, depending on which causal question we ask, is helpful here. Political philosophers like Goodin, O'Connor, and Young object to the stain criterion, which tries to "fix the blame," finding the human act or omission that is stained with fault. But we may also use the lantern criterion, which tries to "shed light" on what happened, seeking an explanation for what appears to be abnormal. Or, most pertinent to assessing global poverty, we may use the handle criterion, which selects the cause in an engineering context so that we can "get a handle" on what is happening in order to have control over future events. These distinctions come from Joel Feinberg, "Sua Culpa," in *Doing and Deserving: Essays in the Theory of Responsibility* (Princeton, NJ: Princeton University Press, 1970), 204-5. For more on this point, see also Christian Barry's argument that historical contribution-based reasons for action (which are similar to my duties of redress, as they rely on a causal or liability framework) are not backward-looking, but are rather "forward-looking in a different way" than the prospective contribution-based reasons advocated by political responsibility theorists like Goodin and Young. Christian Barry, "Understanding and Evaluating the Contribution Principle," in *Real World Justice: Grounds, Principles, Human Rights, and Social Institutions*, ed. Andreas Follesdal and Thomas Pogge (Dordrecht: Springer, 2005), 112-17.

59. O'Connor, *Oppression and Responsibility*, chapters 1 and 3; Iris Marion Young, *Inclusion and Democracy* (Oxford: Oxford University Press, 2000), chapter 2.

60. For more information on how outsourcing has become normal, see Thomas Friedman, *The World is Flat: A Brief History of the Twenty-first Century* (New York: Farrar, Straus, and Giroux, 2005), 103-27.

61. According to the marketing code, infant formula companies are *not* allowed to give free supplies of formula to hospitals, promote their products to health care workers or even to the public, use baby pictures on their formula and bottle and nipple labels, provide new mothers or health care workers with gifts, give free samples to new parents, or promote baby foods or drinks to babies under 6 months old. Labels on their products must also be written in language that even uneducated mothers can understand and include health warnings about their use. International Baby Food Action Network (IBFAN), "Overview: The International Code," *IBFAN*, http://www.ibfan.org/english/issue/overview01.html#2 (accessed September 12, 2006).

62. The history of this issue is provided by International Baby Food Action Network, an advocacy group that promotes nutrition and basic health care for babies around the world. International Baby Food Action Network (IBFAN), "History of the Campaign," *IBFAN*, http://www.ibfan.org/english/issue/history01.html (accessed September 12, 2006). See also Baby Milk Action, http://www.babymilkaction.org/ (accessed on September 12, 2006); Naomi Bromberg Bar-Yam, "The Nestle Boycott: The Story of the WHO/UNICEF Code for Marketing Breastmilk Substitutes," *Mothering*, Winter 1995, available on http://www.findarticle.com/p/articles/mi_m0838/is_n77/ai_17623557 (accessed on September 12, 2006); and Bernard D. Nossiter, "U.N. Dispute Looms on Infant Formula," *New York Times* 1981, http://query.nytimes.com/gst/fullpage.html?sec=health&res=9a04eed71738f937a25756c0a967948260 (accessed September 12, 2006).

63. The right to sustenance is in Article 11 in the United Nations Universal Declaration of Human Rights.

64. Jagdish Bhagwati explains the actions of infant formula makers innocuously, as "a good product" that was marketed poorly. He regards the major moral problem here as merely the companies' inattention to local concerns, for formula was marketed the same in poor countries as it was in rich countries. While he acknowledges that some companies' refusal to participate in the international code of marketing is problematic, he seems to downplay the moral implications of these actions, in particular their intentional disregard for the value of anything other than economic profit. Jagdish Bhagwati, *In Defense of Globalization* (Oxford and New York: Oxford University Press, 2004), 187-88.

65. Andrew Kuper, "Redistributing Responsibilities—The UN Global Compact with Corporations," in *Real World Justice: Grounds, Principles, Human Rights, and Social Institutions*, ed. Andreas Follesdal and Thomas Pogge (Dordrecht: Springer, 2005), 364-70. See also S. Prakesh Sethi's argument that voluntary codes of social corporate responsibility do not currently require enough accountability or have sufficient enforcement mechanisms. Sethi and Melissa Lane agree that in order for corporations to be justly accountable to carrying out these codes of conduct, they must be participatory agents in constructing the codes and determining the content of the moral norms these codes convey. S. Prakesh Sethi, "Corporate Codes of Conduct and the Success of Globalization," in *Global Responsibilities: Who Must Deliver on Human Rights?* ed. Andrew Kuper (New York and London: Routledge, 2005), 221-22; Melissa Lane, "The Moral Dimension of Corporate Accountability," in *Global Responsibilities: Who Must Deliver on Human Rights?* Ed. Andrew Kuper (New York and London: Routledge, 2005), 243-45.

66. Peter French discusses this aspect of roles in corporations in terms of Saul Kripke's concept of "rigid designators." French, *Collective and Corporate Responsibility*, 29.

Chapter 4
Duties of Institutional Justice

A third way that responsibility for global poverty can be justified is according to the justice of global institutions. Duties of institutional justice are duties to change the structures or institutions that distribute social, political, and economic benefits and burdens unjustly, in order to make them more just. Carrying out these duties involves acting within various spheres of life that are governed by these institutions. The spheres of life that can be made more just include political, economic, and social activity.

Responsibility for institutional injustice is sometimes called *political responsibility* to emphasize its distinctly political application, i.e. as an issue of justice. Some aspects of this responsibility are also captured by the term *civic duties*. I prefer the term *duties of institutional justice*, however, in order to highlight what gives rise to the duty or responsibility, i.e. the institutional injustice, and so as not to confuse this model of responsibility with others that might have political application.[1] Moreover, the relevant duties involve more than merely civic action; they also involve economic activity (regarding the action one performs as producer and consumer in the relevant economic institutions) and the actions one takes with respect to being a member of identity groups based on traits such as race, sex, class, and nationality.

These models of responsibility conceptualize poverty as resulting from institutional or structural injustices.[2] The most notable institutional causes of poverty include economic and political practices such as allowing corporate lobbying to influence public legislation unduly, privatizing public land through eminent domain, or demanding coercive terms for accepting badly needed loans such as those given by the World Bank. Structural causes also include social practices and norms that disadvantage certain people based on their position in society, such as according to their race, sex, or class. What justifies responsibility on these models is the need to improve a currently unjust practice. Insofar as poverty results from problematic institutional practices, then, agents living under these institutions have duties to make them more just.

111

Like duties of redress, duties of institutional justice are agent-relative in that they describe the duties that an agent has according to the institutions under which she lives. In other words, these duties apply only to agents insofar as they live under—or share a morally relevant relationship to—the particular institutions that need to be made more just. Conceptualizing poverty in terms of institutional injustice provides agent-relative (particular) reasons for action, based on one's position within the institution; this contrasts with agent-neutral (impartial, universal) justifications for beneficence, but is similar to agent-relative justifications for redress.

On the redress models, what provides the agent-relative reasons for action (i.e., for redressing harm or righting wrongs) is that one played a morally relevant, causally contributing role in bringing about a wrongful harm. As a result of causing this harm, an agent is responsible for rectifying it. In contrast, what provides the agent-relative reasons for action in the institutional injustice models is unjust benefit. An agent who gains undeservingly from an unjust institution has a duty to compensate for her benefit. She is responsible to those who are burdened, not on account of causing their injustice, but rather on account of living under and participating in the same institution. This responsibility involves trying to change the institution to make it just and providing compensation to those who received unfair burdens from the same system.

The kind of justice relevant to the present discussion is distributive justice, in contrast to the corrective justice involved with the redress models of responsibility. Under redress, justice involves correcting for wrongs which should not have occurred in the first place. Such correction requires returning a person's interests, which were set back by the wronging, to the state that they were in before the wrong was committed. When this return of one's interests to the *status quo* is impossible, then correction requires compensation to try to make up for the loss of interests in some way. Although this measure is inferior, and it is very difficult to determine what compensation is fair enough to approximate the original state of affairs, compensation is still necessary if true correction is impossible.

Distributive justice, in contrast, does not try to return to an original *status quo*; rather, it sets a standard for just distribution of resources. Strictly procedural standards describe procedures of distribution of resources that are fair; an example is setting conditions for fair trade. More substantive standards, on the other hand, set goals for outcomes that must be met in order for the distribution to be just; an example is ensuring that all people live above some threshold of wealth and well-being that is designated as the poverty line. An unjust institution is one that violates these standards, involving unfair procedures of distribution or allowing outcomes that do not meet the designated goals. Making such an institution more just does *not* involve returning it to some original state, as in corrective justice, but rather bringing the distribution procedure in line with the requirements of justice. This may involve changing its procedures to operate more fairly (such as changing trade rules to be fair for all parties involved), or changing or augmenting it to ensure that goals are met (such as giving federal money to those who do not earn enough so that they can live above the designated poverty line).

This distributive aspect of institutional justice is shared with many beneficence models of responsibility, providing a framework for understanding what type of action responsibility involves, and what is its purpose. Human rights and consequentialist models of responsibility in particular understand responsibility as a way to meet just standards for distribution of resources. For human rights, justice requires simply meeting people's human rights, so responsibility involves whatever action is necessary to accomplish this; for consequentialism, justice requires achieving certain outcomes—better, best, or sufficient states of affairs—so responsibility involves whatever action will create the desired result. Because institutional justice also uses this distributive conception of justice as its basis for responsibility, these models typically use human rights and/or consequentialist features in their frameworks for responsibility.

What distinguishes duties of institutional justice from duties of beneficence, however, is an emphasis on political action and responsibility rather than individual. Beneficence models are generally discussed in the moral philosophy literature; as I mentioned earlier, few advocates of beneficence acknowledge their political ramifications. Institutional justice models, on the other hand, are generally discussed in the political philosophy literature; analogously, most advocates of political responsibility indicate what role individuals must play with respect to collective and institutional action. Both of these emphases are important, but neither tells the whole story about responsibility with respect to distributive justice without the other. Analysis of the relationship between individual and collective/institutional action is necessary to bridge the gap between these two approaches.

As a result of locating action and responsibility in political systems, institutional justice models are also justified differently than beneficence models. Both emphasize *benefit* as morally relevant, as opposed to the causation of harm emphasized by redress models, but they understand the concept of *benefit* differently. For beneficence models, what justifies responsibility is what an agent can do to create gains for those in need. The bearer of responsibility is seen primarily as an agent who can increase the well-being of others, and she has responsibility on account of this ability. For institutional justice models, on the other hand, what justifies responsibility is what gains an agent has received as a result of unjust practices. Here, the bearer of responsibility is conceptualized as a recipient of benefit, one who did not deserve it and so must compensate for it.

The role of benefit in institutional justice models of responsibility actually makes its basis for justification more analogous to that of redress models. The work that *causation of harm* does for duties of redress is similar to the work that *receiving unjust benefit* does for duties of institutional justice, as both tie an agent to some action or state of affairs that thus provides agent-relative justification for responsibility. In the case of redress, the duty-bearer is the agent that causes some action resulting in wrongful harm. In the case of institutional justice, the duty-bearer is at the end of a causal process brought about by some institution, where she receives systematic benefits while others at the end of the causal process receive systematic burdens. In both cases, the duty-bearer is involved in a causal process whereby harms are brought about, though the role of the duty-bearer with respect to that causal process differs in each.

In the institutional justice models, poverty is seen as a wrongful harm or a special vulnerability to harm resulting from unjust institutional practices. When they receive systematic benefits undeservingly and at the expense of others, agents have duties to make the institutions under which they live more just.

Why Responsibility as Working toward Institutional Justice is Attractive: Accounting for the Moral Relevance of Power and Privilege

Applying the concept of responsibility to global issues like poverty is challenging because there seems to be a conceptual lack of fit between the two. We generally think of moral (not merely causal) responsibility as a concept that applies specifically to moral agents, for carrying out responsibilities and holding agents accountable requires elements of agency. In specifying responsibilities, we assume that identifiable individual or collective action can be taken, which has consequences that are generally felt and intended. Yet global situations like poverty have vague and complicated causes that are often unintended and unidentifiable,[3] and changing these situations demands an amorphously collective response with such a wide scope that its consequences are often unintended and unfelt by their agents. In order for responsibility to be a meaningful concept, it seems that it should belong to specific agents for particular, justifying reasons, and individuals must be responsible *for* particular actions of which they are capable. When we start talking about responsibility for events over which individuals have little control, in a context in which their personal actions seem irrelevant, the consequences of which they cannot predict (never mind intend), and with a scope so wide it seems that they are somehow responsible for "everything," then responsibility starts becoming a meaningless concept. It does not seem to make sense to say that any particular agent is responsible in this way, because responsibility is something that belongs to agents, and in these contexts there seems to be insufficient agency for responsibility to apply. Thus the institutional nature of global poverty strains our ability to apply the concept of responsibility meaningfully.[4]

Some social and political philosophers try to deal with this conceptual lack of fit between institutional injustice and individual responsibility by advocating some form of political responsibility, or what I am calling duties of institutional justice, as opposed to the more traditional models of responsibility as beneficence or redress. These philosophers object to a model of responsibility as mere beneficence because it does not account for the relationships between rich and poor that exist throughout the world. Because beneficence models do not account for the fact that poverty results from the same institutional structures that benefit the wealthy, their view of what action is required to fulfill our responsibilities toward global poverty differs from the kinds of action that institutional justice requires. In fact, many of the actions suggested by advocates of beneficence models actually do more harm than help, perpetuating the same harm that is intended to be alleviated. The best approach to avoiding this danger, and so truly to carry out one's duties of beneficence, is to acknowledge and account for the relationships between rich and poor whereby the rich participate in and benefit from the same institutional arrangements that effectively cause poverty. Since it is their beneficial position within these institutions that give the wealthy the ability to help the poor, actions that leave this position unquestioned do nothing to change the actual causes of poverty, even if they do address immediate needs such as feeding the hungry. Only actions that involve questioning and trying to change these social positions, and the existing relationships of power and privilege, address poverty at its roots.

Proponents of global responsibility as institutional justice also object to applying features of redress models, with its emphasis on causal responsibility and liability ascription, to situations like global poverty because the *institutional* nature of this injustice makes the causal factors involved almost impossible to untangle. If injustice results from an accidental confluence of individual actions that unintentionally produce consequences no one could have predicted, then tracing these accidental causal factors is very difficult and perhaps irrelevant. If no particular agent *intended* to cause injustice, then it is questionable whether any agent had the requisite control to be responsible. This is particularly the case if the burden of acquiring the knowledge necessary to be able to predict relevant outcomes and make an informed decision is very high. Advocates of institutional justice thus argue that intentionality is unnecessary for a certain kind of responsibility, namely to make institutions more just. Participation in and benefit from the institutions that cause poverty is sufficient for this responsibility, because duties of institutional justice regard the obligations that affluent individuals have as a result of their power and privilege, however un-intended and unchosen it is.

How Poverty is Conceptualized:
As Institutional Injustice

Justice in a political context may be understood as interactional or institutional. Interactional or interpersonal justice describes the way agents, both individual and collective, should relate to each other. This interaction occurs in the exchange of claims and duties involved in human rights, as well as in the dispositions held toward others and the actions taken for the sake of others. Institutional or structural justice, on the other hand, applies to the way institutional structures are designed, for they are the frameworks that underlie all interaction between individual humans and collective agents.[5]

Poverty may be a case of structural or institutional injustice in at least two ways. It may result from occupying a social position that makes one more vulnerable to certain kinds of harm, especially those involved with economic welfare. Or it may result from wrongful harm caused not by (individual or collective) agents *per se* but by specific, identifiable institutions. Iris Marion Young describes this first view of poverty as structural injustice. While her analysis focuses on the political nature of poverty (i.e., as resulting from structural factors), it justifies responsibility in a way that is compatible with beneficence, especially in a consequentialist framework, focusing agents' attention on "forward-looking" action that changes structures to be more just. Thomas Pogge describes the second view. While he focuses on the institutional practices that cause poverty, he also identifies the ways in which these practices cause wrongful harm, aligning his institutional justice model with a redress model of responsibility.

The terms *institution* and *structure* are closely related though not identical. Institutions refer to the rules and social practices that are conditions for agents' actions, while structures refer to the positions within society that agents occupy and so which constitute the relationships in which agents stand with respect to each other. Since the two authors from which this chapter primarily derives its accounts of institutional justice use each of these terms exclusively, I follow suit in using the term *structural justice* with reference to Iris Marion Young's account and *institutional justice* with respect to Thomas Pogge's account. However, I prefer to describe the responsibility relevant to global poverty as *duties of institutional justice* because I focus primarily on economic and political duties. While justice also requires us to carry out duties we have to others based on identity traits such as race, sex, and nationality, the justice most associated with alleviating poverty is economic and political.[6]

Justifying Duties of Institutional Justice

What justifies duties of institutional justice models is that one benefits unjustly from the present system of distribution of economic and political benefits and burdens. Those who are "victims" of institutional injustice receive an unfair share of the costs and burdens involved, while those who benefit from the economic and political distribution receive advantages that they do not deserve. What constitutes the injustice in distribution depends on which conception of distributive justice we are using. For example, some may be treated unjustly as a result of unfair processes, such as illegitimate seizure of land or other resources. Or some may be burdened undeservingly by costs that are vastly disproportionate to the benefits that others receive from the same system, such as the gain that the rich receive from mineral extraction compared to heavy losses such as health or even life experienced by the poor. Or some may lose out under the system by not having their basic needs met, for example having no access to basic health care like vaccines for easily preventable diseases; in these cases, standards of minimally decent well-being are not met. Carrying out one's responsibilities with respect to institutional injustice requires making institutions more just, such as by making processes of property transfer fairer, not allowing gains to occur at highly disproportionate expense to the poor, and meeting standards of minimally decent livelihood. In addition to changing these practices, agents also are responsible for compensating those who are burdened unfairly as in the above examples. Those who have the responsibility to change institutions and to compensate are those who benefit undeservingly by the same system that imposes these losses on others.

As on the redress model, what justifies affluent individuals' responsibility toward the poor in institutional justice are the particular relationships they share with respect to the creation and maintenance of poverty. What distinguishes the justification between these two models, however, is that redress aims at rectifying what harm one has *caused*, while political responsibility responds to the unjust *benefit* one receives while others are harmed, when the benefits and harms are caused systematically by the same system of distribution. Affluent individuals need not have *caused* the harm experienced by the global poor; yet they participate in the same system of economic and political distribution that creates advantages to them and disadvantages to others.

There are at least two ways that the power and privilege involved in participating in and benefiting from unjust institutions are morally relevant to ground responsibility. One involves benefiting from an institution that makes some people more burdened by being more vulnerable to the harms of poverty as a consequence of their social position. The responsibility that arises from this involves duties to change institutions so as to reduce or eliminate such vulnerabilities, as well as to reduce the impact of harm that these vulnerabilities allow (both of which are kinds of duties of beneficence). The other way that power and privilege are morally relevant is how they are consequences of institutional arrangements that cause wrongful harm to some people, resulting in conditions of poverty. The responsibility that arises from this often unintended benefit and unchosen participation in such institutions involves duties to ensure that institutions do not cause this wrongful harm (a kind of duty of forbearance) as well as duties to compensate when such harm is caused (a kind of duty of redress). These political and economic duties are aimed at changing government and corporate behavior, as well as the behavior of individuals taken collectively.

Structural Injustice as Vulnerability to Harm

One way to understand structural injustice is as vulnerability to harm, as in Iris Marion Young's account. This vulnerability to harm results from one's social position, in other words by what place in society one occupies, rather than from being an intentional object of unjust practices.[7] Certain people are vulnerable to poverty on this account in ways that other people are not, for example people who have had farming land taken away from them for corporate use, or people who cannot sell their food on the global market because of Western subsidies that encourage over-production and decreased prices. This vulnerability has at least some social causes,[8] and its incidence and correlation with social position are statistically predictable.

What makes these vulnerabilities *structural* is that they result from one's position within society, which conditions her actions and over which she has little control. Young uses the following spatial metaphors to describe social structures:

> Individual people occupy varying *positions* in the social space, and their positions stand in determinate relation to other positions. The structure consists in the connections among the positions and their relationships, and the way the attributes of positions internally constitute one another through those relationships.[9]

These positions both enable and limit individuals' options for action, conditioning what opportunities are available.[10] Some people are thus more vulnerable to certain harms than others based on what positions they occupy relative to others.

What makes the structural vulnerabilities that some people have a case of *injustice* is that they result from an unfair distribution of economic and political benefits and burdens. It is a case of *global* injustice insofar as distribution occurs at the global—or at least transnational—level. When poverty consists of vulnerabilities that are the result of global economic and political institutions that distribute benefits and burdens systemically and unfairly, it is global injustice.

Structural injustices invite a peculiar causal analysis. As they are constituted by interactions of individual and collective agents, structures are dynamic processes, rather than static objects or states. Different structures relate to each other systematically and are often mutually reinforcing. What makes structural processes significantly different from interactions between agents is that they describe the *confluence* of particular agents' actions that may or may not be coordinated or intentional. How agents act with respect to each other (their interactions) is irrelevant here; what matters is the convergence of these actions, and the ways that they influence each other by setting expectations for behavior through the normalization of it. Structural processes are socio-historical conditions that are the products of previous actions, both coordinated and uncoordinated, and they produce effects that are often unintended by the agents that act under them.[11]

One difficulty in analyzing structural injustices is that we are often unable to identify particular agents for causing them. Frequently in situations of structural injustice, all or most agents act well or at least decently; they do not act in blameworthy ways. Agents typically act in ways that make sense to them given their own contexts; yet these ways may constrain and condition the options that others have to act, generally in ways that are unpredictable. In other words, given the context of decision-making and action of the particular agent, one's personal choices and actions may be morally acceptable. Yet any one agent's actions have consequences on others that we are unable to predict or account for, particularly as they conjoin with the actions made by other agents. When we look at our decisions from the individual point of view, we get a very different picture of causal involvement than when we look at our decisions from the social point of view.

Iris Young contrasts the political responsibility required by structural justice with the liability entailing duties of redress that results from causing wrongful harm. She identifies five distinctive features of her model. First, it does not isolate perpetrators because it does not identify particular individuals as responsible, nor is its emphasis on *wrongdoing* or blame. Second, it brings the background conditions that the causal model simply accepts as "normal" and unquestionable under relevant moral consideration, because these background conditions constitute the very structures that create conditions of injustice. Third, the social connection model is "forward-looking" rather than "backward-looking"; since causal webs for structural injustices like global poverty frequently cannot be fairly or accurately untangled, we should understand responsibility as a "forward-looking" process of figuring out what we are able to do to change present structural injustices. Fourth and fifth, forward-looking responsibility to change present conditions is necessarily shared, and it can only be discharged through collective action.[12]

Political responsibility is justified in terms of agents' participation in the structures that causally contribute to poverty; agents are responsible for changing the social and institutional structures that allow and support injustice. Various economic, political, cultural, and religious structures condition everyday life for people. Many institutional structures are so pervasive that they are global and therefore universal in their scope, in that they condition the lives of all people presently living.[13] People share relationships with other people who live under the same social and institutional structures, as the actions of some necessarily have consequences—however unintended or unpredictable—on the options for action available to others.

The relationship between agents' actions and the form that structures take is a dynamic one. What options are available for individual and collective agents to act are at least partly determined by these structures. Since agents necessarily act within structures, actions taken together also influence the form that structures take, since the confluence of different agents' actions comprises the nature of the structures. Thus while any particular agent may not be able to predict what consequences her action has on the options available to others, her particular action, taken together in confluence with the action of other agents, has some impact on others.

The political responsibility required by structural justice involves collective action that must be allocated through task responsibilities.[14] Only collective action can be effective in making structures more just. The corresponding responsibility should not be thought of as non-distributive collective responsibility, but rather as shared responsibility, the outcome of which all individuals are personally responsible for in a partial way.[15] Each individual is thus responsible for carrying out some task responsibilities that result from a division of the moral labor required by structural justice. Which task responsibilities an individual has depend on her particular relationships to the relevant structures that need to be changed to be made more just. These relationships are best described according to what connections she has to others by way of shared institutions (this is also characterized as what interests one has in maintaining or changing present institutions, and what collective ability agents have to effect change), what power she has to effect change in structural processes and their outcomes, and what privilege she has relative to others as a result of her structural position.[16] These three factors—connection (or interests and collective ability), power, and privilege—situate an individual in a particular way to the structure that makes some more vulnerable to harm than others, grounding specific task responsibilities. Young does not further identify the specific roles that individuals can and must take and the specific tasks for which they are responsible with respect to such political, collective action; more guidance with respect to this is needed.

Institutional Injustice as Violation of Human Rights

In contrast to Young's more consequentialist way of understanding institutional injustice as vulnerability to harm, Thomas Pogge understands institutional injustice as a case of wrongful harm caused by specific, identifiable agents. Such a model combines corrective and distributive frameworks of justice. A wrongful harm is an institutional injustice when the action that causes harm occurs within an unjust system of distributing benefits and burdens. An institutional injustice is a wrongful harm when it is an invasion of rights. The agents implicated in this wrongful harm are not generally individuals and sometimes not even collectives, but rather institutions. While on Young's model agents have "forward-looking" responsibilities to alleviate vulnerability and reduce the impact of harm (duties of beneficence), on Pogge's model agents have responsibilities to correct wrongful harms through compensation (duties of redress) and prevention of their future occurrence (duties of forbearance).

An institution is a social practice, set of rules, or other structure that serves as a backdrop for what actions agents are able or expected to take, providing a system of rewards and punishments that create expectations for behavior and penalties for failing to meet expectations.[17] Institutions govern the interactions between individual and collective agents, and they also structure the access that agents have to material resources.[18] The rules, systems, or practices that institutions describe may be either informal, as general social expectations and practices, or formal, as codified principles and procedures. Since they condition individual action, institutions have a normative function. They are more or less just in the ways that they enable or limit action, and they are capable of being designed accordingly.[19] The norms that construct institutions are not merely descriptive but also normative, and they are capable of being changed, such as to be more just, by the individual and collective agents that act within them. Since institutions have this normative function, justice necessarily applies to them.

Because global injustices like poverty are constituted more by the way institutions condition individual actions than by individual transactions, Thomas Pogge argues that the framework of interactional justice is not useful for addressing issues like poverty. Since global poverty has institutional causes such as governmental and corporate policies, it must be addressed at the institutional level. Institutional justice involves reorganizing societies so that individuals can realize their human rights as fully as possible.[20] Pogge defines rights in terms of *secure access* to goods: "The postulate of a human right to X is tantamount to the demand that, insofar as reasonably possible, any coercive social institutions be so designed that all human brings affected by them have secure access to X."[21] These goods may be defined "positively" as material goods, the provision of which sometimes requires active intervention, or "negatively" as expressions of liberty, the respect of which requires forbearance or omission of action.

All agents and the institutions under which they act have obligations to ensure secure access to goods, because interactions between agents, both individual and collective, necessarily occur within institutional contexts. Justice must occur in the institutional sphere because only institutions can provide the backdrop for this secure access adequately. Pogge's conception of rights and the duties they entail thus supports the argument to create particular agencies that have as their goal the provision of necessary goods and the protection and promotion of particular rights. His focus on institutional justice goes farther than this, however. Even collective agents that do not exist for the purpose of providing secure access to goods have duties to not infringe on the rights people have to these goods. In other words, whether or not they are designed to provide goods, all agents and the institutions in which they act have at least "negative" duties to not interfere with people's secure access to the goods to which they have rights.

Institutions cause wrongful harm by infringing upon the ability for individuals to get their human rights met, in other words when they interfere with individuals' ability to have secure access to the goods to which they have a right. Pogge identifies six ways that institutions can wrong the individuals who live under them. First, they can *officially mandate* practices that infringe on people's secure access to goods. An example of this is a government ultimatum, such as the order given on government-sponsored radio for Rwandan citizens to take part in the massacre of nearly 800,000 Tutsis or be massacred themselves. Second, institutions can *legally authorize* such practices, endorsing them even if not requiring them as in the first case. For example, a government may legally authorize the use of media for its self-promotion and the perpetuation of political propaganda even if it does not require it. Third, institutions can *foreseeably and avoidably engender* harmful practices. This means that they engage in a practice despite being aware of the (perhaps unintended) harmful consequences that will result. An example is dismantling a social welfare system to save the government money, knowing that harmful effects such as homelessness and hunger will result. Fourth, an institution can *legally prohibit practices but barely deter them*, in other words not enforce a prohibition, essentially "turning a blind eye," so to speak. For example, governments may have labor and environmental laws, or corporations may have safety or environmental policies, but such laws or policies may not be enforced. Fifth, institutions can *avoidably leave unmitigated the effects of natural defects*, for example not correcting or responding to handicaps that prevent an individual's ability to access or use goods. An example is not providing easily available medicine that will remedy nausea caused by a genetic illness. Sixth, an institution may *avoidably leave unmitigated the effects of self-caused defects*. For example, governments and insurance companies may refuse to pay for medical treatments for conditions caused by what they perceive as individual lifestyle choices such as overeating.[22]

To the extent that these are accurate descriptions of the "actions" (to use the term loosely) that institutions undertake, and to the extent that we differentiate responsibility based on degrees of causal contribution to wrongful harm (as opposed to considering all forms of actions, including omissions, as causally and morally equivalent), these differences suggest differentiated responsibility to rectify the wrongs that result from these practices. In the order of these causal contributions as I have presented them here, the responsibility that institutions have for their redress diminishes. In fact, the farther down the list one goes, the more debate there is in whether institutions have *any* responsibility. For example, many would argue that the last case—of leaving unmitigated the effects of self-caused defects—is not a causal contribution at all, and certainly not a morally relevant contribution, entailing no responsibility on the part of institutions. Whether some "actions" or positions count as a morally relevant causal contribution or not, and where we would draw the line between different degrees of causation and of moral relevance, are questions beyond the scope of the present discussion. Here I just want to acknowledge the diminishing, differentiated responsibility based on degrees of causal contribution.[23]

Pogge recognizes that questions about what "actions" count as morally relevant causal contributions are morally significant, and he intentionally addresses one aspect of them, namely the libertarian beliefs that give rise to them. He frames the institutional injustice of poverty as a case of wrongful harm, or invasion of rights, in order for the duties that correspond to institutional injustice to be compatible within a libertarian framework that prioritizes agent-neutral duties of forbearance and that considers duties involving active intervention (such as redress or beneficence) to be morally required only if they are agent-relative. Institutions at least have duties of forbearance, to not cause the wrongful harms that result in many cases of poverty. When they do cause poverty by interfering with individuals' secure access to relevant goods, institutions have agent-relative duties to rectify that harm by compensating those who have been made poor unjustly.

While traditional liability approaches that ground duties of redress use a diachronic or historical baseline for judging wrongful harm and for making claims of compensation, Pogge uses a subjunctive baseline. People are wrongfully harmed by an institution if they are worse off than they would have been if the institution were more just, i.e. if it respected human rights better. Rather than comparing outcomes of an individual's action with those of inaction, as consequentialists do when they use a subjunctive baseline to justify duties of beneficence, Pogge compares the outcomes of one institutional scheme—the one that presently exists—with those of another—one that would be more just. What constitutes a just institution for Pogge is one that meets people's human rights. An institutional order is unjust, therefore, when it violates or fails to meet minimal human rights standards, when this violation or deficit is foreseeable and reasonably avoidable.[24]

Pogge gives several examples of unjust institutional practices in which First World nations participate. These include the installation of oppressive and corrupt rulers for Western benefit, selling arms to autocrats for economic gain and to help them stay in power, permitting companies to bribe foreign officials and even rewarding it with tax deductions, international resource privileges that allow unjustified ownership and disposal of resources, and international borrowing privileges that allow governments to accrue debt, often without accountability, in the name of their people.[25] Compensation for the wrongdoing that these practices cause consists in changing these institutions so that they succeed in meeting human rights standards, and so meet the requirements of justice. For example, Pogge develops a proposal for the Global Resources Dividend, which gives a small proportion of the profit from selling natural resources to the poorest countries in the world that also show the most promise of using the money wisely to eliminate poverty.[26] Other changes in institutional practices, designed to eliminate violations of human rights and to meet people's basic needs (as expressed by human rights), would follow along these lines. Agents, both individual and collective, are responsible for doing the political and economic work necessary to change institutions accordingly.

In Pogge's framework, agents that act under institutions that violate human rights have responsibilities with respect to these institutions of two kinds: they have duties of forbearance, to refrain from participating in practices that contribute to the violation of human rights, and they have duties of redress, to compensate those whose rights have been violated by the institutions under which agents act. He notes that there are some situations where agents cannot help but benefit from institutional practices in which they do not willfully participate. For example, individuals in affluent countries benefit from the cheap labor and the cheap cost of environmentally devastating resource extraction that produces their food, clothing, and other goods; this benefit consists of being able to purchase these goods cheaply, and so purchase more of them and have more variety of them from which to choose. Even if individuals do not want to benefit from this economic system, it can be nearly impossible not to, as goods made with fair labor or with minimal ecological impact can be difficult to find. Insofar as agents are unable to change their actions within this system to make it more just, they at least have duties to compensate those who are harmed by these practices.[27] For individuals, these duties of compensation may include lobbying government officials to change trade conditions that favor goods made with ecologically sustainable and fair labor practices, and supporting (through financial means, volunteering, and public expression such as joining marches or protests) non-profit organizations that work toward the same end.

Factors that Differentiate Responsibility

All agents interact within and under institutions, and so all agents—individual and collective—are responsible for changing their behavior and influencing the behavior of others, in order to make the institutions that condition their action more just. Individuals play two important roles with respect to institutional justice. They have duties *qua* their institutional identities in at least two respects. In the civic and political sphere, individuals have duties as citizens of particular governments, including national as well as local governments, as well as duties as civic members of various community organizations. In the economic sphere, individuals have duties as consumers, making purchases within certain local, national, and transnational economies, as well as duties as laborers with respect to the production side of the economy (such as duties to join or start labor unions). In addition, individuals also have duties *qua* their roles within collective agencies, especially governments and corporations, to ensure that these collectives fulfill *their* duties of institutional justice.

The factors that differentiate responsibility apply to all agents *vis-à-vis* their position under an institution, but this section focuses on individuals since this is the focus of the book. This section also focuses on the factors that differentiate individual responsibility *qua* institutional identity more than their responsibility *qua* occupational and other roles, mainly because the responsibility of individuals *qua* their roles in collectives was discussed in some detail in the previous chapter.

The kind of responsibility that individuals have on account of participating in unjust institutions varies depending on several factors. Two of these factors—proportionality of benefit and kinds of benefit—regard the way that an individual is situated with respect to the institutions from which she benefits. Four of these factors—intentionality of benefit, kinds of harm, avoidability of benefit, and ignorance—regard the relationship an individual has to the harm experienced by others that results from institutional practices that condition actions for both. These responsibility-undermining and -enhancing features show why and how the responsibility of affluent individuals to create institutional justice is differentiated.

Proportionality of Benefit

Proportionality of benefit is one of the most obvious ways of differentiating responsibility regarding institutional justice. Those who benefit more from unjust economic and political systems, such as the super-rich, the top 1% or even 5% of wealth-holders in the world, have greater responsibilities toward the global poor than the "middle-class" affluent who work long hours to pay their bills. Even though the bills of the latter may include paying off a luxury car or vacation, their share of benefit is much less than that received by the wealthiest in the world whose children live off of trust funds. The wealthiest in the world have greater responsibilities partly because of consequentialist reasons that they have greater means (including both money and time) to respond, but also because of justice concerns that they have more to gain from continuing the *status quo* system of distribution that benefits them so tremendously at huge expense to others. It is not merely the inequality of wealth that justifies their greater responsibility, in other words, but the fact that such vast wealth is obtained *at the expense of* others' poverty.

It is not merely the richest who have responsibilities toward the poor, however. In many cases the richest have the most or the best justified responsibilities, but my intention in focusing the book on the responsibility of "middle-class" individuals is to not allow excuses that one does not have the greatest means (i.e., is not among the richest), or is not clearly causally implicated (i.e. does not have the most power) to excuse one from responsibility altogether. Those who have the most resources, power, and privilege have the greatest responsibility. But those who have fewer resources and less power and privilege still have some responsibility.

In fact, since this book focuses on the responsibility of affluent individuals, this chapter concerns the duties of institutional justice that those who receive benefits have. Advocates of institutional justice, however, note that *all* people have duties to make more just the institutions under which they live, not only those who benefit the most but also those who systematically receive the most burdens from them.[28] Moreover, it is important also not to reify the group of people who systematically receive more benefits or more burdens. Some people overwhelmingly receive more of one than the other. But many also receive some of both, in different contexts and regarding different goods. All of these people have duties of institutional justice, though the kind of action this responsibility may take, and the power and ability to effect change that one may have, vary depending on one's social position with respect to the institution. While I write as if I assume that duty-bearers are those who benefit by institutional practices, those who do not benefit, or who do not benefit wholly, also have duties of institutional justice, though the nature of these duties varies depending on their situatedness with respect to the institution.

Kinds of Benefit

Different social positions situate agents differently to poverty, making the nature of one's benefit with respect to others' impoverishment different. Middle-class consumers in Western nations like the United States, corporate executives of transnational companies (many of whom are from Western nations like the United States), government officials in Third World nations with sweatshops, and sweatshop managers all benefit from the exploitation of sweatshop workers in Third World countries. The nature of the benefit that each receives differs, however, because each shares a different relationship to the sweatshop workers, with respect to participating in the unjust institutions that exploit them. Some of these agents play some sort of causal role in contributing to injustice, while others profit unintentionally, perhaps unknowingly, and perhaps even without being able to do otherwise.

Benefiting from injustice may involve contributing to it, in several ways. First, regardless of whether agents played any role in its initial cause, they can perpetuate injustice by preventing the restoration of justice. For example, sweatshop managers who dismiss employees who try to unionize prevent the restoration of justice in this way. Second, agents enable injustice by encouraging others to establish and maintain unfair practices. Corporate executives who pressure government officials to not create or enforce labor standards, by threatening to move their business elsewhere if they do, enable injustice this way. Third, by taking advantage of those who are vulnerable, and making victims of injustice worse off than they already were, agents can gain at the expense of others. Government officials who bargain with corporations to bring business to their countries, for the mere sake of adding state revenue, benefit at the expense of others when they take advantage of the desperation of their poorest people to put them to work in sweatshops.[29]

But benefiting from injustice may also involve mere profit, without any intention or knowledge of one's participation in an unjust system, and possibly without even having any other options for action. The middle-class consumer who buys products made in sweatshops benefits by being able to buy cheaper— and therefore often more—goods like clothing as a result of the unjust institutions that allow workers to be exploited as cheap labor, often violating their rights. The middle-class consumer almost certainly does not *intend* to take advantage of the people who made her clothes, and often she does not even know that she is doing so. When she does find out, she may feel remorseful and may even look into other options for clothing, but find that it is difficult if not virtually impossible to find affordable clothing that is made with fair labor standards.

The duties of institutional justice that each of these agents has are different because of the nature of benefit that each receives as a result of being situated differently with respect to the injustice. Agents that play causally contributing roles with respect to institutional injustice have direct duties to compensate for injustice and to prevent future injustices. For example, government officials should refrain from taking advantage of their most vulnerable citizens; corporate executives should encourage the creation and enforcement of fair labor standards by bringing their business to those countries that have them; sweatshop managers should allow their employees to unionize. Agents that benefit unintentionally have duties first to learn about what injustices they benefit from in their economic and political activities. As they educate themselves, they have duties to try to reduce their participation in unjust activities as much as possible, such as by choosing to buy used clothing rather than new and by simply buying less. But because they can never completely remove themselves from participating in unjust institutions, they also have duties to change the institutions themselves. There are a variety of actions individuals can and should do to enact change collectively, including educating others about institutional injustices, participating in political campaigns to elect officials who will work toward justice, and getting involved with political action oneself. All of these different actions are examples of the actions required by institutional justice, and different agents are able and expected to undertake different actions depending on their situation. Middle-class individuals cannot change labor laws in foreign countries; government officials cannot reduce the consumer demand for certain products made in a certain way, namely cheaply. But both of these actions are important and should be undertaken by the appropriate agents. In sum, an agent's responsibility for institutional justice is differentiated depending on her social position.

Intentionality of Benefit

Some critics of duties of institutional justice may argue that only those who benefit intentionally from the injustice of others have some corresponding responsibility; those who profit accidentally have no corresponding responsibility, as they could not have helped their benefiting. Their benefit was purely a matter of luck, not the result of violating duties that were owed (such as duties of forbearance).[30] Just as causation of harm may occur intentionally or accidentally, benefiting from injustice may also be intentional or accidental. And just as we tend to judge intentional causation of harm more harshly than accidental causation, we are inclined to judge intentional benefiting from injustice as worse than accidental benefit, which has less if any moral relevance to responsibility.

Lack of intentionality does not let those who benefit accidentally off the hook of responsibility, however. The kind of responsibility an agent has in each case differs because intentionality and moral luck have different moral relevance. This distinction is analogous to the different ways that we view responsibility for causing harm, depending on whether intentionality played a role.

In liability approaches of responsibility which ground duties of redress, intentionality in causing harm is morally relevant when evaluating the fault of an agent. An agent is at fault—and so has fault liability—when certain conditions of her agency with respect to the action are met, such as whether she intended to cause the harm that she did. If an agent did not intend to cause harm, or intend to do the action that she did do, then she may not be at fault for the action—even though she may still be liable for it. She may have strict liability, or liability without fault, if she played a causally contributing role to the wrongful harm that ensued; as a result, she may have corresponding duties of redress to right that wrong. Her responsibility under strict liability differs in kind—justifying compensation that rights the wrong and returns the interests that were set back by her action to the state they were in previously—from the responsibility she would have under fault liability, which could justify retributive punishment on account of her "deserving" it.

A similar distinction can be made regarding the responsibility that arises from benefiting from injustice. Responsibility for intentional benefit is analogous to fault liability, where the motivations of the agent are morally relevant and can be assessed—and, if appropriate, punished. This is because intentional benefit involves not merely profiting from injustice, but actually contributing to and maintaining it, willingly. This willingness to participate in perpetuating harm to others for one's own benefit invites moral assessment of the agent.

Accidental benefit, in contrast, is analogous to strict liability, where assessment of the agent is irrelevant; what matters are the action and the relationship between the agent and the outcome of her action. Responsibility is not a judgment of the agent (such as for the sake of punishment), but rather a judgment of the action; compensation is justified only on this basis. Playing an intentional causal role by contributing to and maintaining injustice is thus not necessary to ground responsibility for making institutions more just; only the fact that one gains at the expense of others is relevant. Just as causing wrongful harm is sufficient for grounding strict liability and corresponding duties of redress, benefiting undeservingly is sufficient for grounding duties of institutional justice; intentionality is not necessary.

Kinds of Harm

Sometimes those who perpetuate institutional injustice argue that practices that take advantage of others' vulnerability are not unjust if they also create benefits for those who are vulnerable. In other words, if someone gains enormously from a practice (such as corporate profits that result from saving money through sweatshop labor), and those who are taken advantage of by that practice also benefit slightly by it (for example, by being able to work in a sweatshop instead of in the sex industry), then that practice is not unjust. Since that practice takes advantage of others' vulnerability, however, then it is unjust regardless of what overall harms and benefits actually accrue to the individuals who are being taken advantage of. Those who argue otherwise confuse rationalization of their practices with moral justification of them.

Intentionally benefiting from someone's vulnerability may be understood in terms of *exploitation*. Exploitation involves using someone for one's own ends in a wrongful or blameworthy way, regardless of whether one's treatment of the other actually harms her. "Using" someone involves profiting unjustly from one's relationship with that person, or taking unfair advantage of some characteristic of the person or a feature of her circumstances.[31] Taking unfair advantage of someone involves degrading her, or failing to respect her inherent value. Exploitation as degradation may mean neglecting the requirements for another's well-being, taking advantage of an injustice done to her, or commodifying (treating as an object with a market price) an aspect of being that should not be commodified.[32]

Exploitative actions are not necessarily harmful in the sense of setting someone's interests backward; it is perfectly compatible for an action to be both exploitative and also one's best option.[33] Since consent and even harm are not the final determinants in exploitation or unjust benefit, the other most morally relevant factors are the context of gain and the proportion of gain.[34] If a situation provides the best option for someone, but in the context of only a few and only really bad options, this does not make the situation justified. For example, if a sweatshop moves into an area where women's other options are to work in the sex trade or to survive only barely by working in agriculture, then the fact that working in a sweatshop is a *better* option does not mean that it is a *fair* option. In fact, if a sweatshop is installed in that location in part because its managers know that women have few other or better options, then it can be argued that this exploits the economic need of its potential workers.

Likewise, even if the person being exploited actually benefits from the situation, this does not justify it. We might argue that sweatshop workers benefit from their arrangement because they do make money, sometimes enough to support their families, and this is a less degrading job than an option like sex work. Yet sweatshop work may still be unjust if it violates human rights standards. Because rights regard the agency and dignity of a person, no corresponding benefit can justify or correct a human rights violation. Moreover, the benefits received by one party with respect to the situation might be vastly disproportionate to those received by another. If sweatshop workers make a pittance compared to owners' and managers' profits, never mind the profits of corporate executives, their gain is disproportionately small. The disproportionate gain of those who profit from such an arrangement makes the relationship an exploitative one and the benefit an unjust one. Regardless of whether a practice sets back people's interests or is the best available option, if it is exploitative it is still unfair and thereby warrants duties of institutional justice.

Avoidability of Benefit

Just as intentionality is not necessary for having duties of institutional justice, neither is it necessary that one's benefits be avoidable. An agent may not be able to help participating in unjust institutions; for example, she cannot help but participate in various economies and live under some government. Nonetheless she still has duties to compensate for her benefits by working to change those

institutions to be more just. It is not wrong to contribute to or profit from institutional injustices—such as by participating in economic practices that one cannot
help—as long as one also acts to make those institutions more just, in other
words to compensate in an on-going way for the continual benefits one receives
through that participation.[35]

What is at the heart of the suggestion that unavoidable benefit should mitigate responsibility is the belief in the conceptual connection between responsibility and control. A common intuition is that a person is responsible only for
that over which she has some control. If a person cannot control whether she
benefits from unjust institutional practices, then, on this belief, she would not
have any responsibility toward this injustice. But what we mean by "control" is
highly controversial. In cases where we have very limited control over events,
responsibility still applies. For this reason, the fact that one cannot avoid benefiting from injustice is not an excuse for not taking responsibility.

Regardless of what little control we have over events, we always have some
degree of control over our mental states, namely our attitudes, dispositions, and
reactions (unless we are too rationally incompetent for responsibility to apply at
all). Our dispositions are necessarily tied to our social experiences, including the
beliefs and practices of the social groups to which we belong. This identification
does not require a strong sense of solidarity, for example an explicit affirmation
of beliefs such as about the appropriateness or justness of present economic and
political arrangements, but it may be an unconscious acceptance of dominant
beliefs and practices. In other words, voluntary acceptance of present conditions
is not necessary; it is sufficient that we find ourselves living under these present
conditions in order to have a duty to react to them.

The relevant duty here is to become more self-aware of our own beliefs and
behaviors, to judge them critically, and to disassociate from dominant harmful
beliefs and practices. Howard McGary argues that if a person does not sufficiently disassociate herself from the harmful acts in question, and her failure to
disassociate herself from the wrongdoing was not a part of a reasonable strategy
to prevent further or greater harm, she has sufficient identification with the
harmful activity of her group to share in collective guilt.[36] While McGary's argument regards racism, his view might be extended to argue that affluent individuals share in collective guilt for global poverty insofar as they do not become
self-aware of the roles they play in contributing to and benefiting from it and
insofar as they do not dissociate from these practices as much as they are able.

The duty of dissociation is limited in its application, however. Trying to
avoid benefiting from injustice, so as not to be implicated in the structural
causes of poverty, is ultimately impossible. The duty of dissociation suggests
that people should try to have clean hands by trying to escape from the dirty,
immoral practices of global economic and political institutions. This is not an
uncommon response by affluent liberals who do care about injustice but think
that the right approach to it is to try to not participate in it—instead of trying to
address it directly. This is problematic because it allows people to believe they
are off the hook of responsibility if they avoid supporting a harmful practice

rather than looking at the larger context for that practice. For example, affluent people may try to avoid buying goods made in Third World countries without examining the broader issues of power and privilege surrounding fair labor standards. What is morally relevant is not just that one participates in unjust practices, but also that one has the *luxury* of choosing *not* to participate in certain ways—when most of the world has no such option. Only people who are privileged have sufficient means to try to distance themselves from global injustices; the rest of the world can only dream of having enough resources to be able to have such an option.

Part of the problem here is that dissociation can allow people to believe they are doing their part by removing themselves from unjust practices, so exercising control over their actions and taking responsibility for themselves, but this is an illusion. Global economic and political institutions affect all people even if to different degrees. Just because one does not buy goods made in a Third World country does not mean that one therefore has no relevant connection to the economic problems that are involved with the production of such goods. Global institutions in part enable affluent individuals to have enough wealth to be able to buy more expensive goods. People who eschew material goods in general, such as those who live a "simpler" life[37] still cannot escape the effect of global institutions. The ways that they can even "choose" to live such a lifestyle are conditioned by the general wealth of the country under which they live. Even if they live separate from the general consumerist demands of capitalist democracy, their choices are reactions *to* a predominant institution, not a complete separation from it, for a rejection of institutional ties occurs within a structural context from which they cannot fully escape, but can only change their relationship toward.[38] And of course, those who live the "simplest" lives often do not "choose" such a lifestyle at all, having to make do with little as a result of being subject to the constraints of poverty, especially in the rural areas (including areas in affluent nations) romanticized by the "simplicity" movement.

Having hands that are clean from the influence of global economic and political institutions is truly impossible, and the attempt to attain them is a way of deluding oneself that one can be pure and therefore off the hook of responsibility. It is true that benefiting from unjust institutions is unavoidable; no one can have clean hands by not participating in unjust economic and political institutions, because there is no real way to opt out of these institutions that have such global reach. But that does not mean that because people cannot help participating, they therefore have no responsibilities; because the affluent necessarily benefit, they necessarily have responsibilities as a result. Their responsibilities are to make their participation as just as possible by changing the conditions of their participation—the institutions under which they act—to make them more just.

Ignorance

A common and reasonable excuse that affluent individuals make to mitigate their responsibility is ignorance. It is very hard to know enough about many of the particular circumstances about which we are supposed to make rationally informed judgments regarding how to act. Even if one is aware of the moral relevance of one's actions, such as the terrible working conditions of sweatshops and the ways that our ability to buy cheap goods comes largely from these conditions, it is still difficult to know what effect one's actions will have with respect to such indirect consequences, or to know what reasonable alternatives might exist.

My simple answer to this problem is that affluent individuals do have a duty to learn what they can about such situations, at least in a broad way, so that they have at least some moral awareness of their actions. Acquiring this knowledge can be very difficult, especially since exploiters do not want those who aid them in their practices to know about the harms they cause. After all, corporations do not want their consumers to know about the harms that result from the practices that benefit them and their consumers. A clear example of this is the way that corporations hire companies that provide shoddy audits of sweatshops for the sake of appearance only and create fake but authentic-appearing documents of working conditions; rather than using the demand for factory oversight to create better working conditions, many corporations and the factories to which they outsource simply become better at concealing human rights abuses.[39] The very real constraints on obtaining knowledge about factors that exacerbate poverty must be acknowledged. Nonetheless, individuals can do their best to seek out various alternative news sources that provide perspectives other than what is available in mainstream media and advertising. Seeking out knowledge, and trying to make it more available for ordinary people, is part of what responsibility for institutional justice involves.

After people acquire this knowledge, we should expect them to act upon it in some appropriate way. When possible, they should change their behavior, such as to buy goods that are produced under fair labor conditions and are traded according to fair trade standards. When such changes are not possible because of very constraining conditions (such as extremely limited income that prohibits the costlier purchases of more ethical goods), individuals still have duties to respond in other ways, such as by complaining to offending companies, educating others, reducing one's overall purchases as much as possible, etc. If individuals fail to react in some way to injustice upon learning about it—for example, if they decide that their undeserving benefit is worth more to them than the costs they pass on to others, or if they are simply too lazy to bother to change—then we may have good reason to condemn them.[40] It seems reasonable to expect individuals to change their behavior or otherwise react upon learning about their participation in the schemes that create injustices, and individuals should be held accountable for this expectation of change or reaction.

Limitations with Applying
Duties of Institutional Justice to Global Poverty

Even granting that certain aspects of poverty result from unjust distribution of benefits and burdens, it can be difficult to see how responsibility arises from this institutional framework of justice. The main problem in justifying responsibility according to the institutional justice framework is that the agency required to make institutions just is unclear.

Inappropriateness of Ascribing Agency to Institutions

The problem with locating responsibility for meeting human rights within an *institutional* space rather than within the realm of human—individual or collective—action is that institutions themselves do not have agency. Consisting of social relationships that enable social practices, rules, and expectations, they are "instruments to perpetuate power"[41]: static conduits rather than active doers. Since responsibility is predicated of *agents*, but institutions are not themselves agents, it is unclear how institutions can have or carry out responsibility. Some philosophers do in fact write about the agency of institutions as if they are full agents on a par with individuals,[42] but perhaps these philosophers conflate institutions with conglomerate collectives, mistaking a set of social practices (such as economic practices undertaken by the International Monetary Fund) with the collective that engages in these practices, having decision-making and action-delegating procedures (such as the aspect of the IMF that acts in granting loans and that makes decisions about who the recipients will be and under what conditions they receive the loans). While agents undoubtedly engage in institutional practices, attributing real agency to institutions themselves is mistaken.

This lack of agency in institutions is why some critics object to the ascription of institutional responsibility. For example, Michael J. Green objects that Pogge's claim that institutions violate "negative" duties is overstated.[43] Green uses the term *institution* differently than Pogge, as he acknowledges, to mean collective agencies such as governments rather than rules or practices. On either meaning, however, his objection does not hold. Any entity with some amount of agency is the kind of thing that can have duties, especially duties to refrain from specific action. If collectives have any capacity for agency, then they are capable of at least "negative" duties. Although Green wants to confine the application of rights and corresponding duties to individuals, there is no legitimate reason to do this besides mere tradition or intuition.

Even if institutions mean rules or practices, however, they are capable of being organized to respect or violate rights. While institutions are not themselves the agents that do infringe or uphold rights, they are comprised of agents that perform the actions that lead to this infringement or upholding of rights.

What Green's criticism correctly suggests is that even within a framework of "negative" action, we need some account of the agency relevant. For in order for institutions systematically to *not infringe* on human rights, agents must act intentionally to design or change them to be just in this way.

The agency involved with institutional responsibility remains mysterious. What is significant about the relationship between individual and collective agents and the institutional structures in which they act is that the kind of agency involved is a compromised one. Even as they condition what options are available for action, institutions are constituted by interactions between individual and collective agents. These agents may meet the criteria to be considered full or sufficient agents within their own realm of interaction—but, when their actions are combined with the actions of others in a typically unintended and uncoordinated way, the confluence of actions and the way such actions are carried out may not meet the criteria of full or sufficient agency. This is a problem of understanding agency at different levels. At the micro, individual level, the agents involved have sufficient voluntariness, knowledge, rational decision-making, etc. for their actions to be the actions *of agents*; at the macro, institutional level, the structure itself does not act or create outcomes with sufficient voluntariness, knowledge, rational decision-making, etc. The way that agents act *within institutional structures* constitutes a strange middle space between pure agent-causation (in which agents have full or sufficient control in producing specific outcomes to be considered an agent or have sufficient agency) and pure event-causation (in which agents play no role or have insufficient control or agency in producing specific outcomes).

While individual and collective agents do act within institutions, it is not their actions *qua* particular agents that result in harm; rather, it is the confluence of their often unintended and uncoordinated actions that results in the harms that give rise to human rights claims. The strange middle space between agent-causation and event-causation is constituted not by agents *qua* particular individuals or collectives, but rather by agents *qua* their roles and more generally the positions that they occupy within structures. Thus the agency required for carrying out institutional responsibility, and in particular for meeting human rights, is that involved with roles.

Pogge provides a helpful way to understand this role responsibility and its corresponding agency with his distinction between interactional and institutional justice. His definition of a right is meant to account for institutional activity and effects that does not involve interaction between specific agents. He says, "By postulating a human right to X, one is asserting that any society or other social system, insofar as this is reasonably possible, ought to be so (re)organized that all its members have secure access to X...Human rights are, then, moral claims on the organization of one's society."[44] In institutional responsibility, individuals do not have responsibilities to other individuals *qua* agents (as on the interactional justice model), but they do have responsibilities to the institutions under which they live *qua* their institutional identity. Individual responsibilities with respect to institutional injustice thus involve making sure that the institutions are designed in such a way as to guarantee the fulfillment of individuals' human rights; individuals have responsibilities according to their specific roles within the institutions under which they live.

Another way to account for role responsibility is with task responsibility. Since institutional justice entails collective action, the moral labor required for fulfilling this collective responsibility can be divided among the relevant agents. Task responsibility means that a person is responsible for her *share* of the overall collective responsibility to make institutions more just. In contrast to a deontological account that understands responsibility in terms of carrying out specific actions involved in responding to rights claims (as seems to be the case for Pogge's account), the consequentialist account of task responsibility (as presented by Robert Goodin and Iris Young) understands it in terms of creating specific outcomes. Individuals are thus partially responsible for ensuring that specific outcomes required by justice are attained. [45]

This relationship between individual action and the institutional responsibility entailed by institutional justice, or task responsibility and the collective responsibility entailed by institutional justice, helps answer the seeming conflict that results when applying responsibility meaningfully to global justice. Responsibility is something predicated only of agents, and some people think it applies chiefly to *individual* agents. But if this is so, how can we speak of institutions as being a "space" of justice and responsibility? The answer is that it is the role of institutions to provide the context for justice, but it is individuals' responsibility to ensure the justice of institutions. Justice and responsibility apply to institutions only derivatively, based on the moral claims that individuals can make against institutions (and that institutions, lacking the moral status of a human being, cannot make against anyone), and on individuals' fulfillment of their duties to make sure that institutions meet those rights claims. [46] Institutional justice thus both requires and sustains responsible individual action.

Individuals can claim rights against others. Since institutions condition all individual action, they must be designed so as to respect these human rights. But institutions are not themselves agents. And so individuals have indirect duties toward other individuals regarding global justice. These are duties to make institutions just, and this is what comprises the responsibility entailed by institutional justice.

Contrasting the duties individuals have directly to other individuals with those individuals have to institutions, which are also indirect duties toward individuals, Pogge further explains the distinction between interactional and institutional justice and responsibility as follows:

> On the interactional understanding of human rights, governments and individuals have a responsibility not to violate human rights. On my institutional understanding, by contrast, their responsibility is to work for an institutional order and public culture that ensure that all members of society have secure access to the objects of their human rights. [47]

The significance of this re-conceptualization of human rights, justice, and responsibility is its grounding of duties that are agent-relative rather than agent-
neutral. Individuals have only relative duties to make just the particular institutions under which they live; on Pogge's institutional justice model, they do not
have duties with respect to institutions under which they do not live. Yet the
rights that individuals can claim are still universal or cosmopolitan in scope;
they are rights that can be claimed by all humans. All institutions that are in a
position to enable or inhibit a person's access to a good are required by the demands of justice to enable that access as best as they can. But individuals have
duties with respect to these institutional responsibilities only relative to the particular institutions under which they live—and their responsibilities are differentiated depending on their particular roles and power within these institutions.

Pogge does not explain what constitutes the kind of institutional responsibility and individual agency that allows for institutional justice to exist, nor do
Goodin and Young provide any explicit account of how task responsibilities are
allocated from collective responsibility. In distinguishing between interactional
or interpersonal justice and institutional or structural justice, advocates of institutional justice argue that since philosophers have wrongly focused on interactional accounts, we need to shift the dialogue toward institutional conceptions of
human rights and justice. Pogge suggests that the two conceptions are not re-
ducible to each other, and the nearly exclusive focus on interactional justice is
misguided, for while it may be relevant to some degree, institutional justice is of
greater concern. But he explains this distinction and its significance in all of four
pages,[48] and Goodin and Young do not do better in clarifying the relationship
between individual action and institutional responsibility. These brief accounts
overlook the fact that in order for institutions to carry out their responsibilities to
ensure secure access to human rights, or otherwise create conditions of justice,
they must have the requisite agency for responsibility, and this requires individual and collective (especially government and corporate) activity. In other
words, interactional responsibility and justice is necessary for institutional responsibility and justice. For the purposes of his project, Pogge wants to refrain
from taking a position on the kinds of interactional duties (for example, as requiring "positive" versus "negative" actions) that institutional responsibility
requires.[49] Yet for the purposes of my project—which examines what is the affluent individual's responsibility toward global poverty, given that it generally
has institutional causes and requires collective action—details about which interactional duties are required, and by whom, are essential.

Applicability of Institutional Justice Models
of Responsibility

In order to see how responsibility for institutional justice works, let us look at an
example in which collective action to make institutions more just has been at

least partially successful. In the late 1990s and early 2000s, college students became increasingly concerned about where their college apparel was made and under what labor conditions. Aware that much clothing is made in sweatshops, i.e. in factories which are labeled as such because they routinely violate human rights standards about worker health and safety, concerned students wanted to make sure that their colleges and universities were not complicit in these reprehensible working conditions. Students at many colleges and universities successfully pressured their schools to ensure that their clothing was made under fair labor conditions by agreeing to have the factories where their clothes were made monitored by the Worker Rights Consortium (WRC), which checks factories for human rights violations.

To get their schools to pay attention to the issue and act justly, students used methods like making presentations to student government and administration, staging public demonstrations including speeches and visuals, writing letters and editorials to campus news media, and protesting unresponsive administrators such as by staging sit-ins in their offices. Over the course of a decade, many campuses responded by agreeing to have their colleges join the WRC. For example, in 2006 the University of California agreed to a Designated Suppliers Program, which requires clothing to be made only in factories monitored by the WRC. The program also guarantees that all clothing makers are paid a living wage for their work, which may only be a difference of US$0.50/day—making a large difference to a worker who made US$0.50/day to start with (as this now doubles her income) but a barely noticeable difference to a buyer who now has to pay $0.50 extra for the sweatshop that bears her university's logo.[50]

One might ask how sweatshops contribute to poverty, and so how it is that students are benefiting from a situation of poverty that entails duties of institutional justice. Some theorists maintain that sweatshops are an important step *out* of poverty even if their working conditions are less than ideal. At a national level, factory work is a step toward national development, away from the poverty of subsistence farming and primitive hunting-and-gathering forms of survival. At an individual level, factory work provides women with independence and choices about how to spend their small income.[51] Seen in these ways, sweatshops seem to help people out of poverty rather than keep them in it. This argument suggests that college students should buy more apparel, supporting the livelihood of more women, rather than buying less in a misguided attempt to save people from impoverished working conditions.

This argument is misguided, since what critics object to is not factory work but sweatshops. Factory work is not itself degrading; what is degrading are conditions that involve a "race to the bottom" to maximize profits at the expense of health and safety concerns (for example, working twelve-plus hours per day, seven days a week, with no bathroom breaks); these conditions often violate human rights. Moreover, taking advantage of poor women's cheap labor is unethical even if it also benefits them; just because a woman's only other option is the more degrading job of sex work, or the more harmful condition of starvation, does not make factory work justified. Many women submit to work in factories that they believe will offer reasonable working conditions, only to find themselves in a sweatshop, bound to work there through indentured-servitude-type arrangements. For example, in the late 1990s, Chinese women were lured to the American territory of Saipan in the Mariana Islands, promised "American" jobs working in the textile industry. They expected American labor conditions but found themselves kept behind barbed wire, forced to work excessive hours under inhumane conditions (including being forced to have abortions if they got pregnant).[52] Their paychecks often bounced, making them unable to pay back the exorbitant fees they owed the recruiters who brought them to the island. Even if they wanted to leave, they could not, because they could not afford to do so; they had no money and nowhere to go.

Working in a factory may be one way out of poverty, but working in a sweatshop often contributes to poverty, trapping women into a situation that they cannot leave, deteriorating their physical and mental well-being to the point where functioning and survival are difficult. Factory work is not intrinsically degrading; it can provide economic independence for individuals and contribute to regional economic development. But exploiting people's vulnerabilities basically to force them to work under the inhumane working conditions which constitute what we mean by the term "sweatshop" is unethical. People who benefit from the cheap labor resulting from the worst working conditions have a responsibility to make these working conditions fairer.

Regarding the present example, students saw that human rights violations resulted from unjust economic institutions such as purchasing clothing from the cheapest vendor possible, as universities usually do. They educated themselves about these unjust working conditions, and realized that they were connected to these conditions through their consumption of the products of this labor. They also worked hard to educate other students and administrators about why this was an important issue, explaining the ways in which human rights were being violated, how universities were connected to this violation, and why people in the universities should care. In pressuring the universities to join the Worker Rights Consortium, students worked to make an unjust institution more just. Through their collective action, they did bring the issue to public attention, pressure some apparel companies to agree to independent monitoring of their factories, and hold their universities accountable for the ethical consequences of their economic purchases. While they did not, of course, *solve* the problem of sweatshop labor, they did make a significant, noticeable difference to the problem. Their collective action mattered. And what individuals did to contribute to that collective action mattered as well.

The sweatshop movement began largely with college students but did not end there. Recently, progressive cities including San Francisco and Berkeley have adopted "Sweatfree" ordinances that declare the cities will not purchase goods made in sweatshops when an alternate good made with fair labor can be found. Companies like the Gap and Nike, embroiled in some of the worst controversies about using sweatshops in the 1990s, have volunteered to have their factories monitored and made public critical reports that demonstrated widespread human rights violations, which these companies have promised to stop condoning. Social pressure helps; these companies care about their public image, and if they are seen as complicit in human rights violations, they will act to change that image—and hopefully the underlying reality.[53]

College students benefit as much as any other consumer from the cheap prices on their goods brought about by cheap labor; they thus have as much responsibility as any other consumer to address this benefit. The university which buys their apparel benefits from the cheaper costs of contracting with the companies that provide these cheaply made goods as a result of unjust labor conditions. As members of their university, therefore, college students have a special interest in ensuring that their university—the collective in which they are a member—acts justly.

The kind of benefit that one receives from an arrangement matters in what kind of responsibility an agent has toward that arrangement. It is true that university leaders and apparel company executives benefit the most from the use of sweatshop labor in making university clothing, for university administrators are responsible for minimizing costs of the university and maximizing returns (e.g. contracting for cheap goods and then selling them at a profit), and executives of clothing companies increase their profit by cutting costs through cheap labor. These profits are substantial, and the benefit is intended even if the harm to sweatshop workers is not. Apparel companies like the Gap benefit from injustice very clearly, sometimes encouraging or at least condoning factories to violate safety and health standards that will increase productivity and profit, and sometimes by taking advantage of vulnerable people who have no other options for work, exploiting them with these terrible working conditions for their own profit. When companies refuse to acknowledge or change these practices, they perpetuate injustice. Universities also benefit when they turn a blind eye, so to speak, ignoring the injustices in which they are complicit. Because each plays a different role with respect to the human rights violations of sweatshops, each has a different responsibility. University administrators are responsible for learning about and acknowledging the ethical consequences of their economic decisions, and for not contracting with companies that violate human rights. Company executives are responsible for not violating human rights, and for rectifying those rights violations that occur.

As conglomerates—collectives with the requisite decision-making and action-delegating procedures to be agents—corporations and universities have collective responsibilities as a whole to change their practices to be more just. In particular, companies like Gap and Nike have duties to engage in corporate social responsibility. Voluntarily committing to codes of conduct like the Global Compact, a set of principles for corporate social responsibility developed by the United Nations, and voluntarily agreeing to enforcement mechanisms like the Worker Rights Consortium, which monitors whether such principles are enacted, are important ways of demonstrating this corporate social responsibility. Universities do their part by agreeing to do business only with companies that agree to such codes of conduct and enforcement mechanisms. Voluntary approaches may be insufficient; if this is the case, then laws that govern such codes and their enforcement should be created. Such laws would probably need to be made at the international level to be effective, requiring a more powerful system of international law and enforcement than currently exists. In any case, collectives of all kinds, including corporations, non-governmental organizations like universities, and governments at all levels, have relevant duties to promote justice.

When leaders of these collectives fail to act responsibly, other individuals must take responsibility to put pressure on their leaders to do the right thing. So when university administrators and company executives fail to act responsibly, it is appropriate that students take responsibility to do their part in changing unjust institutions to make them more just. Students benefit less than company officials and university leaders, and their benefit is largely unavoidable in a global economy where most of their goods, especially clothing, are made under questionable labor conditions. They make less of a contribution to unjust practices than leaders who make decisions about actions that have greater effects. Students benefit accidentally, not intending to contribute to harm through their action of purchasing apparel, and not necessarily desiring that the clothing will be cheap. For all these reasons, students do not have the responsibility that a university administrator has to not contract with offending companies, or that a company executive has to not allow its clothing to be made under sweatshop conditions. But they do have a different kind of responsibility specific to their social location, to what power they do have: as students, they have a collective student voice that can put pressure on university leaders, which can put pressure on company executives, to make ethical decisions. Students fulfill their responsibility with respect to sweatshops by acting *vis-à-vis* their role as students, trying to change the institutions which condition their action—here, their universities—to make them more just.

So What Should Affluent Individuals Do?

Let us examine what kind of agency and what form of collective responsibility students in this example have. As individuals living under a specific institution—here, the university—students share in a common lot of receiving the educational and other benefits that their university offers. Students' relationship to their university is different from workers' relationship to the corporation in which they work, for students are not responsible for carrying out duties attached to roles in the same way. With respect to the students, then, the university is not a conglomerate collective with its own agency; it is a set of practices and procedures in which the students take part, and that enables and limits students' action. The form of collectivity that the students have with respect to the university (*vis-à-vis* their role as students) is what I call a congregation.[54]

A congregation is a collection of individuals who share some form of solidarity. The form of solidarity most relevant here is that of sharing in a common lot, or receiving common benefits and burdens. Congregations have collective responsibility to change the institutions that govern what benefits and burdens they receive to make them more just. Individuals have responsibilities according to what roles they play within these congregations and under these institutions. One institutional role that some individuals have is that of student; but there are other institutional roles that accord individuals with responsibility for institutional justice. All individuals living in a democratic, capitalist society have at least the institutional roles of being a citizen and a consumer.

Note that individuals have agency collectively here in a different way than they do *qua* individuals or *qua* their roles within collectives that themselves have agency (i.e. conglomerates). The agency that individuals have *qua* their institutional identity is a form of agency that is easily overlooked by philosophers and others assessing responsibility for global problems like poverty that have institutional causes. For example, Ser-Min Shei argues that the relatively affluent cannot be said to harm the poor through their support of and participation in the "ongoing global order," whether that harm is understood in individual or collective terms. At the individual level, individuals do not cause discrete, identifiable harmful effects with their actions; at the collective level, affluent individuals in no sense constitute a community and so can in no way be said to act intentionally, presumably a precondition of acting with harm.[55] But this assumes that the only kind of collective that has agency, and can therefore be responsible, is one that has intentions (and decision-making and action-delegating procedures)—in short, one that is a conglomerate. This is simply false. Individuals can share in collective responsibility that stems from their institutional identities. While the group itself is not an agent in the way that a conglomerate is, individuals that comprise the group do have agency, as well as the ability to form a group that does have this agency, and they have reasons to act responsibly based on their membership in this group.

The form of solidarity relevant to affluent individuals with respect to global poverty is sharing in a common lot. Affluent individuals share with other affluent individuals the common lot of receiving benefits in a regular, systematic way from an unjust system of distribution of political and economic benefits and burdens. What this common lot consists of is not only the actual benefits received, but also the way that these benefits provide strongly motivating reasons to maintain this system against the poor who are harmed by it. Affluent individuals thus share common interests with respect to the global distribution of economic and political benefits and burdens that advantages them and disadvantages the poor. They have duties of institutional justice to change the economic and political institutions that allow this systemic injustice.

The issue of sweatshops affects not only individuals as students, but also individuals as consumers and as citizens in general. In fact, many goods that consumers buy are made with unjust practices that cause or exacerbate the poverty of certain groups of people. A great many consumer items that one can think of—not only apparel, but also toys, books, cookware, and electronics—are made with cheap labor in factories, some of which have labor conditions that make them sweatshops. While boycotting all of these goods is probably impossible, affluent individuals can at least learn which manufacturers and brand labels are the worst in relying on sweatshops, and try to buy goods that are created under fair labor conditions as much as possible. Repairing rather than replacing goods, and learning to do with less rather than more are also ethical responses to consumption. Although the current global economic system requires ever increasing consumption to keep up with its frantic race toward greater profits, this level of consumption is unsustainable and will result in environmental catastrophe without intervention.

Some goods that are brought to market through unjust practices can simply be avoided. Most diamonds in the world are mined from a region in Africa that is controlled by diamond warlords and funneled to DeBeers. This mining fuels wars such as those in Sierra Leone, Angola, and the Congo in which child soldiers are used, mutilation is a common punishment, and slave labor is used for mineral extraction; these diamond wars probably also contribute to terrorism.[56] Unless a diamond's source can be traced, affluent individuals who wish to act justly should not buy diamonds. Most heroin and cocaine crops are similarly controlled by drug warlords who have their own militaries defending their production, harvesting, and distribution of their drug. While there are many reasons for affluent individuals to stay away from heroin and cocaine, one of the most compelling is probably the desire to not support the conditions of war surrounding the drugs. Oil is not currently a product that can be avoided, but the wars surrounding control over oil extraction suggest that alternatives to oil—for fuel and energy, as well as for the goods we make out of oil (especially plastics)—must be found.

With other practices, it is less clear what should be done. For example, toxic waste dumping and eminent domain are both practices that corporations and governments engage in, and which cause or exacerbate poverty, but what individuals should do with respect to these practices is more difficult to determine. Companies and governments often dump waste, especially toxic waste, in the poorest areas, ruining their living environment and their health, contributing to illnesses like cancer, destroying their access to hygienic water and food, sometimes even directly killing people. Governments often take land from people for their own purposes, or to give to corporations for development; this practice, which is almost never done to wealthy people, impoverishes the poor further by depriving them of their resources. While the offending governments and corporations have duties to rectify the wrongs they have caused, and to stop engaging in such practices, individuals who live under these governments, or who consume products or services of the corporations engaging in these practices, also have duties. At the very least, individuals have institutional duties to educate themselves and others about such practices, and to lobby their government representatives as well as corporate boards to not take these unjust actions.

Ethical consumption, including many of the above examples of what individuals should do, only goes so far. Just as importantly, and perhaps more effective in addressing injustice at the institutional level, individuals need to be politically involved. They should pressure their governments to pass laws that promote fair and non-exploitative labor standards around the world, including laws that favor goods made with fair labor standards and laws that boycott companies or countries that are guilty of the worst human rights violations. Politicians should pass laws regarding goods that involve wars and other bloodshed, including laws that prohibit the sale of "blood diamonds"; politicians should also re-evaluate the effectiveness of the international drug wars, and invest in developing renewable sources of energy. In order to retain their ability to legislate ethically, governments also need to renegotiate trade agreements that do not give corporations, banks, and other economic bodies more power than political governments.[57] International law should be broadened and enforcement mechanisms given more power. Non-state actors like corporations need to be recognized as agents of great power, sometimes greater power than governments,[58] and be brought into the relevant discourse of power; after all, politics and economics are no longer two separate arenas of power, if indeed they ever were.[59]

Individuals need to educate themselves and others on these and related issues and be informed voters. Although voting should be seen as a duty (as it is in Australia, which legally requires all citizens to vote) and not merely a right (as it is in the United States), voting is not the end of individuals' political duties. Individuals must also get involved with politics in a more active way, including working on campaigns and even running for office themselves. As with beneficent actions, individuals' political efforts should start at the most local levels, such as running for school board, while making broader and even global connections.

Conclusion

Institutional justice regards a just distribution of political and economic benefits and burdens. Poverty is unjust insofar as it results from, or is exacerbated by, unjust distribution of these benefits and burdens. All agents, both individual and collective, have duties of institutional justice to make the institutions which govern their actions more just. Individuals have duties of institutional justice *qua* their institutional identities as citizens and consumers, as well as *qua* their roles within collective agencies. The roles that individuals occupy include occupational roles within collectives like corporations, chosen positions of responsibility within collectives such as non-governmental organizations (such as environmental advocacy groups) or governments (such as school boards). Many individuals have occupational roles within which to act that include different kinds and degrees of responsibility, and some individuals choose to take on responsibility in voluntary positions. Whether or not individuals have these kinds of roles, however, *all* individuals have roles within institutional structures, including—at least in a democratic, capitalist society—being a citizen and consumer.

Individuals have a variety of duties *qua* their institutional identities as citizen and consumer, including civic duties of being educated and involved with political decision-making, as well as duties of ethical and sustainable consumption. These duties have a wide scope and are only partially dischargeable, as no individual can ever "complete" the requirements to be a good citizen and an ethical consumer; fulfilling these duties is an ongoing process with which one engages all her life. Some of these duties are strict and not discretionary, such as the duty to vote or the duty to not buy easily avoidable goods that resulted from bloodshed (such as diamonds). Other duties involve some discretion in how to fulfill them, such as the duty to get involved with politics (for some people, working on a campaign is the most they are capable of, while others are capable of running for office), or the duty to learn about how goods are made so that one can buy ethically (some people have the time and ability to do extensive research and the means to pay more for more ethical products, while others have more limited means). As with beneficence, institutional justice requires the collective action of many agents to make changes together, so individuals share in responsibility for institutional justice, and the responsibility of any single individual is only a portion of the entire collective responsibility.

A great deal of poverty is caused or worsened by institutional injustice. If agents would change institutions to make them more just, much poverty would be alleviated. Responsibility for global poverty requires individuals to act in ways that change political and economic institutions to make them more just.

Notes

1. A secondary motive, I must admit, is also to create a classification analogous to the titles of the other models of responsibility described previously ("duties of...").

2. As I shall explain, institutions and structures are not strictly equivalent, although for the sake of convenience, at least with respect to responsibility, I subsume both concepts under the term *institutions*.

3. For discussion on the vague causes of global poverty, see Debra Satz, "What Do We Owe the Global Poor?" *Ethics and International Affairs* 19, no. 1 (March 2005), 48-50.

4. See also Samuel Scheffler, "Individual Responsibility in a Global Age," in *Boundaries and Allegiances: Problems of Justice and Responsibility in Liberal Thought* (Oxford: Oxford University Press, 2001), 32-47.

5. For two examples of this contrast, see Thomas W. Pogge, *World Poverty and Human Rights: Cosmopolitan Responsibilities and Reform* (Cambridge: Polity and Malden, MA: Blackwell, 2002), 64-65; and Iris Marion Young, *Inclusion and Democracy* (Oxford: Oxford University Press, 2000), 92.

6. The terms "institution" and "structure" also suggest different connotations. "Institution" is often used interchangeably with a specific kind of collective agent, namely a "conglomerate" such as the World Bank or the United States government. Strictly speaking, the World Bank and U.S. government are both collective agents, with decision-making and action-delegating procedures, as well as institutions that include formal poli-

cies and practices. This common conflation makes the term "institution" sometimes confusing. Yet the term "structure" also carries historical baggage tied to Marxist and socialist ideology, suggesting some link to structuralism. Possibly because of this historical baggage, many contemporary philosophers prefer to use the term "institution" as commonly used within contemporary political liberalism. Despite their problems, I use both terms depending on their context and whose theory (Pogge's or Young's) I am mainly addressing.

7. Iris Marion Young, "Responsibility and Global Justice: A Social Connection Model," *Social Philosophy and Policy* 23, no. 1 (January 2006), 114; Young, *Inclusion and Democracy*, 34-36, 98.

8. This vulnerability may also have individual causes such as poor personal judgment, but it is insofar as it has social causes that make this harm a case of structural injustice.

9. Young, *Inclusion and Democracy*, 94.

10. Young, "Responsibility and Global Justice," 112-113; Iris Marion Young, "Equality of Whom? Social Groups and Judgments of Injustice," *The Journal of Political Philosophy* 9, no. 1 (2001), 12.

11. Young, "Responsibility and Global Justice," 113-114; Young, *Inclusion and Democracy*, 91-96.

12. Young, "Responsibility and Global Justice," 119-124; Iris Marion Young, "Responsibility and Global Labor Justice," *Journal of Political Philosophy* 12, no. 4 (December 2004), 377-82.

13. See Pogge, *World Poverty and Human Rights*, 112-16.

14. Young, "Responsibility and Global Justice," 123-26; Young, "Responsibility and Global Labor Justice," 384-87.

15. Young, "Responsibility and Global Labor Justice," 380.

16. Young, "Responsibility and Global Justice," 127-30; Young, "Responsibility and Global Labor Justice," 385-87.

17. J.L. Mackie, *Ethics: Inventing Right and Wrong* (New York: Penguin Books, 1977), 80-82; John Rawls, *A Theory of Justice* (Cambridge, MA: Belknap Press, 1971), 55.

18. Thomas W. Pogge, "Human Flourishing and Universal Justice," *Social Philosophy and Policy* 16, no. 1 (Winter 1999), 337; Thomas W. Pogge, "Three Problems with Contractarian-Consequentialist Ways of Assessing Social Institutions," *Social Philosophy and Policy* (Summer 1995), 241.

19. Andrew Hurrell describes institutions in the following way: "International institutions are made up of two elements: first, clusters of connected norms, principles, and rules (constitutive, transactional, and societal); and, second, clusters of norms organized into stable and ongoing social practices." Andrew Hurrell, "Global Inequality and International Institutions," in *Global Justice*, ed. Thomas W. Pogge (Oxford: Blackwell, 2001), 36.

20. Pogge, *World Poverty and Human Rights*, 64-65. See also Stefan Gosepath, "The Global Scope of Justice," in *Global Justice*, ed. Thomas W. Pogge (Oxford: Blackwell, 2001), 145-68. Hurrell, "Global Inequality and International Institutions," 32-54; and Onora O'Neill, "Agents of Justice," in *Global Justice*, ed. Thomas W. Pogge (Oxford: Blackwell, 2001), 188-203.

21. Pogge, *World Poverty and Human Rights*, 46.

22. Thomas W. Pogge, "Human Rights and Human Responsibilities," in *Global Justice and Transnational Politics: Essays on the Moral and Political Challenges of Global-*

ization, ed. Pablo De Greiff and Ciaran Cronin (Cambridge and London: MIT Press, 2002), 167-68; Pogge, *World Poverty and Human Rights*, 41-42. Terminology is Pogge's; the first example comes from Bill Dong; the other examples are mine.

23. I also want to suggest that more work needs to be done in this area by philosophers who do ethics, political philosophy, and philosophy of mind. While philosophers frequently bridge ethics and philosophy of mind to discuss action, agency, and responsibility, these concepts also relate to political philosophy and need to be analyzed accordingly.

24. Thomas W. Pogge, "Severe Poverty as a Violation of Negative Duties," *Ethics and International Affairs* 19, no. 1 (March 2005), 55-56 and 60.

25. Pogge, *World Poverty and Human Rights*, 22; Thomas W. Pogge, "Priorities of Global Justice," in *Global Justice*, ed. Thomas W. Pogge (Oxford: Blackwell Publishers, 2001), 18-21.

26. Thomas W. Pogge, "A Global Resources Dividend," in *Ethics of Consumption: The Good Life, Justice, and Global Stewardship*, ed. David A. Crocker and Toby Linden (Lanham, MD: Rowman and Littlefield, 1998), 510-519. Alexander Cappelen develops a more controversial proposal along these lines, regarding all resources, not just natural resources. He argues for an international liberal egalitarian transfer scheme which would equalize the fiscal capacity of nations by transferring resources so that all nations are able to provide the same level of public goods. Alexander Cappelen, "Responsibility and International Distributive Justice," in *Real World Justice: Grounds, Principles, Human Rights, and Social Institutions*, ed. Andreas Follesdal and Thomas Pogge (Dordrecht: Springer, 2005), 226.

27. Pogge, "Severe Poverty as a Violation of Negative Duties," 61 and 69.

28. Pogge, "Severe Poverty as a Violation of Negative Duties," 81-83; Young, "Responsibility and Global Labor Justice," 381.

29. Norbert Anwander, "Contributing and Benefiting: Two Grounds for Duties to the Victims of Injustice," *Ethics and International Affairs* 19, no. 1 (March 2005), 42.

30. Anwander, "Contributing and Benefiting," 40-41.

31. Joel Feinberg, *Harmless Wrongdoing: The Moral Limits of the Criminal Law, Volume Four* (New York: Oxford University Press, 1988), 176-210; Alan Wertheimer, *Exploitation* (Princeton, NJ: Princeton University Press, 1996), 207.

32. Ruth J. Sample, *Exploitation: What it Is and Why It's Wrong* (Lanham, MD: Rowman and Littlefield, 2003), 57.

33. Sample, *Exploitation*, 87.

34. Feinberg, *Harmless Wrongdoing*, 203.

35. Thomas Pogge agrees with critics like Norbert Anwander on this point. Pogge, "Severe Poverty as a Violation of Negative Duties," 69.

36. Howard McGary, "Morality and Collective Liability," in *Race and Social Justice* (Malden, MA: Blackwell, 1999), 87-91.

37. The "simple" life is a lifestyle movement that includes such things as buying minimally and buying goods that are reused or recycled whenever possible; using energy-saving devices; making or fixing needed objects, etc. Ironically, the movement toward the "simple" life has become a cottage industry in itself, producing numerous books, newsletters, and magazines that promote and brand this as a particular lifestyle. See the extensive literature on "the simple life" for more information about what this lifestyle involves, including: Duane Elgin, *Voluntary Simplicity: Toward a Way of Life that is Outwardly Simple, Inwardly Rich: Revised Edition* (New York: Quill, 1993); Juliet B. Schor and Douglas B. Holt, Eds., *The Consumer Society Reader* (New York: New Press,

2000), especially section 7; Jerome M. Segal, *Graceful Simplicity: The Philosophy and Politics of the Alternative American Dream* (Berkeley, CA: University of California Press, 2003); and Paul L. Wachtel, "Alternatives to the Consumer Society," in *Ethics of Consumption: The Good Life, Justice, and Global Stewardship*, ed. David A. Crocker and Toby Linden (Lanham, MD: Rowman and Littlefield, 1998), 198-217.

38. I am thinking of people who might "choose"—using this word problematically, since what constitutes meaningful "choice" is highly controversial and whether such choice here is meaningful I question—to reject society's expectations for them by living outside of the mainstream, such as by being homeless, using illegal drugs, or participating in criminal activity. For an ethnographic, sociological discussion on why people "choose" to reject mainstream norms and structures in this way, see Philip Lalander, *Hooked on Heroin: Drugs and Drifters in a Globalized World* (Oxford and New York: Berg, 2003).

39. "Secrets, Lies, and Sweatshops," *BusinessWeek* (November 27, 2006), http://www.businessweek.com/magazine/content/06_48/b4011001.htm (accessed April 21, 2008).

40. Peter French calls the expectation that an agent should change her behavior upon learning that it causes harm, and the moral judgment that accompanies a failure or especially an unwillingness to change this behavior, the "Principle of Responsive Adjustment." Peter A. French, *Responsibility Matters* (Lawrence, KA: University Press of Kansas, 1992), 12.

41. Alessandro Pinzani, "'It's the Power, Stupid!' On the Unmentioned Precondition of Social Justice," in *Real World Justice: Grounds, Principles, Human Rights, and Social Institutions*, ed. Andreas Follesdal and Thomas Pogge (Dordrecht: Springer, 2005), 195.

42. For examples, see Christian Barry, "Understanding and Evaluating the Contribution Principle," in *Real World Justice: Grounds, Principles, Human Rights, and Social Institutions*, ed. Andreas Follesdal and Thomas Pogge (Dordrecht: Springer, 2005), 120; Michael J. Green, "Institutional Responsibility for Global Problems," *Philosophical Topics* 30, no. 2 (Fall 2002), 85; Onora O'Neill, "Global Justice: Whose Obligations?" in *The Ethics of Assistance: Morality and the Distant Needy*, ed. Deen K. Chatterjee (Cambridge and New York: Cambridge University Press, 2004), 242-59; and Onora O'Neill, "Agents of Justice," in *Global Justice*, ed. Thomas W. Pogge (Oxford: Blackwell, 2001), 188-203.

43. Green, "Institutional Responsibility for Global Problems," 88-89.

44. Pogge, *World Poverty and Human Rights*, 64.

45. See Robert Goodin, *Utilitarianism as Public Philosophy* (Cambridge: Cambridge University Press, 1995), chapter 7; and Young, "Responsibility and Global Labor Justice," 384-87.

46. Gosepath, "The Global Scope of Justice," 147.

47. Pogge, *World Poverty and Human Rights*, 65.

48. Pogge, *World Poverty and Human Rights*, 64-67.

49. Pogge, "Severe Poverty as a Violation of Negative Duties," 66.

50. Peter Dreier and Richard Appelbaum, "Campus Breakthrough on Sweatshop Labor," *The Nation*, June 1, 2006, available on *Global Exchange*, http://www.globalexchange.org/campaigns/sweatshops/3959.pf (accessed on September 20, 2006); Global Exchange, "Sweatfree Bay Area," *Global Exchange* 2006, http://www.globalexchange.org/campaigns/sweatshops/sfbayarea.html (accessed October 18, 2006).

51. Jagdish Bhagwati, *In Defense of Globalization* (Oxford and New York: Oxford University Press, 2004), 83-86 and 175; Jeffrey D. Sachs, *The End of Poverty: Economic Possibilities for Our Time* (New York: Penguin Press, 2005), 11-12.

52. ABC News, "Women Forced to Work," *20/20 Special Investigation*, April 1, 2000, transcript available on *Global Exchange*, http://www.globalexchange.org/campaigns/sweatshops/saipan/abc040100.html (accessed on October 9, 2006).

53. For information on the Sweatfree ordinances, see Global Exchange, "Sweatfree Bay Area." For information on the Gap's and Nike's voluntary agreement to have their factories monitored, see Peter Dreier and Richard Appelbaum, "Campus Breakthrough on Sweatshop Labor"; and Global Envision, "The End of Gap Sweatshops?" *Global Envision*, July 8, 2004, www.globalenvision.org/library/8/639 (accessed on September 20, 2006).

For an assessment of how working conditions have changed and of how companies have fared as a result of voluntary codes and monitoring, see David Vogel, *The Market for Virtue: The Potential and Limits of Corporate Social Responsibility* (Washington, DC: Brookings Institute Press, 2005), chapter 4.

54. I owe the name of this model to Dr. Mike Myers at Washington State University.

55. Ser-Min Shei, "World Poverty and Moral Responsibility," in *Real World Justice: Grounds, Principles, Human Rights, and Social Institutions*, ed. Andreas Follesdal and Thomas Pogge (Dordrecht: Springer, 2005), 147-48.

56. For details, see Greg Campbell, "Blood Diamonds," *Amnesty International USA* 2002, http://www.amnestyusa.org/amnestynow/diamonds.html (accessed October 10, 2006).

57. It is appalling that the World Trade Organization has the right to prohibit legislative boycotts. In response to a WTO agreement which the United States signed but which individual states did not, a court struck down Massachusetts' official boycott of goods made in Burma, a country with terrible human rights violations. See Fred Hiatt, "Massachusetts Takes on Burma," *Washington Post*, Sunday, January 31, 1999, 7(B), available on *Online Burma/Myanmar Library*, http://www.burmalibrary.org/reg.burma/archives/199902/msg00071.html (accessed October 10, 2006); Public Citizen, "MA Burma Procurement Law Challenged at WTO," *Public Citizen*, http://www.citizen.org/trade/issues/burma/articles.cfm?ID=11103 (accessed October 10, 2006). Trade agreements like this one need to be renegotiated so that the WTO, an organization comprised of various economic bodies in the world, does not have more power (in a legal sense) than a legislative body like the state of Massachusetts.

58. Of the 100 largest economies in the world, 51 are corporations and only 49 are states. Cited in Andrew Kuper, "Redistributing Responsibilities—The UN Global Compact with Corporations," in *Real World Justice: Grounds, Principles, Human Rights, and Social Institutions*, ed. Andreas Follesdal and Thomas Pogge (Dordrecht: Springer, 2005), 362-63.

59. For more on the relationship of economics to politics, see Pinzani, "'It's the Power, Stupid!'" For more on the importance of acknowledging the political agency of non-state actors like corporations and NGOs, see Kuper, "Redistributing Responsibilities"; and O'Neill, "Global Justice: Whose Obligations?"

Chapter 5
Responsibilities of Affluent Individuals

On any account of poverty, no matter how we understand its causes, the responsibility for addressing it is largely collective. Insofar as poverty is simply deprivation, the aid that is most efficacious, that most adequately meets people's human rights, and that most appropriately expresses universal human benevolence consists in collective action by governments and private charities. When poverty is the result of wrongful harm, the agents liable for the harm are responsible for redressing it by rectifying the conditions that contributed to poverty; while individuals rarely have so much power they can be said to have caused poverty in the morally relevant way, governments and corporations frequently do. And insofar as poverty is the result of unjust institutional practices or unjust social and economic structures, the agents that have the most power to ensure that institutions and structures are just and to change them when they are not, are, once again, governments and corporations; though individuals also have some power through their collective actions as citizens and consumers. Whether the relevant collective agents are conglomerates—such as governments, corporations, and (non-profit) non-governmental organizations (such as private charities)—or whether they are congregations—that is, the collection of individuals that share in a common lot, namely of sharing in the socio-economic benefits of affluence—collective agents are primarily responsible for global poverty simply because they have more power with respect to causing or changing the conditions of poverty. In light of the power that collective agents have, it can be hard to see what role individuals play regarding global poverty. How individuals share in collective responsibility must be identified.

This chapter begins by summarizing the three different forms of collective responsibility discussed in the previous chapters. Since the three models of responsibility primarily justify collective, rather than individual, responsibility, the particular forms of collective responsibility that are justified must be explained, and the particular ways that individuals share in these forms of collective responsibility must be clarified. The next section looks at problems that arise in trying to determine an individual's role or share with respect to these forms of collective responsibility. In response, I suggest some ways that an individual's contribution to collective responsibility does matter. Next I discuss the scope of responsibility and argue that the duties an individual has should be made specific. Finally, I suggest a list of duties that individuals have with respect to global poverty, particularly with respect to the collective action that global poverty demands.

Why Collective Responsibility?
Review of Who is Responsible and Why

To say that individuals share in collective responsibility, or that collectives have responsibilities toward global poverty, can mean several different things. There are many forms of collectives, and correspondingly many kinds of collective responsibility. This section reviews three relevant types of collectives and forms of collective responsibility, in order to clarify the relationships that individuals have toward these various collectives and their corresponding forms of responsibility.

A conglomerate is a collective that is itself an agent, having decision-making and action-delegating procedures that allow it to "think" and "act" just as a person does, and having goals and mission statements that serve as its "intentions." Corporations, governments, and non-governmental organizations are examples of conglomerates. As agents, conglomerates have the same kinds of duties that individuals do. Because they can act in a way that has morally significant causal effects, including the ability to cause wrongful harm or injustice, conglomerates have duties of forbearance to avoid causing harm, duties of redress to rectify wrongful harms, and duties of institutional justice to not participate in institutional practices that violate human rights. Because they have more power and wealth than other agents, especially individuals, conglomerates may also have duties of beneficence to help those in need and duties of institutional justice to change institutional practices to be more just.[1] Corporations and governments have much more power than individuals, so their actions have greater causal reach in their effects. This enables them to cause greater harm and to violate human rights more easily, but it also allows them to make more significant changes that promote justice or increase benefit. As a result of this power, conglomerates have greater responsibility than individuals.

A conglomerate has non-distributive collective responsibility, meaning that as a whole it can have duties to act or be held liable for wrongful actions it has performed, just as an individual can; but individual members that occupy roles within the collective do not personally share in these responsibilities. Such individuals do have role responsibilities, however, both in the pre-moral sense to carry out expectations attached to their roles, and in the moral sense to act justly within their roles and to do their best to ensure that the conglomerate as a whole acts justly. Individuals occupying roles within collectives share in the non-distributive "collective" responsibility of conglomerates only in the context of their roles, as parts contributing to the whole. To say that individuals share in collective responsibility in the context of their roles within conglomerates, then, is to say that they have special pre-moral as well as moral duties with respect to acting within and on behalf of the conglomerate as a whole.

In contrast to a conglomerate, an aggregate is a collective that does not have its own agency; it consists in the summation or collection of agents sharing a common trait. An example of an aggregate is a random collection of individuals sharing a trait such as spatio-temporal location, in which the individuals each have agency, but the group as a whole does not. A random collective can share distributive collective responsibility insofar as each is equally responsible for what any should do or should have done; if it is necessary that someone in the group should save someone from dying, then every member of the group is equally responsible for doing the action, even if only one such person is necessary. In random collectives, there is no particular justifying link between the agent who carries out the duty and the recipient of the action, for it does not matter which particular agent acts, as long as at least one in the relevant group—those who are capable, given the relevant trait which they share—does.

Who is responsible to fulfill duties of beneficence depends on what ability agents have; agents that share some relevant ability are grouped together as a random collective. What identifies particular agents as responsible is that they share the relevant trait that gives them sufficient means, or greater means than others have, to help. The means to help is an accidental or contingent trait when it is viewed as something that one "just happens" to have (as opposed to constituting or arising from a more particular relationship with those who would be helped, as is the case in the collective described below). Insofar as the appropriate agents are individuals, the relevant trait that justifies their aid is relative affluence. Insofar as the appropriate agents are conglomerates (collectives that themselves have agency), the relevant traits that justify their aid are having sufficient wealth and power to help, and having a designated role to do so (such as part of their mission statement). Governments and non-profit non-governmental organizations are primary examples of these collectives, as these may be designed or justified for the sake of helping those in need; for example, one role of governments is to ensure that people's human rights are met or not violated, and agencies like United Nations Children's Fund (UNICEF) and Save the Children have as one of their missions to meet the needs of specific populations such as children. These agents share in collective responsibility by being equally responsible for doing their part to use their means to help those in need. While the actions of all such agents may not be necessary to fulfill these duties, responsibility nonetheless distributes to all because each shares the relevant trait(s) on the basis of which responsibility is assigned. To say that individuals share in collective responsibility in the context of their personal moral agency, then, is to say that they have the same distributive responsibility to help those in need as other individuals do, based on their relative affluence.

A third kind of collective is another type of aggregate, what I call a congregation. Like random collectives, congregations are collections of individuals that share a trait that is the basis for their grouping. This trait serves as the basis for ascribing collective responsibility for the group because possessing this trait is morally relevant enough to justify sharing responsibility. While in random collectives individuals are grouped together based on sharing an accidental or contingent trait like spatio-temporal location, in congregations individuals are grouped together based on sharing a different kind of trait, one that serves as the basis for solidarity or at least sharing in a common lot, such as racial identity or religion. In the case of global poverty, the trait of sharing benefits from a system that distributes them unjustly—for example, having the economic benefit of being able to buy goods cheaply while others produce them for extremely low wages and under unfair working conditions—is the morally relevant trait that justifies sharing in collective responsibility. Congregations thus describe institutional relationships between various individual and collective agents (conglomerates) whose actions condition, and are conditioned by, these institutions.

When affluence results from receiving benefits from a system that distributes them unjustly, it cannot be understood as grouping people together in a merely accidental or random way as described above. Affluence groups people together based on their positioning within the structures that distribute benefits and burdens. Affluence is a relative concept, so that one is affluent more or less compared to others. There is no single class of affluence, but many classes; membership depends on what particular benefits (being of a certain socio-economic class, or having access to certain kinds of political power, for instance) agents receive from the relevant institutional structures. The ability to share in a common lot of affluence applies to both individual and collective agents (conglomerates), because both act in ways that condition and are conditioned by institutional structures that distribute benefits and burdens in a systematically unjust way. Because conglomerates like governments and corporations engage in shared institutional practices, and are enabled and constrained by institutions in the same way that individuals are, they are members of congregation on account of sharing the morally relevant features, and so they share in the collective responsibility that this trait justifies.

Since a congregation is an aggregate, agents (whether individual or collective) comprising the congregation share distributive collective responsibility because each member of the group is responsible on account of possessing the morally relevant identifying feature that makes her a member of the group. Solidarity or sharing in a common lot form a different and perhaps stronger relationship between individuals and the group than sharing accidental or contingent traits, and they justify a different kind of responsibility. In random collectives, individuals share in distributive collective responsibility on account of possessing a trait that makes each person capable of doing the morally necessary action—a contingent matter of fact. Responsibility depends on how far the causal effects of one's actions reach. In congregations, in contrast, agents share in collective responsibility on account of possessing a trait that allows each to contribute to harm or to benefit unjustly—a less contingent feature since it is more tied to one's identity. Responsibility is based on features of one's identity, and whether these features are chosen or even desired is irrelevant. Since each agent in the group shares the identifying trait—here, the trait of living under certain economic and political practices that benefit some and burden others unjustly—each shares the same relationship to the harmful practice as a whole, and so each is responsible for her portion in changing the moral nature of the trait that is the basis for responsibility. Just as individuals who receive preferential treatment for having white skin have duties to change social practices so that white skin does not offer such privileges, agents that benefit unjustly from certain economic practices are responsible for changing these economic practices so that they do not distribute benefits and burdens unjustly.

The major criticism of the collective responsibility of congregations regards what counts as relevant causation. One may object that individuals do not contribute to harmful institutional practices because they do not cause identifiable harmful effects with their actions;[2] what causes harm is not any one individual's actions but the confluence of many agents' actions together. But this confluence means that all agents contribute, even though the action of any one of them is not sufficient to have a particular effect. In other words, any particular agent's actions are not sufficiently causally responsible for institutionally harmful effects; but particular agents do conjoin with other agents to act collectively in ways that do in fact cause harm. The responsibility that results is not distributive in the same easily identifiable, causal way that is associated with random collectives; but each individual nonetheless shares some portion of the overall responsibility to change the nature of the group as a whole. To say that individuals share in collective responsibility in the context of their institutional identities, then, is to say that they share some portion of the overall responsibility to change the nature of this basis for their identities (i.e. to change the nature of these institutions) so that it is no longer a morally relevant feature justifying normative response (i.e. so these institutions are more just).

In comparing and contrasting conglomerates, random collectives, and congregations with each other, I want to make clear that none of these forms of groupings or justifications of collective responsibility are "better," stronger, or prior to the other; they are simply different bases for justifying different, noncommensurable, and generally compatible forms of responsibility. The aim of this book is to examine what responsibility affluent individuals have toward global poverty, *given* that poverty generally has structural causes such as corporate and government practices, and *given* that poverty is generally a political problem requiring collective action. Taking these features of poverty into account, the responsibilities that arise must be collective in nature—making individuals' responsibility toward global poverty some form or forms of sharing in collective responsibility. In arguing for a pluralistic model of responsibility that affluent individuals have toward global poverty, I claim that individuals have duties based on their personal moral agency, their roles within collectives, and their institutional identities. Each of these duties arises from the particular way that individuals share in the different forms of collective responsibility explained throughout the book and summarized here—random collectives, conglomerates, and congregations—which are justified according to the three forms of responsibility considered throughout this book—beneficence, redress, and institutional justice.[3]

Problems with the Agency Involved in Collective Responsibility

Individuals have responsibilities with respect to the various collectives of which they are members, namely to do their part in making sure the collectives carry out *their* responsibilities. The agency of the individual can be understood in terms of the role responsibility she has based on her position within the collective—not merely a pre-moral responsibility to fulfill expectations, but also a moral responsibility to act well. There are several problems with ascribing moral responsibility that attaches to roles, however, since individuals have, or at least seem to have, very little agency relative to the collective. These problems all seem to diminish the responsibility an individual has given her constraints and thus complicate what role an individual can play with respect to collective responsibility.

Givenness of Roles

One problem for individual agency with respect to collective responsibility is that individuals often have no choice in whether to occupy certain roles; these roles are just "given" to an individual. This is particularly true of the roles an individual occupies by virtue of her institutional identity, as the particular citizenship that a person has or the particular roles that a person plays within various economies are largely unchosen. It is true that individuals can become citizens of countries other than the ones in which they were born, and it is also true that individuals can shift their placement in economies depending on their occupations and how well they do with the resources they have. However, these changes are not easy, and they do not result from mere "choice." If I am very poor, I cannot simply "choose" to become wealthy; I must have opportunities and resources available to me of which I am capable of taking advantage.

The problem with articulating the responsibility of individuals with respect to their institutional identities is that responsibility is predicated of agents, yet the kind of voluntariness or control that agents have within their institutional roles is necessarily limited. An individual's voluntariness is constrained by structures in at least two ways: her control is limited relative to the outcomes determined by institutional structures, and she is also subject to the moral luck of being in a particular social role. Yet if an individual has any responsibility related to collective action, even if her only responsibility is with regard to her role, she must have some relevant freedom to have control over her action—or the carrying out of her role—such that she acts as an agent. Only if she is an agent in the relevant way can she take responsibility.

Institutions condition what options are available to us in our actions, both limiting and enabling the set of options available to us. Political institutions include laws and policies that constrain our behavior in some ways and provide us with opportunities in others. Economic institutions create the conditions for our productive and consumer lives, both limiting and enabling our choices in work, how we spend money and time, and general quality of life. As individuals, we largely cannot choose *that* we play roles with respect to these political and economic institutions. We may be able to move to different places and live under different governments, or we may be able to change our career paths and livelihoods, but even the most dramatic changes still occur *given* the existing institutional structures. Some options are easier for us to choose, and others simply impossible, depending on what structural conditions obtain, over which we have little control.

As individuals, we have limited (if any) choice in the existence of particular institutional structures and of how we occupy roles within these structures. For example, we may work for a particular corporation because it provides the most benefit for the kind of work for which we are skilled—but this may not be a "choice" in the sense of choosing among suitable alternatives, for often there are few comparable alternatives.[4] Our options may be even more constrained as citizens and consumers, for we cannot choose *not* to be citizens and consumers, particularly in liberal, capitalist democracies. The irony in such roles is that the hallmark of living in a liberal state with capitalism democracy is the value of choice, but often the differences between available options seem irrelevant so that the "choice" between grocery items or political candidates seems arbitrary. As individuals, we often do not have enough knowledge to make informed decisions, so that we are unable to choose the best among possible policies. Within roles, especially occupational roles, we are often not allowed much room to make any individual choice, as we are supposed to follow orders or at least cohere to expectations, or we may lose our position. In various ways we find ourselves in political and economic roles, the positions of which we did not choose to occupy in any deep or meaningful way, yet in which we are expected somehow to be responsible.

Replaceability of Role Holders

One way to think about roles within collectives and institutions is as placeholders in which the specific identity of the person occupying the role is replaceable with another. In some cases, this replaceability does not accurately describe the nature of roles; people do sometimes turn their roles into something of their own creation, leaving their own unique mark on them, acting within their roles largely in the same way that they would act as individuals. This occurs most easily and most often when roles are voluntarily chosen. To the extent that the particular individual in a role does not matter, however, responsibility that attaches to the role is less meaningful because the individual has no reason to think that the responsibility applies *to her*. After all, she can simply be replaced with someone else who will be expected to act in the same way. When individuals are replaceable in roles, the role—and one's action within it—starts looking like a cog in a machine rather than a position of agency capable of responsibility.[5]

Anonymity of Roles

Closely related to the problem of replaceability is the problem of anonymity. To the extent that individual identity of the role holder does not matter, one's identity and action within a role are anonymous. It does not matter *who* occupies the role, or what she does, since she can be replaced. This anonymity treats all individuals who are potential role holders as the same, eliminating any freedom that individuals have to be themselves as unique individuals and to follow their own conscience, to be accountable to action. By precluding them from accountability, anonymity allows people to perform actions in their roles that they would not do as individuals, permitting terrible deeds to occur. This is because anonymity allows people to lose "face-to-face confrontation" with other people, making the consequences of their actions seem less real, and resulting in a loss of personal responsibility.[6]

This problem is compounded by the fact that even corporations, which provide many of the roles that individuals occupy, are themselves anonymous in the sense that their particular identity does not matter to their overall goal of profit maximization. The obsession with maximizing profits, especially in the stock market, changes the nature of a corporation so that it is no longer a business entity, but rather merely "one of a number of diversified streams of risk and return."[7] As such, the actual business that a corporation engages in—the actual products it makes or services it provides—is inessential to a corporation's identity, as it can be replaced by other products or services that create greater profit. The particular identity of a corporation, and the values that it embodies through that identity, erode according to the demands of profit maximization. Although the phenomenon of branding makes a corporation's identity more pronounced in some ways, by associating the name with an image, a logo, and/or a mission, the break in linkage between the corporation and the goods or services it provides makes it essentially anonymous, replaceable with other streams of revenue to the stockholders who see it as just another way to maximize profits. This anonymity makes it very difficult for corporations to be held accountable for their actions, as they use for the justification of their actions the defense of profit maximization. For the individual who works in a corporation, the diminished agency and personal responsibility that she experiences as a result of the anonymity and replaceability of her role is worsened substantially by the fact that the source of that role, the corporation, is itself anonymous and replaceable, and therefore not easily accountable for its actions.

Inevitability of Causal Processes

If roles are anonymous and their holders replaceable, then the consequences that result from the action expected from those acting in roles can seem inevitable. Even if one does not perform a given action herself, she may be unable to prevent its occurrence, making *her* particular performance of it morally inconsequential. Individuals often say in defense of morally reprehensible actions they perform *qua* their roles, "If I didn't do it, someone else would have." The more that roles seem to have an existence of their own, independent of individual human influence, the more that they seem to have a causal process of their own, independent of human agency. Again, they really start seeming like cogs in a machine, just a way for inevitable causal processes to occur like machinery. Event causation that is independent of agent causation (i.e. causal processes that occur without human agency or intervention involved) can seem like processes over which humans have no control. And the more inevitable causal processes and outcomes seem, the more it seems that humans are *unable* to have any control over them. Responsibility for these actions and outcomes seems irrelevant.[8]

Diffusion of Responsibility

Because collectives like corporations and governments have multiple levels of decision and action, responsibility is greatly diffused. This presents several problems. Diffused responsibility means that the responsibility that attaches to any one role, even those at the top levels, is low. Having multiple levels of decision and action make it too easy to evade responsibility by blaming someone else for a faulty action, whether that someone else is at a lower level (the person who "did" the action) or a higher level (the person who "decided" on the action). The greater number of people involved who could carry some of the responsibility, the less that any one of them has any, or at least seems to have any.[9]

The aggregate nature of agents acting by virtue of their institutional identities makes the responsibility that any one agent has even more diffused. Under a given set of institutional practices or social structures, individuals and collectives act in ways that are largely uncoordinated with each other and that often have unintended but far-reaching effects, especially when the effects of any given agent's action are added to the effects of other agents' similar action. Under institutions, agents act in confluence with other agents, so that the particular action of any given agent and its particular effect are usually unidentifiable. Determining the particular responsibility an agent has, either in terms of liability for harm or responsibility for making conditions more just, is very difficult, therefore, if not impossible.

Insignificance of the Individual

The nature of collective action is such that it supersedes the action of any particular individual. When collective action is necessary, an individual's action is not sufficient and may not even be necessary. If the whole of collective action is required, then the portion that is an individual's action is by itself insufficient. Additionally, there are many situations in which any particular individual's action may not be necessary to contribute to the collective action of the whole, especially when collective action is taken from the top-down. For example, if U.S. politicians vote to send more aid to Africa, their billions of dollars in foreign aid makes my $50 contribution to the U.S. Fund for UNICEF unnecessary and insignificant. Or, in the context of environmental concerns, if politicians increase fuel standards of vehicles substantially, or if motor vehicle companies voluntarily enact such fuel standard increases on their own, then my taking the bus to save my portion of contributing to energy consumption and pollution becomes unnecessary and insignificant. In other words, an individual's contribution simply does not matter in the context of substantive collective action, especially when such action is dictated by relevant government or corporate leaders. It still somehow seems *good* for me to send money to UNICEF or to take the bus if I can, but what accounts for this good when the action is neither sufficient nor necessary for collective change is unclear. Perhaps it makes me a better person, in the virtue framework of morality. But if this is the case, what bounds me to perform these actions is my interest in having a good character, not what the moral tragedy of a condition like poverty or environmental destruction demands from me. When individual action is neither necessary nor sufficient for collective change, it is unclear what duties, if any, that one has with respect to global poverty.

Perpetually Dirty Hands

The globalization of the world's economies means that just about everyone has "dirty hands" in contributing to institutional injustices. In the previous chapter, I argued that no one can have "clean hands" by refusing to participate in unjust social and economic practices, because many of these institutions have such far reach that "opting out" is impossible. The fact that we are *always* morally implicated in injustice, however hard we try to do good in the world, makes us seem impotent as agents. For example, anyone who owns stock in a 401(k) or 403(b) retirement plan tends to own stock in most of the major corporations of the world. Even if I boycott Nestle for pushing their infant formula on mothers too poor to use it in a healthy way, then, or even if I refuse to shop at Wal-Mart for being the worst offender of creating a retail monopoly and relying on sweatshop labor to lower prices, I almost certainly own some stock in both corporations. Although my share is only a tiny fraction of a company's investments, I am still a shareholder, even in companies that I wish to boycott as a consumer.

The aims of the different aspects of my identity—as consumer and as a worker with retirement benefits who thereby becomes a shareholder—now become contradictory.[10] It is unclear how an individual can effect change when she is always implicated in injustice, despite her best intentions; it is equally unclear how—or whether—an individual can resolve this tension between different aspects of her identity.

Impotence of Agents

As a result of all these factors, individuals who act within roles can feel impotent, that is they feel as if they have no power or control over the actions that they are expected to perform and the outcomes which are supposed to result. In other words, it seems that they do not have sufficient agency to be responsible in any meaningful way. If this is true, then role responsibility reduces to the responsibility for carrying out the expectations attached to a role. When roles do not correspond to what morality requires an individual to do, problems arise concerning to what extent an individual is able to act contrary to role expectations in following her own conscience, and to what extent we should hold her morally accountable for such action.[11]

Acting *qua* individual and not *qua* role in such cases may be morally praiseworthy—e.g., we may applaud whistleblowers—but in many cases it is hard to blame those who do not do so. When individuals have little power to transform their roles, it may be unreasonable to expect them to act outside of their constraints as a matter of duty. One way to resolve this problem is to acknowledge an asymmetry in how we evaluate these kinds of cases, where we praise those who follow their conscience rather than obey orders but do not blame those who do not.[12] Yet this solution allows for terrible injustices to occur, and for people to act horrendously in their roles in ways they would not do as individuals. The desire not to blame others for not resisting temptation to act wrongly in social or occupational roles seems to condone terrible harms.[13] Passing moral and legal judgment is crucial for humans to make sense of the rightness and wrongness of their actions, motivating them to figure out how to act more justly and morally in the future, and punishing them for acting badly in the past. As a result, an asymmetrical stance of praise and blame is an unsatisfactory way to resolve potential conflicts between responsibility to role expectations and responsibility to ethical considerations. But the problem still remains.

Compartmentalization of Self

As contemporary life becomes more and more modernized and bureaucratic, the roles that individuals occupy seem to become less constitutive of their selves. An individual separates her self, with its unique identity and corresponding moral agency, from the anonymous roles she occupies, each with its own set of expectations for appropriate action. Often, she encounters others only in their roles, and so knows others only *qua* their roles, not *qua* themselves as individuals. As individuals exchange roles through the various facets of their life, their individual identity becomes "dissolved into their various roles."[14] Within each role, the individual plays a part, but as she changes roles she plays a different part, and the parts often do not add up coherently; the demands of each part frequently contradict each other. In some cases, an individual loses a sense of her unique identity altogether, identifying wholly with the array of roles she occupies; when this happens, she also loses a sense of herself as a moral agent.

When an individual acts as a moral agent, she reflects critically on her actions and their contexts, stepping back from her roles and evaluating them normatively from some standpoint external to the roles themselves. In compartmentalization, however, spheres of activity are insulated from each other so that ethical considerations in one sphere do not carry over into other spheres, and there is no sphere of activity in which this critical reflection is possible. This compartmentalization of self into the various bureaucratic roles that one occupies gives an individual the excuse that she does not have to reflect critically on the nature of the roles she occupies or the moral quality of their expectations on her. She objectifies her actions as separate from her, stemming from her role rather than from her *self* as a moral agent; this allows her to detach herself from the moral nature of her actions. She understands the responsibilities she has *qua* her roles as merely a pre-moral responsibility to fulfill the expectations of the roles, without appreciating her responsibility as a moral agent. As a result, she has no context for understanding the moral nature of her actions. This lack of awareness about the moral nature of her actions is what leads Hannah Arendt to refer to such behavior as "the banality of evil."[15]

How Individual Agency in
Collective Responsibility Matters

As these problems show, an individual can feel as if she has no ability to act on her conscience when occupying roles or fulfilling social expectation, and in fact an individual's particular action often does not make much of a difference, if any, within bureaucratic and institutional structures. Given these very real constraints, it is difficult to see why an individual should see herself as an agent and not merely a cog in the machine, and how she is able to do so.

There are a few ways to address this. Causation explains why the action of any given individual occupying a role matters, why causal processes are not inevitable, and why a person's involvement in them is not truly anonymous. For many people, however, this answer is not sufficiently motivating. Social philosophy provides other ways to think about the meaningfulness of individual agency and responsibility within roles. Our individual action seems to matter more when we respond to particular others such as by entering into relationships with them, as communitarians argue, and when we see our action as extensions of our identity, as virtue theorists argue. Moreover, when we examine the ways in which we always have some element of free choice in our action, as in the existentialist view, we find that we are not as impotent as we may feel. In fact, focusing on the tasks for which a person is responsible by virtue of her roles is the most pragmatic way of showing how individual agency matters. Collective responsibility can be discharged only when individuals carry out their portion of the shared responsibility as it attaches to their roles.

Particularity of Action: Causal Response

Role responsibility is a problematic concept largely because of the nature of roles as seeming to support inevitable outcomes of causal processes and in which the individuals occupying them are replaceable and anonymous. The concept of over-determination in causal theory helps us understand this nature of roles, and points us to ways of seeing our way out of these problems.

Over-determination helps explain the anonymity of roles and social positions, underscoring the reasons why responsibility is difficult to apply to structural injustice and why role responsibility especially is problematic. Both as victims of injustice and as agents of responsibility, our particularity and uniqueness vanish, so that both our suffering and our actions are defined by what position we hold within social structures, by our roles, making irrelevant who we are as individuals. A person in a given role may be expected to act a certain way, knowing that if she does not carry out these expectations, someone else will replace her in the role. *Her* particular agency in the situation seems irrelevant because the action will occur regardless of whether *she* does it.

Yet how an individual occupies a role does matter, and an account of causation as a basis for moral responsibility can explain why. When there are multiple sets of sufficient causal conditions, we can identify *"the* cause" as what is necessary *post factum* or necessary in the circumstances.[16] In other words, *"the* cause" is what is necessary given that it is the only sufficient condition that is present, such as what actually *did happen* or who actually *did act* in a certain role. Even if others would have acted instead, the agents that did act are morally responsible for *how they did act* because their actions were necessary *post factum* and causally relevant. If moral responsibility is a meaningful concept such that we act as agents and are not mere cogs in a machine, then what actions we carry out in our roles or what experiences we endure through our social positions is morally relevant. Even if others would have acted or suffered if we had not, our particular actions and experiences, and the fact that they were *ours*, matter.

Moreover, regardless of whether someone else could have or would have done the same action, the law treats human agents as individual human beings, with a moral conscience and the ability to make a decision about whether to act rightly or wrongly. The excuse that one acts *merely* as a functionary in her role and not as an individual moral agent is akin to a criminal pointing to crime statistics and arguing that *someone* had to commit the crime, and it was only an accident that it was she; she was merely performing her criminal role, doing what was statistically expected.[17] Of course this strikes us as ludicrous. No one acts *merely* as a functionary in her role; when individuals act in roles, they also remain moral agents and thus also have the capability to, and consequently should, act *qua* their moral agency.

Causal relationships show us both what institutional actions lead to poverty, so that we can determine what actions we can and should take in response, and also how we fit into structures, so that we can see what roles we do play and what scope of action we have relative to these roles. We can carry out our moral responsibilities by reflecting critically on what is demanded of us, understanding its moral context, and understanding ourselves as moral agents who are necessarily causally connected to others through our decisions and actions.

Particularity of Response: Communitarian Response

The feeling of impotence or powerlessness commonly arises when an individual feels that her actions make no difference to the outcome, that things will happen a certain way regardless of *whether* she acts or not, and regardless of *how* she acts. Philosophers commonly respond to this worry with facts, such as by arguing that an individual's actions *do* matter, for example sending even $1 to Oxfam can buy enough salt packets to prevent a few children from dying of dehydration brought about by diarrhea.[18] But such a consequence cannot be seen or felt. While philosophers may reply that this worry expresses an unreasonable concern, that vividness or the felt consequences of response is a motivational issue that should not matter to moral action, the fact is that for most people they do. People are not rational machines made up only of calculating minds. The affective side of being human makes us want to see how our actions have some effect in the world, to feel that we play some relevant role in causal processes. Philosophers are wrong to reject this as morally insignificant, particularly for consequentialist reasons: since many people do not act unless they can see the effects of their action, and since doing some of one's duty is better than doing none of it, it is important for many people that their actions have some perceptible effect.

One solution to this problem is to draw on the relational aspect of self that communitarians emphasize. When we have choices in how to direct our response, we can choose to direct our response to those causes to which we feel most connected for personal reasons, even if the reasons are somewhat morally arbitrary according to strictly impartial criteria. Moreover, we can enter into relationships with people that allow us to see and feel the consequences of our actions. Some agencies that do charity work recognize the value of people seeing the consequences of their action by entering into relationships. This is why organizations like Save the Children have children write letters to donors.[19] This also explains the appeal of microfinance organizations like the Grameen Foundation and Kiva, which match particular, identifiable loan requests of poor entrepreneurs with particular donors. By providing small loans that carry high success rates of repayment, relatively wealthy donors can see satisfying results from helping particular, identifiable others within the familiar business model that allowed them to prosper themselves.

Consumer decisions are another relevant example. People may feel that whether one buys food from the national supermarket chain or from the local farmer's market does not matter in the general scheme of things, because the decision does not change the general structure of how food is distributed and who makes money from it. Broadly speaking, this is true, for one's individual action usually does not make a noticeable difference to the structure as a whole. But if a person chooses to enter into a relationship with local food producers, then she can see some results from her action. For example, if a person buys produce regularly from a local farmer, her regular purchase does make a difference to that farmer. For some people such an effect is not significant enough to feel that one is making a difference. But for other people seeing such an effect makes one feel that one's action matters much more significantly than, for example, writing a letter of protest to a transnational company. In my view both actions are appropriate, though I cannot assess the degree of "difference" either action makes. But when individuals are choosing among possible actions, the ones in which they feel like they make a difference are important because these are actions they *will* perform, and they provide a way to prioritize response. Entering into relationships with people is one way that this can occur.

For many people, political problems like poverty are so broad and overwhelming that the only way they can feel as though their action matters at all is to particularize the problem, to narrow in and focus on particular individuals or a particular sub-group. As long as individuals feel that they are merely cogs in a machine, in which their action falls into some amorphous black hole, they have no reason to act at all. This is not only a motivational issue; it has real consequences that affect the way we assess a situation morally. If they have no reason to change their behavior, people will likely continue to act in ways that perpetuate the *status quo* and that contribute to unjust structural practices. In order for their particular action to matter, to have reason to care and to take responsibility for changing behavior, individuals need to feel connected to other people in morally significant ways. What makes structural injustice and political responsibility such difficult concepts to apply at the individual level is their broad nature, the way that we cannot trace individual action to consequences, or unjust situations to particular causes. In order for individuals to be involved in political responsibility, even if by this we mean only that individuals act in collective and institutional roles, they need to see some particular, causal consequences in which they have some meaningful effect on particular individuals. Humans are not cogs in a machine. We are agents. In order for any responsibility to apply, including political responsibility, we need to be able to see and feel our agency in a meaningful way.

Involvement in Role Descriptions: Constructivist Response

In arguing against impartial duties to assist those in need, some philosophers note that there is a "common-sense" intuition that our most pressing duties are the special obligations we have to particular others.[20] Most people prioritize their obligations to family members and compatriots, for instance, over those to "distant strangers." Role responsibility provides us with a way to understand how we have duties to these "distant strangers"—not as impartial, universal duties to all in equal need, and not with respect to relationships with other particular individuals, but rather with respect to the relationships we share with others by virtue of the roles we have within collectives and institutions.

Since we occupy multiple roles, with responsibilities that often come into conflict—for example our responsibilities as parents may conflict with those we have as consumers—it can be difficult to figure out how to prioritize these responsibilities and why. A simplistic assertion of the priority of either partial or impartial duties over the other will not resolve the conflict, as each takes priority in different situations. Dealing with conflicts in duties requires making differential analyses. Moral priority depends on the particular context of decision-making, and this requires some empirical analysis of the relevant situation, the roles an individual occupies, and the potential responsibilities that stem from these roles. This consideration involves making act and role descriptions of such issues as what actions led to the present situation, who was involved in contributing to it and benefiting from it, and who is in a position to respond and how.

Role descriptions are made in the same constructivist way as act or causal descriptions: with infallible reasoning based on incomplete knowledge, therefore open to revision. Making these role descriptions is an act of power, so it matters who makes them. When power is concentrated in the hands of a few at the top, or so diffused that it seems to be meaningless, the result tends to be to preserve the *status quo*, which makes role descriptions susceptible to the same worries of conservativism that action descriptions are. Like action descriptions, however, the creation of roles and their expectations is a process open to debate and revision. In order to share power in constructing roles and their moral responsibilities, we need to maintain a sphere of public discussion and action. Some of our most important duties are thus political duties to maintain public spheres and to increase public awareness, interest, and discussion on social, political, and economic issues, as well as to make global connections with these issues.

The development of roles and their standards is not simply an act determined from the top down. Except perhaps in the most totalitarian societies, role creation and individual accountability develop dialectically with each other. Making role descriptions of what we expect people to do is not merely a *descriptive* process of accepting some standards as given, but also a *prescriptive*, normative process of evaluating and revising expectations of how we think people should act in particular roles. Our moral judgments are grounded in community standards, but holding people responsible also has the power to change what we expect from people.

Focusing on What Choice and Power We Do Have: Existentialist Response

In order to not feel impotent, we must focus not on the enormity of the political problems we face but on the ways in which we do have choices and actions. In this existentialist view, our freedom is necessarily situated; despite limitations on one's freedom of choice and action, an agent can have sufficient control over her behavior to be responsible for it. We always have choices in how we respond, despite the fact that we are situated within specific circumstances, identities, and roles that we do not choose; we always have some morally relevant control over our mental states. Individual action leading to harm is not necessary to relate an agent to harm; individuals can still be responsible with respect to group identities and roles within collectives that they did not choose if they sufficiently identify with and contribute to the harmful behavior or practices in question. As a result, our responsibility is to become more self-aware of our own beliefs and behaviors, to judge them critically, and to dissociate from the harmful beliefs and practices that are dominant within our social groups.[21]

This response includes the evaluation of our social roles. Philosophers have traditionally discussed role responsibility in individualist terms, as if a role reduces to the individual's choice and conscience. This is a narrow way of understanding the nature of roles, however, since roles are made meaningful by social contexts that condition our choices and action. An individual occupying a role is not essentially alone with her individual conscience; she is part of many larger, overlapping social structures, and her responsibilities to the interests of each, when they conflict, involve a "difficult balancing act."[22] Yet in order for the individual to remain a moral agent, she must retain enough of a sense of her self independent of her role within a collective or institutional structure, in order to be able to evaluate what she is called upon to do and how to do it. She may decide that following orders and working within the system, perhaps trying to gain a position of greater authority, is the best way to change it—but *she* must make this decision, and she is responsible for it.

Although a person makes decisions and performs actions given a particular context, the self is also sufficiently individualistic to be able to make moral evaluation and have the kind of control relevant to being a moral agent. The individual is able to step back from the social, political, and economic factors that structure her identity and behavior in order to evaluate and respond to them. This is often a very difficult process of negotiating between different, overlapping, and sometimes conflicting interests. Yet being moral agents and taking moral and political responsibility requires this of us. We must acknowledge the tensions within our social identities, values, and roles, and work with those tensions by reflecting upon them critically.

These tensions are dynamic, for they will change as we shift our understanding of one aspect of our identity to make it more cohesive with other aspects, or as we change the nature of one of our roles so that it is more consistent with our overall values, or as we strengthen or weaken the moral weight of some of our values based on reflection upon them. Being a moral agent involves recognizing these tensions, and reflecting on them and living with them. The ideal of lining up all of one's values, roles, actions, and social identities so that they are all internally consistent with each other is not only a problematic ideal, potentially leading to dangerous forms of fundamentalism and fanaticism, but also almost impossible to attain, especially in our highly complex and highly bureaucratic modern world. While we should not aim for perfect consistency, we also should not ignore the moral aspects of the parts of our actions and roles that do not fit with how we want to think of ourselves.

Willful ignorance is a choice one makes to limit one's moral agency—a choice that is itself an exercise of moral agency and thus for which one is responsible. In response to unethical behavior, individuals commonly give the excuse that "I was just doing my job," when one's job required one to do something extremely unethical. This excuse arises from the self that is compartmentalized into different roles, the functions and values of which are kept separate from each other. This divided self allows a person acting as a corporate executive to make a decision—such as allowing vast pollution that will endanger the lives of very poor people (such as contaminating drinking water)—that he would never condone in his roles as father and churchgoer; in the first role his main function is to maximize profit whatever the consequence, while in the latter two roles he cares very much about the well-being of other people.[23] The functions and values of these roles easily conflict with each other, but such an individual is deluding himself to think that keeping their functions and values separate will avoid conflict; all this separation does is to mask the conflict willfully. Since compartmentalization of the self requires intentionality and self-discipline, the excuse of the divided self—that one was just doing one's job in a certain role—does not hold. The divided self is complicit in its compartmentalization, and so shares in responsibility for having diminished one's moral agency.[24]

Agents—not only individuals, but also collectives—are thus at least partially responsible for willful ignorance of the consequences of their actions, even when those actions are made within the contexts of particular roles or under certain social constraints. For example, many affluent individuals put themselves in a position of chosen ignorance, choosing not to learn about the unjust conditions that allow them to buy certain goods, such as the sweatshop labor that went into making their clothes, or the civil wars that went into the mining of their diamond. When the information is available and easily accessible—and today, with the Internet, most information is very easily accessible—there is no excuse to not learn about the ethical effects of one's decisions, especially the consumer decisions that arise from being part of a global economy.

Existentialists remind us that we always have choices to respond to tragic or unjust conditions, regardless of our causal role in them. Willful ignorance allows us to ignore those conditions and delude ourselves that we therefore have no responsibility toward them; but willful ignorance is itself a choice. We can and should choose to learn more about how we connect to others globally through our political and economic decisions. The conflicts in our identities and values may make it difficult to know what the best thing to do about this knowledge is; for example, is it better to support one's local economy and buy local products made under high labor standards, or is it better to buy products imported from places with low labor standards but where people need the money more desperately to escape from dire poverty? There is no simple or obvious answer to a question like this. Exercising our moral agency means thinking through the relevant issues and trying our best to figure out what to do with that knowledge. We do have power through these choices.

Focusing on Task-Responsibility: Pragmatic Response

There is a pragmatic dimension to the role individuals have with respect to collective responsibility. Many duties are not fully dischargeable by any single agent, especially by a single individual agent. Allocating tasks to individuals acting in their roles, so that an individual's chief responsibility is to do the tasks expected of her, is a way for collectives to discharge their moral duties more completely.

Dischargeability regards the degree to which a duty can be satisfied or fulfilled, based on the extent of action that it implies and the ability for humans to complete it. Completion of action and satisfaction of duty implies a relationship between the duty and the goals at which it is aimed. Full dischargeability involves aiming at a goal that one can either meet or not meet; in other words, the success of one's action is an all-or-nothing matter. In contrast, partial dischargeability involves a receding target. Here one aims at a goal that is an ideal impossible to attain completely, but which one can try to attain as much as possible.[25]

Whether a duty is fully dischargeable depends not on how narrow or wide its scope is, but rather on what resources the designated duty-bearers have. The greater means that an agent has, the greater the ability she has for discharging a given duty. For example, donating 1% of one's income sounds like a fully dischargeable duty, but it only is so insofar as one can survive without 1% of her income; for some very poor individuals, this is impossible, so the duty cannot be discharged. On the other hand, providing adequate nutrition to those who need it in a given area sounds like a duty that can at best be partially discharged, but an agent or group of agents that has great means, such as a well-funded governmental agency or a non-governmental organization, would be capable of fully discharging this duty despite its great demand.

Note that an individual rarely has the means to discharge a duty of wide scope fully; usually she can fulfill these duties only partially, by focusing on a single task that is part of the larger duty. For these duties of wide scope, then, an individual is not responsible for discharging the duty fully, but she shares partial responsibility for fulfilling particular tasks that are within her means. For example, an individual is most likely incapable of providing food for all who are needy in her region; but—if she is relatively affluent—she most likely does have sufficient means to make regular donations to the area food bank. Even if she is incapable of discharging a duty fully, she can share partial responsibility by partially discharging the duty through her specific task-responsibility: of donating to or volunteering at the food bank as much as her means will allow her to do.

In contrast, collective agents may discharge duties of wide scope fully because they have greater means to act than individuals; they have greater resources of time and money to draw upon, and more "heads" and "hands" to plan and execute actions than a single individual. In order to get collective action done, and to fulfill collective responsibility, groups must allocate particular tasks to individuals that act as the "heads" and "arms" of the collective agent. These individual actions must be coordinated so that they result in carrying out the overall collective responsibility. For example, a food bank that has sufficient resources on hand may be able to discharge fully the duty to provide adequate food to those in the area who need it, if it can coordinate the actions required to distribute the food. Individuals who work or volunteer at the food bank share specific task-responsibilities that are required for the food bank to fulfill its overall duty, such as determining who needs the food, planning a distribution scheme, and transporting the food to those in need. Coordination of carrying out task-responsibilities that contribute to the overall collective responsibility involves designating tasks and tracking the behavior of each individual who acts within or under the collective, so that each individual is accountable to the group. The kinds of groups most capable of this coordination are conglomerates, because they have the decision-making and action-delegating procedures that make them agents in their own right.[26]

The responsibility of the individual thus involves task-responsibility, in some cases supervisory-responsibility, and, when relevant, an initiating-responsibility that involves joining or starting the kinds of groups that have the power to take coordinated, collective action on account of having the requisite agency. Individuals within groups have responsibility to carry out the specific task that the group designates to them. For example, if a person's role within a food bank is to solicit funds by advertising the needs of the hungry, then she is responsible for creating these advertisements and marketing them in appropriate venues. Some individuals within groups act as supervisors, making sure that those responsible for fulfilling tasks do their job. But individuals also have an additional responsibility with respect to collective action. Since collective action can only occur when individuals act within their roles, individuals must partake in collective activity, i.e. to join relevant collectives if they are not already members, and/or to organize needed collectives that do not presently exist. If a food bank is needed in a certain region, then individuals cannot simply use the excuse that there is no food bank to let them off the hook of being responsible for providing, in a coordinated way, access of food and nutrition to the needy; individuals then are responsible for starting such an organization.

Initiating a group is important because individuals have more power acting within a group than alone. Individual action summed together in an uncoordinated way will usually not make a significant difference. Even if I boycott sweatshop-produced clothes, and you boycott sweatshop-produced clothes, and the person down the street from me boycotts sweatshop-produced clothes, this does not generally add up to a noticeable difference; it will not make companies think twice about using sweatshop labor, or make governments decide to enforce labor standards. This is why random collectives are generally not morally responsible for actions or omissions: individuals added together lack the power to decide what action to take and the power to act with intention. But individuals as individuals do have the power to start a group that has the decision-making and action-delegating procedures that allow it to act with intention to produce a desired outcome (such as meeting people's nutritional needs) through coordinated efforts. When such collective action is necessary, individuals have a responsibility to create the kind of group that is needed to carry out the action.[27]

Individuals thus have duties to turn congregations into conglomerates. Individuals who share in a common lot of benefiting from economic structures that allow them to have jobs and relative affluence have a duty to turn the loose grouping, based on the identity of relative affluence, into a more formal group that is capable of making decisions and acting to change unfair structures. We considered earlier in the book that when existing agents cannot be identified as having duties to meet people's human rights, we must design the agencies that we need to fulfill morally pressing duties, particularly to meet people's basic needs. The role of individuals here is to take responsibility for organizing such agencies, or at least ensuring that others, those with more political power and economic resources such as government and corporate leaders, do so.

These considerations show that individual agency does matter to alleviating global poverty. Even though the primary agents responsible for addressing global poverty are conglomerates and institutions, individuals play important roles within these groups. Individuals have responsibilities *qua* their moral agency (such as to educate themselves and others), task-responsibilities *qua* their roles in groups, supervisory- and initiating-responsibilities where relevant, and political and economic responsibilities *qua* their institutional identities (such as to maintain active public spheres, to be involved in politics, and to be knowledgeable voters and consumers). The next section explains why the particular duties that affluent individuals have should be specified as much as possible, and the section following that offers a suggested list of these duties.

Why Duties Should Be Specified

Epistemological reasons make it difficult to specify the duties that affluent individuals have toward global poverty, particularly the duties that I am classifying as beneficence or structural justice, as these have a broader scope of action than what is often required for redress.[28] There are several reasons why acquiring sufficient knowledge on which to act is difficult, and these problems affect the ways that we are able to describe—or specify—our duties. These reasons include the following:

> *Identifiability of the actions and agents*: We are uncertain which actions and by which agents are necessary and will produce the desired outcome.
> *Amount of actions and number of agents*: Even if we can identify the correct actions and agents that are necessary, we are unsure how many agents or how much action is required.
> *Unpredictability about the process*: We are uncertain about which causal relationships are relevant, whether logically necessary or sufficient, so that we do not know which combination of a particular number of particular agents acting in specific ways will affect the process such as to produce the desired outcome. The process to obtain any given outcome is necessarily vague.
> *Vagueness about the outcome*: In fact, we may not even know what specific outcome it is that we desire; at most, we may only have a general idea, such as "to reduce poverty," without having a specific conception of what that should look like.

Since we lack knowledge about what causes poverty and what is required to alleviate it—and even what comprises it—trying to identify these components of which we have insufficient knowledge may seem to lead to logical incoherence or absurdity. Because the actions that alleviating poverty require are vague and indefinitely multiple, it seems absurd to specify which actions count. Any specific list will necessarily exclude some actions that are necessary or sufficient. Any list of relevant actions will also vary from case to case of poverty since different particular situations have different causes and probably entail different responses that would appropriately or effectively alleviate it.

Despite these problems, there are great advantages to specifying duties. This section argues that the actions contained or implied by a duty should be described as specifically as possible. The main reason is that specification provides action-guidance in at least three ways.

Expectations and Evasion of Responsibility

One worry is that it is too easy for agents to evade responsibility when the actions that are expected of them are not spelled out. Some people seem to think that if no duties are specified for them to do, then they must not have any relevant responsibilities. The link between not specifying duties, and using that as an excuse to evade responsibility, is primarily a motivational concern.[29] Although some philosophers may think that motivational worries are not something with which moral philosophers should concern themselves, I disagree. Motivation, like empirical problems involved with what kind and how much knowledge and resources agents have, is a morally relevant concern. Like empirical issues, motivation affects what action agents can, should, and are likely to take; it also affects what outcomes are likely to come from particular moral and political theories. In other words, moral theories that do not even try to account for empirical and motivational factors are likely to be so idealistic that they have little or no bearing on actual action. In order for morality to be applicable to real life, hence to be action-guiding and meaningful, it must address these issues at least to some degree.

If duties are left vague so that agents do not have specific guidance on what actions the duties require for their fulfillment, there is no way to check that the right is being interpreted in a more or less accurate or appropriate way, and there is no way to enforce the fulfillment of its corresponding duty. For example, a government may decide that the right to food merely involves that sufficient food is stocked in supermarkets without ensuring that all people have sufficient means to buy it. This interpretation does not seem to fit the spirit of the declared right, but there is no way to evaluate it when the right is so vague. Vague rights and duties have no substance, and so they are not action-guiding.

Evasion of responsibility is not only a concern for *assigning* responsibility but also for *taking* responsibility, as expectations are important in motivating us to act. We are part of moral communities that form expectations for us about what is appropriate, required, or forbidden behavior. These expectations suggest not only blame or liability, but also praise when we meet or exceed expectations. This does not address just a motivational problem, but it also speaks to our conceptions of morality and agency. When we know what others expect of us, and we care about being respectable members of a moral community, then we try to *take responsibility* as much as we can in the relevant ways in order to meet or even exceed expectations and therefore earn others' respect.

Epistemological Aspect of Expectations

Expectations for actions provide not only standards for being members of moral communities but also epistemological requirements for action. In addition to providing motivating reasons to act, standards for action also help give agents the knowledge necessary for taking appropriate action and for using as guidelines according to which they can evaluate their actions. Critics may think that standards are relevant only to "backward-looking" assessments of responsibility such as attributing liability, serving only to provide reasons for holding liable or blaming agents for non-performance of action. Yet standards also inform agents of what is expected of them so they are capable of taking responsibility.

Agents evade responsibility, however unintentionally, just by not knowing what is expected of them. In order for a concept of responsibility to be action-guiding, then, it must set some standards by specifying at least some appropriate actions so that agents have enough knowledge on which to act and in order to evaluate for themselves the kind and extent of action they perform. Even *taking* responsibility involves acting according to some standards or expectations.

Selection and Prioritization of Action

Besides not having enough knowledge of what actions are expected, there is another reason, almost an "opposite" one, for why agents may evade responsibility in a non-blameworthy, especially unintentional, way. Agents often feel so overwhelmed by the vast scope of what they can and should do in response to a problem like global poverty that they do not act at all. The previous concern is a problem of not having enough knowledge on which to act; here the problem is of having too much knowledge, or at least having too many possibilities for appropriate action, so that one does not know how to prioritize one's action and so gives up entirely. Moral philosophers tend to ignore this problem as somehow irrelevant to philosophical concerns, perhaps because it seems to deal with motivation and personal psychology rather than morality and action. Yet empirical and motivational considerations *are* relevant for morality to be truly action-guiding and therefore applicable to real-life. Specifying the actions that a duty involves allows a way for agents to identify what is expected for them to do so that they feel like their task is more manageable.

For example, some philosophers may object that the fact that moral response *seems* ineffective is morally irrelevant, if in fact moral response *is* effective.[30] The objection here is that this is an epistemological problem in which agents need to acquire the relevant information, or a psychological problem in which agents just need to learn how to *feel* more capable or effective in their actions. Yet this is also a moral problem of how to select and prioritize actions from an unreasonably large or indeterminate set of morally required or appropriate actions. Agents need some way to identify these relevant actions and some criteria for ranking or choosing among them. Selection and priority of obligatory action are indeed moral issues.

What an Individual Should Do

It should be clear by now that what an individual should do with respect to global poverty is not simply to give money to charity, as some philosophers writing on this topic have seemed to suggest. In fact, giving money to charity, though not unimportant, is one of the less significant actions an individual can and should do. What individuals are most responsible for are actions that involve changing the way that power is distributed, so that those who abuse their power by harming the poor, whether through direct causation or through support of institutional practices that have a harmful effect, are unable to continue doing so. Because individuals have less power individually than they do collectively, their actions accomplish the most good when they are done through collectives of the three kinds described above. The actions that individuals should do are mostly those that are their portion of the collective responsibilities in which they share.

Actions that the affluent individual should take to address poverty must be identified somewhat specifically for the reasons above. Since we do not have enough knowledge to make a full description of what is required, actions cannot be specified fully. However, this empirical fact does not imply that any attempt to describe the actions required is absurd. Rather, attempts to identify specific actions can be made to the extent that we have the relevant knowledge. In other words, as we acquire more knowledge we can revise our description of which actions are necessary; this may involve adding more actions to our "list," changing their nature, or even removing them if we find later that they turn out to be counter-productive. Although actions cannot be described completely, they should be described as specifically as possible based on whatever knowledge we do have, leaving space for amendment as we learn more.

In this reflective and collaborative spirit, I offer a suggested list of duties that affluent individuals have toward global poverty. This list is of course open to revision as we continue to discuss and clarify relevant duties based on further understanding of what constitutes poverty and what roles affluent individuals play with respect to its causes.

Educate Self

The most important thing that a person can do to begin carrying out her responsibility toward global poverty is to educate herself about situations of poverty, including their causes and people's needs, and about her connections to poverty. These connections include her social location and the ways that her political and economic behavior, as well as her occupational and other organizational roles, contribute to, or alleviate, poverty. Learning about the existence of poverty, understanding what makes it an issue of morality and justice, and understanding oneself as the kind of moral agent that has some responsibilities to address it, are all preconditions for carrying out any of the other duties that affluent individuals have toward global poverty.

This education consists of many facets. One of the most important aspects is simply being aware of what goes on in the world, by paying attention to the news and reading the international affairs section of the newspaper instead of skipping it in favor of the domestic news. Another section of the newspaper that should not be skipped is the business section; although this section is often written for business leaders, one can read between the lines to understand how business decisions and practices affect various groups of people. Understanding basic economics, as well as world history and contemporary foreign affairs, are also important. Reading popular but scholarly books by economists, historians, policy analysts, journalists, and other analysts can help in this regard.

Education is an on-going process, and the duty to educate oneself is a duty that can never be fully discharged because there is always more to learn. Although technically there are a finite number of situations of poverty and related tragedies and injustices, the global world is so vast that there are always other situations about which one can get more information, and for any given situation, one can always learn more about its causes and solutions. As people around the world become more and more connected through various economic, political, and cultural practices, the world becomes smaller and "flatter."[31] As a result, the affluent are more causally and structurally implicated in poverty, and they are also more capable of feeling benevolent and acting beneficently toward the poor. Learning about these causal and structural connections, and the common humanity that unites all poor and affluent alike, is the first step in carrying out any of the more specific duties one has toward global poverty.

Educate Others

As a person educates herself, she finds that she alone cannot take action to effect change without the coordinated efforts of others. But other individuals and collectives alike are only capable of acting responsibly if they are educated about the existence and prevalence of poverty, if they understand the moral nature of poverty such that it demands response, and if they see themselves as the appropriate moral agents who should act to make that response. After educating the self, the next most important duty for an individual to carry out with respect to global poverty is to educate others. This duty is a crucial political duty.

By "educating others," I mean the obvious sense of educating other individuals privately, such as by talking about poverty and responsibility with people one knows, or educating individuals publicly, such as by creating a public display about poverty at a library, by manning an educational table at a civic event, or by organizing educational events such as the viewing of a relevant movie or documentary. But the duty to educate others does not stop with "others" who are individuals—it also includes educating "others" that are collectives, especially powerful collectives like corporations and governments. Attending and speaking at city council meetings, writing letters to companies requesting that they change their practices to be more mindful or just to the poor, and speaking with elected representatives are some examples of this. Educating others can also involve working with a non-profit organization such as a local food bank to make connections with agencies that do related work, such as drug counseling centers and homeless shelters (at the local level) or food banks in other regions or even in other nations (at the global level). Educating others is an important way to change social expectations about how individual and collective agents should act; through educating others, therefore, a person has power in changing action descriptions and responsibility ascriptions.

Note that educating others should not commit the paternalistic error of taking a preachy tone. Most people are put off by attempts to teach them in ways that assume they are woefully ignorant. A person should undertake the duty to educate others always with the understanding that she has more to learn as well, and she can learn from the very people she wishes to educate. The duty to educate others is really more like a duty to engage in dialogue about poverty. To avoid being paternalistic and essentialist, this duty is best carried out in the spirit of mutual learning, and with a primary intention to keep poverty, and its causes and solutions, in the forefront of public discussion.

This duty has a very wide scope and can never be fully discharged, because there are always more people and more groups that can learn more, and always more knowledge about poverty and its causes and solutions that can be learned; moreover, there are always more connections to be made between different agents and agencies that can share in carrying out responsibility. Since the demand of this duty can be particularly daunting, it is probably best for an individual to choose one or a couple of areas of poverty to focus on, such as poverty and genocide in a region like Darfur, the relationship between poverty and immigration to affluent countries like the United States, or the correlation between poverty, unsustainable development, and environmental destruction in developing nations like China as well as in developed nations like the United States. Focusing one's energies on learning a lot about just a couple of situations of poverty, and educating others about them in a focused, knowledgeable way, makes the duty to educate others more manageable.

Vote Knowledgeably

Individuals need to use their knowledge about poverty for political and economic ends by being informed voters and consumers. While in most countries voting is a legal right (and some individuals treat it as a privilege, ignoring the reasons why voting is so important as to be a right), voting is also a moral duty. Voting is the cornerstone of democracy, as it is the most direct way that every citizen has a voice in the various governments under which she lives. Democracy is a form of government in which all its citizens share power by having a voice in what laws and policies are made. When a person neglects to vote, this expresses disregard for citizen voice; when many people neglect to vote, democracy falls apart. The most important political duty that individuals have, therefore, is to vote, and to do so knowledgeably.

Individuals need to be aware of where candidates stand on issues that relate to poverty, which of course includes not only obvious issues like homelessness, but also issues that relate to poverty in less obvious ways, such as rules governing business and stock transactions, patent law and intellectual property, trade relations between countries (especially those with repeated human rights violations), and—within one's own country—the medical healthcare system, treatment for mental illness, and the criminal justice system. Learning about candidates' stances and voting records, and learning about policies that voters may directly vote for (such as through ballot initiatives), will ensure knowledgeable voting. Through this voting, every individual has at least a small voice in what laws and policies her governments should adopt. If the majority of voters agree with her, her views will be represented in government policies, and she may be able to have some indirect effect on governmental action taken toward poverty.

Through voting, she also pledges her support for the democratic process, guaranteeing that she will continue to have some political voice. We cannot underestimate the importance of exercising this fundamental right and duty, for without democracy governments are not accountable to their citizens. Only with citizen voice in policy-making will governments pay attention to citizens, especially the concerns of the most disadvantaged people.

Consume Ethically

Affluent individuals need to apply their knowledge about poverty not only to the political but also to the economic sphere, to be responsible consumers. In many affluent countries, individuals are encouraged by their culture and even by their government to consume as much as they can, in order to keep the economy rolling. Every time individuals make a purchase, the amount of money that they spend is added to the nation's Gross Domestic Product, a figure that represents each country's economic expenditures. The GDP is seen as a marker of the health of a nation's economy. Since an economy is seen as stronger the more that this number rises, federal governments encourage consumer purchases to continue making this number rise. This leads to many problems which I will not go into here, including spending beyond one's means, which results in increasing individual and national debt that threatens to destabilize some nations' economies in the future. The cult of the rising GDP also contributes to the belief that affluent consumers can and should purchase ever more goods, with no end in sight, and that the major goal of well-being for people in developing nations is to attain the same level of consumption that people in developed nations have. Both of these beliefs are impossible to realize.

Continually increasing levels of consumption, especially by the affluent, are bad for poor people for at least two reasons. First, since goods depend on natural resources for their materials and manufacturing, ever-increasing levels of consumption are unsustainable. As the environment gets destroyed, poor people who are not integrated into globalized economies have fewer and fewer resources available to them for survival. While there are other reasons for caring about environmental preservation besides the livelihood of poor people, we have to keep in mind that environmental degradation and poverty are inextricably linked. Poor people have the least ability to escape pollution, unsanitary water, filth, and disease, because they cannot afford to live in the nicer, less polluted places that rich people have claimed for themselves. Poor people also have the least political power, so their living areas are the most likely to be targeted for the dumping of waste, and they are the least likely to be cleaned up after extraction of natural resources like minerals. Being stuck in a hazardous environment makes poor people even poorer, diminishing the few resources they might have for survival, and often leading to avoidable illness and death. These are all situations from which affluent people have the means to escape.

Increasing levels of consumption are bad for poor people not only for destroying their living environment, but also for the role that their labor plays in acquiring natural resources for goods and in manufacturing these goods. Poor people are routinely taken advantage of for their cheap labor. When people are desperate enough, they will do anything to try to survive, including moving to a different country, working at all waking hours, and selling their children to human traffickers. These are not actions people would choose to do if they had other options and were not so desperate in their attempt at survival. The fact that people will do these actions out of desperation does not make these actions the result of meaningful choice. Companies and governments that take advantage of what people are "willing" to do in desperation are exploiting them. And groups that *force* individuals to provide cheap or free labor, such as through threats of violence (as experienced by those who work in diamond mines in Sierra Leone) or through physical containment or economic deception (as experienced by those who work in sweatshops in Saipan) are violating human rights in the most obvious, offensive manner. I want to reiterate that I do not object to factory or manual work in general; what I object to is work that violates human rights and/or exploits people's desperation. Increasing levels of consumption increase the demand for cheap labor, for in the globalized world the competition is so much fiercer to sell goods at the lowest prices yet pull in the highest profits.

Given these considerations, what an individual does as a consumer matters. Her singular contribution is so miniscule that it seems irrelevant, but her action taken together with the actions of other consumers is powerful. After all, the confluence of actions taken by consumers drives consumer trends, and makes companies successful or drives them out of business. If an individual's decisions as a consumer did not matter, companies would not spend billions of dollars on advertising, and especially niche marketing, their products. An individual's actions as a consumer are miniscule, yes. But they still matter.

Ethical consumption can take various forms. One currently popular form involves supporting social causes through one's purchases. For example, for several years people have been able to buy certain items that are pink or have a pink ribbon on them, and a portion of the purchase price supposedly goes to groups that promise to "fight" breast cancer in one way or other. Recently, a group of companies formed the Red Campaign to "fight" disease in Africa by creating red items, including clothing and cellphones, which can be purchased by socially minded individuals; a percentage of the proceeds goes to the Global Fund to Fight AIDS, tuberculosis, and malaria. Movements to support social causes through consumption are largely driven by celebrities who endorse the cause much as they would endorse a product. U2 singer Bono calls this form of consumerism "punk capitalism," which is "enabling companies to profit by supplying consumers with items they covet, at the same time making generosity hip and easy." In this vision for ethical consumption, affluent individuals can solve major social and global problems simply by spending enough money through consumer purchases. In this spirit, Bono recommends that individuals should "shop until it stops."[32]

This kind of consumption is not as ethical as it may appear. In some cases, the price of the item increases by the amount that is donated, so that the individual making the purchase is still making the donation, not the company from which she is buying the product.[33] More problematically, this approach can actually exacerbate some of the problems it is trying to help. Asking consumers to buy more pink or red products is like asking individuals to take higher paying jobs so they have more money to send to Oxfam: if those higher paying jobs actually contribute to poverty (such as selling diamonds in a jewelry store and thereby supporting the diamond trade), then the intention behind them is thwarted. Similarly, addressing poverty and diseases like AIDS and malaria requires measures such as ensuring basic healthcare, stopping environmental devastation that destroys stable ecosystems, stopping civil wars that destroy living environments and livelihoods, and finding a way to grow food sustainably. Making unnecessary consumer purchases, which use up natural resources that are often harvested and then manufactured in harmful ways, at worst thwarts these goals and at best misleads consumers into believing they are doing something worthwhile instead of focusing on the deeper issues. If a person would like to support the "fight" against AIDS, she would do better to send a check to the Global Fund and save the resources she would use up through her unnecessary purchase.

In addition to these consequentialist concerns is a moral question about what the relationship should be between one's economic self and one's political self. The form of "ethical consumption" that involves supporting causes through one's consumption of consumer items is seen as a form of active citizenship. It provides an affordable and easy way to participate in civic activities, without requiring substantive sacrifice of time, energy, or money. But in the process, it also reconceptualizes aid as voluntary contribution, rather than as morally required, socially shared duty.[34] This is problematic for the reasons described throughout this book: it ignores the causal and structural factors that contribute to poverty.

The problem with privatizing public issues is that this makes social causes subject to the same economic forces as business, where causes have to compete for attention. They become subject to advertisements and marketing just as goods and services are, and they must be fashionable in order to be successful in achieving their aims. Funding decisions become more a matter of fashion rather than worth. This is evidenced, for example, in the disproportionate funding given to AIDS research and breast cancer research in the United States, both of which are very fashionable causes, especially among the wealthy and powerful. The least fashionable causes, of course, are chronic problems that require long-term action and potentially dramatic change in political and economic institutions. Important moral and justice issues like poverty should be addressed not according to fashion, however, but rather according to their moral urgency.

Present levels of consumption by affluent individuals are unsustainable and make the world a worse place for everyone, but especially the poor. If the affluent really want to have a positive effect through their purchasing decisions, they are better off reducing their levels of consumption and making ethical decisions about the products they do have to consume. Keeping up with fashion trends or the latest technology is pointless; accepting this fact will not only reduce frivolous consumption that uses up resources and quickly turns to waste, but it will also save one's budget and make one happier by reducing the stress of trying to keep up with others economically. Many household goods and major consumer items, like cars, can be purchased used; this gives resources a second life before they end up as waste, and it also saves money.

When individuals must buy something new, they should do research about the policies of the companies from which they are considering buying, about the materials used in making the item, including the processes used to acquire the materials, and about the conditions of manufacture. Individuals have duties to inquire into these issues as much as they are reasonably able to do so; items that have greater social and environmental impact, such as automobiles, require more research than items with lesser impact, such as pencils. Of course it is not possible to do extensive research about the manufacture of every single item that one buys, but individuals should do extensive research about significant purchases and gradually acquire information about lesser purchases.

Let us not deceive ourselves into thinking we can "dissociate" from consumer society entirely, or try to have "clean hands" by making everything ourselves or buying only ethically "pure" items. This is, of course, impossible. It is unrealistic for everyone to grow their own food, make their own clothes, repair all items that break down, and/or buy goods or services directly from individuals who do these things themselves. I am not asking people to turn back time and live a romanticized, self-sufficient, pastoral lifestyle. Nonetheless, I do think that it would be helpful for individuals to be slightly less specialized in their labor and to be able to do *some* of these things, to some extent, and to re-conceptualize the good life apart from rampant consumerism. The smaller ecological "footprint" that each individual takes up—the fewer resources that each of us consumes and the less waste that each of us creates—the more that is left for others, and the cleaner that is what is left. The duties that we have as consumers are not merely to make ethical decisions about which items to buy—but also to rethink our relation to consumption: to consume less, to find value in one's own labor (not merely in one's job, but in the everyday activities that make up a life), and to revalue things that cannot be bought and sold, like community and companionship.

Invest Ethically

How people invest their money as shareholders matters at least as much as how they consume goods and services. People have duties to gather information and make ethical decisions about the companies in which they invest as well as the companies from which they buy products. Any individual who is a stockholder is a shareholder in a company, including all individuals who own retirement accounts like 401(k) or 403(b) accounts in the United States. A person who is a shareholder occupies a certain role with respect to the company in which she holds stock; she is a part owner, and by providing funds to the company through buying its stock she also has a say in the company. A critic may argue that publicly traded companies are more prone to unethical behavior, as their primary mission must be to satisfy shareholders by making as much profit (at whatever cost to other values) as possible. Even if this is true, the fact that a company is publicly traded also allows individuals some power with respect to their ownership in the company, giving them a voice in the direction of the company. Individuals ought to use that voice as much as they are able, and to use it to guide corporate actions to be ethical—in particular, to not violate human rights and to engage in practices that alleviate rather than contribute to poverty.

One form of ethical investment is to choose companies that carry out social corporate responsibility. While most investment portfolios pick companies to invest in based purely on economic performance, some investment firms, including the Calvert Group and the Interfaith Center on Corporate Responsibility, choose companies according to ethical performance as well. Many people see economic decisions as independent of, or even beyond the reach of, ethical values; for many people, maximizing economic profit is the only goal of financial decisions, regardless of what ethical consequences result. We have seen what this thinking leads to: a rationalization of unjust practices that exploit people or even violate their human rights. These socially conscious investment firms show that capitalism is compatible with social and religious values, however. In this version of capitalism, economic profit does not *trump* all other values; rather, it is one value among others, all of which are considered in pursuing one's financial goals.

Another approach to ethical investment is to avoid investing in companies that commit the most egregious violations of human rights. This divestment is similar to the way nations impose sanctions against a country for highly unethical practices. It is a way to prevent money from getting into the hands of people who would use it to cause great harm; if they do not have money from investments to fund their projects, they cannot engage in them. Many Americans practiced divestment against companies that operated in South Africa under apartheid in the 1980s; currently some Americans are divesting from companies doing business in Sudan under the regime that is presently sanctioning genocide. Although critics may object that divestment is pointless, arguing that if "we" do not invest in these companies, then someone else will, this objection is ludicrous. If most people do not invest in these companies, then this will make it harder for these companies to find the investors they need to fund their projects, creating a lot of pressure for them to change their actions.

A third approach to ethical investment takes a different form: rather than divesting from companies that cause wrongful harm, this approach directs shareholders to buy shares in such companies in order to have a say in what they do. A shareholder, no matter how much or how little stock she owns, has the right to attend and participate in shareholder meetings. These meetings are difficult to attend, since they are held throughout the country if not the world and on an infrequent basis, making this an impractical suggestion for most individuals as a way to have power over the direction of a company. But for socially conscious groups of individuals, who have formed for civic and institutional reasons such as to address poverty and/or environmental degradation in a specific neighborhood, becoming shareholders is a way for such a group to have a voice over how a particular company acts in a specific area. When a group's energy is focused on a particular company's actions, becoming a shareholder is a useful way to have more of a say over what the company does than other actions such as writing letters or arranging a boycott.

The ethically-minded capitalism that ethical investment and consumption supports is the version of capitalism that I would like to see. It allows for consumption, profit, and economic growth, but not for the ever-increasing levels of consumption that are unsustainable, or for the pursuit of profit regardless of other costs such as egregious human rights violations or crimes against humanity like genocide. It values consumption, profit, and economic growth as goods—though not the most important goods—among many. It values some forms of consumption, those which are sustainable and which promote justice, more than other forms, those which are frivolous, wasteful, and result from injustice.

Get Involved with Politics

Although a person's political duties start with voting, they do not stop there. Voting and ethical consumption are individualistic actions, which, although important, only go so far. Making a difference requires getting involved at the structural level to work on changing institutions as well.

In addition to voting, a person has duties to get involved with politics in other ways, including talking with and writing letters to her elected representatives to let them know where she stands on issues, working with groups to lobby legislators to pass laws and policies that will help the poor, working on political campaigns to get good candidates elected, and running for political office herself. Voting is vitally important, because it is necessary for democracy to work. An individual will have more power in politics if she does more than just vote, however. In order to persuade government officials to pass laws and create policies that will help the poor, she must communicate with these officials about the relevant issues and/or become one herself. Getting involved with politics is also the most significant way that individuals can change social expectations and action descriptions, as well as responsibility ascriptions.

This duty can never be fully discharged, as there is always more political work to do. The scope of this duty is thus imperfect, as a person should do as much as she is able to do. Which specific actions she performs as part of this duty is of course discretionary. All political actions such as these listed above are necessary, yet she is not able to do them all, so she has some choice in which ones she does. I recommend that people start out small with the actions that are easiest to do, such as writing to and talking to elected representatives, and then work their way to slightly more difficult and time-consuming actions, such as working on political campaigns, with an ultimate goal of running for a local elected position, such as school board member. Some people will enjoy the process and find themselves able to go further, running for higher offices, being involved with drafting local or even national policies. Others will find the process daunting and find themselves too shy or too busy to do more than write a quick letter to a congressperson. Any level of political involvement is good, and better than none; all are valuable for the process of democracy to work. I challenge individuals to push themselves to get involved with politics at some level that is slightly greater than their comfort level and see where it takes them.

Ensure that Collectives Carry Out *Their* Duties

Many of the most significant actions that address global poverty must be taken by collectives, not individuals. But individuals have duties with respect to the roles they occupy within these collectives, to ensure that the collectives of which they are members carry out *their* duties. Collectives can act only when individuals perform roles within them, and so they have the agency necessary to carry out their responsibilities only when individuals act in their roles. With respect to the roles they occupy, individuals have several duties, including: acting in one's role as ethically as possible, changing the nature of the role as much as one can in order to ensure that the collective to which one belongs promotes justice rather than injustice, leaving roles and dissociating from groups that promote injustice when there is no opportunity to change them. These duties all require that an individual also maintains her awareness of herself as a moral agent independently of her roles.

An individual occupies many roles based on different spheres in her life, including family and work, as well as her memberships in various communities. Some of these roles are largely unchosen, such as the places she occupies within her family, or the national identity into which she was born. Other roles are more voluntary, such as what job she has, or to what hobby or civic organizations she belongs. Regardless of whether a role is chosen or not, an individual has duties to carry out the actions associated with that role as ethically as possible. This means that she must critically reflect on what actions are expected of her, including the reasons for those actions and their likely outcomes.

When unjust actions are associated with her role, she should try to change the nature of that role as much as possible, so that she can perform what is generally expected of her in the most ethical, justice-promoting ways possible. When the group to which she belongs acts unjustly or creates unjust policies, she should speak out against this injustice and refuse to perform the associated actions. She should do everything she can to try to convince the decision-makers who prescribed the actions of their injustice, pointing out not only the bad consequences and/or exploitation that victims experience, but also the bad consequences the group will experience as a result of contributing to injustice.

How an individual chooses the roles that she is able to choose also matters. Individuals should try to choose occupations that allow them to contribute to society in just ways, avoiding occupations that commit wrongdoing or contribute to poverty and related injustices. While it is easier to promote justice in public service jobs than in jobs in industries where profit is the primary goal, there is no necessary correlation here. A person can promote injustice in public service jobs, such as when she takes advantage of vulnerable populations with which she works. And a person can promote justice in profit-driven industries, such as in selling affordable basic medical supplies to poor communities, when public and private interests are both promoted, and when profit is not the *only* value that drives one's decisions. In order to carry out justice within these positions, a person ought to have as at least one of her major goals to contribute to the community and to promote justice—which will, indirectly, alleviate poverty. Again, this involves re-conceptualizing capitalism so that maximizing profit is not the sole value of businesses; and it involves re-conceptualizing one's role within such a business so that profit is promoted alongside social justice.

When a person's role requires her to act unjustly with no alternative, she should consider leaving the role and dissociating from the group that expects her to act unjustly. For example, there is no ethical way to perform the racist actions expected of a Ku Klux Klan member, and probably no way to change the orientation of the group from the inside to make it more just. Some roles are very difficult to leave, making dissociation problematic. For example, when a person has few if any alternatives, it can be very difficult to leave a job, even if the job requires of her what she knows to be unethical actions, such as making weapons for use in war. When this is the case, an individual must simply try her best to change the nature of unjust roles or to leave unjust roles in pursuit of just ones. In order to do the latter, she must learn about other options available to her and how to pursue them, such as through education. The options that an individual has may be very constrained; and the poorer that she is, the more constraints she has. Nonetheless, individuals remain moral agents and must figure out what options they do have before resigning themselves to the ones they have. In the end, keeping a job that has bad consequences for oneself may be better for the individual herself if her other options are significantly worse; in this case, it may be more appropriate for other people to try to change the nature of the company, such as through political and consumer actions.

Underlying all of these duties that an individual has *qua* her role within collectives is also a duty for an individual to maintain her awareness of herself as a moral agent, meaning that she should critically reflect upon the moral nature of the actions that are expected of her. She should not get so consumed by her role that she loses sight of who she is underneath the role. She should be aware of how she would evaluate her actions ethically if they were in a different context, outside of the role. She should try to be consistent in how she views her actions, and try to act consistently to reflect her underlying sense of morality. When she sees inconsistencies in her behavior, she should reflect on the cause and nature of that inconsistency and use that to figure out whether she should change her behavior in some way.

The scope of these role-related duties is different than that of most other duties. Individuals have perfect duties to not commit wrongdoing within their roles and imperfect duties to not allow their collectives to promote injustice as much as they can. Agents have little discretion in carrying out these duties, because they must act ethically with respect to *all* their roles, and ensure that *all* of the groups to which they belong act justly. Their dischargeability depends on the particular roles that an individual occupies. In some roles individuals find it easy to act ethically and ensure that the groups to which they belong promote justice; in other roles, this is harder. For example, it may be easier for a nurse to act ethically and promote justice through her occupation than it is for someone who works for an energy company that drills on land that it does not own to which it has mineral rights, that has a history of environmental destruction, and that profits from selling a necessary good to the public. The worker at the energy company should learn about the company's policies, history, and willingness to change based on new knowledge; if she can have a voice in making sure the company acts for the public's interest as much as for its own, then she may be able to help ensure the company promotes justice rather than injustice. Everyone has these kinds of duties *vis-à-vis* their occupational and social roles; but some roles are within collectives that are more prone to acting unjustly and committing wrongdoings, and in these roles it is harder—but not impossible, and still very important to try—to ensure their justness.

Contribute to Society through Roles

In addition to the duties she has to act justly within the various given and chosen roles that constitute her life, an individual also has a duty to take on certain roles primarily for the sake of addressing poverty. Through these roles she takes on some task-responsibilities that are her portion of the shared responsibility that she has by virtue of her institutional and civic identities. Being a member of a collective that takes on this shared responsibility is a way to formalize the particular tasks allotted to her morally.

The roles that she should take on are social and civic roles that will help her contribute to social justice by meeting people's human rights or making institutions more just. Examples of these kinds of roles include working in a food bank or homeless shelter, volunteering with a city department such as Health and Human Services or with a hospital's community wellness program, and being on a board of directors for a relevant organization. The scope of this duty is of course imperfect. A person can never fully discharge the duty, for there are always more social and civic roles that she can take on, but she must do as much as she is able to do. Which kinds of roles one takes on, and how many, is also discretionary.

If the groups or agencies that are required to carry out duties of making institutions just or meeting people's human rights do not exist, individuals also have duties to help form these groups. This action is much more demanding of one's time and energy, of course, and is not for everyone. But the fact that the need for forming some relevant groups exists means that some individuals must take it upon themselves to work toward that end. Individuals who have the greatest means to form such a group—i.e., those who have the most time and the most resources, such as college students who have flexible daily schedules and who have access to student funds and fundraising abilities—have this duty most strongly. College students can form a campus group to gather coats and winter gear for a homeless shelter, or to educate students about genocide in Darfur; church members can form an action committee to gather and deliver food to the food bank, or to educate churchgoers and the general public about AIDS in Africa. This duty is similarly imperfect, only partially dischargeable, and discretionary.

I want to say a word about the level of commitment that some of these duties of political, civic, and social involvement require. Some people's lives are so busy with working and raising children that they have no time left over for taking on community roles like this. But people's level of activity and commitment changes through different periods in their lives. For some people, raising ethically minded children who grow up to care about the world, and who want to make a difference in it, is the most important thing that they can be doing for the many years it takes to raise children. But at other times in their lives—before having children, after children leave the house, as their work hours reduce, and/or as they retire—people will have more time and fewer commitments, and they then can turn some attention to their communities. Of course, it is also good to be involved while raising children, as contributing to one's communities makes the world a better place for one's children to inherit. In addition, by being socially involved, parents model the kind of commitment to the community they want their children to have; and when they have their children help them, their children learn the value of community involvement directly. People's abilities to contribute to the community will vary throughout their lifetimes, but they should really try to fulfill political, civic, and social duties to whatever extent that they are capable.

Support Charities

In addition to the duties individuals have *qua* their occupational and other such roles, and to the duties they have *qua* their institutional identities, individuals also have duties of beneficence that arise purely out of their identities as moral agents. These duties of beneficence are captured best by the broad, imperfect (and only partially dischargeable and highly discretionary) duty of helping others whenever and to whatever extent that one is able. Because the need is so great, this duty can be discharged only partially by any particular agent; because there are so many people and so many relevant causes that are needy, how this duty gets fulfilled by any particular agent is also highly discretionary.

Beneficent duties to help others by supporting charities in various ways are not necessarily the most important of an agent's duties; educational, civic, consumer, and role duties are at least as significant, if not more so. Education is the precondition of all the other duties; role responsibilities are necessary for collectives—whose action has greater impact than individuals, and so can do more harm that needs redressing as well as do more good that creates justice—to carry out their responsibilities. Political involvement and ethical consumption are important because they involve structural change that addresses many of the root causes of poverty. Yet beneficence still matters, because many of the agencies that directly work to alleviate poverty rely on charitable donations and volunteers. Without beneficence, this needed work would not get done. Institutional change, government aid, and ethical corporate behavior are absolutely necessary to address poverty at a deep, long-term, structural level. But as long as institutions remain unjust, as long as governments of rich nations do not give the foreign aid they promised in the Millenium Development Goals, and as long as corporations do not uniformly refrain from committing wrongdoings, poverty will remain. So until these changes occur, the agencies that work toward alleviating poverty in the short-term need the resources that allow them to respond. This means that individuals—as well as corporations and other collectives—must donate as much money and time as they are able to some of the agencies that help the poor.

Almost everyone is capable of helping others in at least a broad way; those who are relatively affluent have some capability to give money or volunteer time to those who are most needy. Those who have the most money and/or time also have the most to give, and so have the greatest obligation to give. For most middle-class individuals in a developed country like the United States, beneficence requires that she give at least some portion of her income to worthy charities such as Oxfam or UNICEF, or to microfinance organizations like the Grameen Foundation or Kiva. Microfinance organizations provide a good alternative to people wary of charities, as they allow an individual to provide a small loan (usually less than US$200) to a very poor entrepreneur (usually a woman) who will use the loan to start a small business; since these loans have high success rates of repayment, they are a good way to receive tangible results from giving money to particular individuals with identifiable needs. The exact portion that ought to be given to charities or microfinance programs is the subject of much debate among philosophers who focus too much attention on the scope of agent duty rather than the scope of recipient need. I refuse to enter this debate except to say that we should look into our hearts and ask ourselves, truly, how much we are able to give.

In addition to the usual philosopher's suggestion that we donate money, I also strongly encourage us to donate time. For middle- and lower-class individuals who have a hard time making ends meet no matter how much they make,[35] volunteering may be an easier way to act beneficently. While most individuals cannot take time off from the rest of their lives to travel to distant countries and help the poorest people in the world build wells and sewage systems with groups like the Peace Corps, they can always find organizations in their own communities that need their help as well. It is true that the poorest people in the world are often the most ignored by would-be benefactors. But it is also true that there are worthy causes everywhere, and that people are often more motivated to help those who are members of communities close by, like the town in which one lives, and that people can often do more good by focusing their energies locally. In some cases it is in fact better to start locally with problems such as homelessness or lack of food, volunteering with shelters or food banks, as long as one also makes global connections, learning about how experiences of homelessness in different areas of the world relate to each other and have similar structural causes, and even making connections with people working on homelessness in other parts of the world. Especially for volunteering, the slogan "think globally, act locally" is apt. Volunteering should not replace giving to charities, who need money to run their operations no matter how many volunteers they have. And local action should not replace global efforts, or the poorest in the world would remain ignored. But both time and money are necessary to make a difference, and both local and global actions are important. Individuals certainly have some discretion in deciding which actions are most appropriate for them to do.

Conclusion

As many philosophers note, the responsibility that affluent individuals have toward global poverty is difficult to specify, carry out, and assess. This is because the relevant duties are mostly imperfect in scope, only partially dischargeable, and involve some discretion in determining which actions one should take. This does not make the relevant duties optional, however. Duties toward global poverty are not supererogatory; they are morally required. Various duties are morally justified, and have normative force, for different reasons. Individuals are not licensed to choose among which of the duties they prefer to fulfill, as if all responsibility toward global poverty is a matter of choice to take up as one wishes or not; this would conflate morality with consumerism. Rather, individuals have *all* of these duties, but within the scope of each one they have some choice in deciding how to fulfill that particular duty, depending on how much room there is for discretion and how partial the dischargeability of the duty is.

Often a person interprets the imperfect scope of duties toward poverty—as "doing as much as you are able"—to mean not doing much at all. She pats herself on the back for sending a $20 check to UNICEF and considers herself having done—that is, having fully discharged—her annual duty to poverty. She ignores the many other actions, and the different kinds of duties, to which she is obligated to contribute her portion of the shared responsibility. They seem too difficult, too unnecessary, and too insignificant.

Individuals must look deeply inside themselves to see what they are capable of. They must assess their limitations honestly and forgive themselves for not doing what they truly are unable to do, whether because they are responsible for too many other commitments at the moment, or because they themselves barely make ends meet, or perhaps because they are not mentally capable of taking on some of these actions. But they should not merely make excuses for themselves. Being moral agents requires us to make these critical reflections about our values, our actions, and our limitations and capabilities. It requires us to consider honestly what we can and ought to do.

Ultimately this determination is up to us as individuals. Some duties can be assessed and enforced by others, particularly in a court of law; for example, companies, governments, and individuals are liable for actions they perform that cause wrongful harm to others, justifying duties of redress or sometimes punishment; agents can also be blamed and sanctioned for failing to meet social expectations of appropriate behavior. But changing social expectations for what counts as morally appropriate or required behavior, and determining how much and what kinds of actions that these imperfect duties require of us, is at some level ultimately up to each one of us to determine as individuals. What we determine individually adds up to form some collective decision about what the social expectations should be for how individuals fulfill imperfect duties. Individuals need to acknowledge their moral agency and begin the process of looking deeply inside themselves to assess their capabilities and limitations in light of what is morally required of them.

How to balance these duties toward global poverty with each other, and with other obligations that one has, is difficult. With respect to balancing duties toward global poverty with each other, we can use Thomas Pogge's concept of compensation to help guide us. We must do some of these actions, but for the duties of imperfect scope it is hard to know how much we must do when we have so many other obligations, and when the demandingness of many of them is open to interpretation. Pogge notes that if we cannot help but participate in a system that causes harm to others, we can at least compensate for the harm to which we vicariously contribute.[36] Similarly, if we do not have time or energy to carry out all of the imperfect duties in substantive ways, particularly if we are in periods of our life in which we have other demanding obligations (such as raising children or taking care of elderly parents), we can compensate for our failure to carry out some of these duties by carrying out others more robustly. For example, if I do not have time or energy to get too involved with politics or to take on social and civic roles, I can compensate by working in an occupation that is socially beneficial and that, at least indirectly, works to alleviate poverty. Or, if I am stuck in a job that is socially harmful, such as making weapons or working in the office at a human rights-violating energy company, and I have no other options at the moment to change jobs, I can compensate by taking on social and civic roles and running for government office, trying to change the institutional practices that make these occupations harmful. The various duties that an individual has toward global poverty must be balanced with each other, as well as with her other obligations; sometimes the form of balancing that is appropriate is compensating in one area for what she is unable to do in another.

In balancing different important moral obligations with each other, however, no matter how one resolves the tension between these competing duties, there is always a *remainder* left over. Most moral dilemmas that people face are not easily resolvable. Ethicists who pit two important obligations against each other and argue that one is the morally "right" act to take at the expense of the other, or who suggest that a person must do a terrible deed in order to prevent an even more terrible event from occurring, do a disservice to ethics by misrepresenting the moral nature of the actions involved. Moral decisions are usually not this easy. There is usually some sacrifice no matter what action one chooses to do, and it is sometimes truly impossible to resolve moral demands satisfactorily. Another way to put this is to say that whenever one makes a decision with respect to some specific person, every other person that one *could have* responded to in that moment is disregarded. In responding to a specific person (or cause), then, one also is *not* responding to all the others to whom she could be, and who are probably just as deserving of her moral attention. Response is thus always, and necessarily, selective and exclusive.[37]

The fact that moral response is always exclusive, and therefore never as fully responsive to those who are worthy of our attention as we would like, should not be used as a way to rationalize ignoring the many who are needy, however. Instead, it should be used as a way to acknowledge the difficulty in directing one's moral attention with respect to so many different and important moral demands. However one chooses to act, there will usually be a remainder, something left over that "should have" been done but could not have been done because of what was done in its place. The proper acknowledgement of the remainder is the experience of regret—not only regret for being forced to act badly in a particular set of circumstances, but also regret for being unable to do actions that nonetheless have obligatory force. What morality requires of us, but that circumstances such as conflict or greater moral urgency make us unable to do, we at least ought to regret. [38]

Of course, the problem with feelings like regret is, what should a person *do* with it? How can feeling regret, or guilt, or a similar feeling have any moral relevance since it has no power in effecting consequences? Regret needs to be accompanied by a commitment to do what one is currently unable to do later, when circumstances change. What we should do but cannot do now, we should aim to do (or do better) in the future, as much as it is in our power to do so. In balancing our various moral obligations, therefore, we should do as much with respect to poverty as we are currently capable, acknowledging what we cannot do, and aim to do better in the future as the facts of our lives shift along with their moral demands. The fact that we are unable to do everything needed to

solve poverty—the fact that we, individually, can never alleviate poverty completely—does not mean that we should therefore do nothing to address it. The
imperfect scope of most of our duties means that we must do *something* to alleviate poverty, and what the scope of that "something" is depends on factors such
as our ability and resources, and our particular connections to specific cases of
poverty. We do have discretion in determining the exact scope of action that
these duties require of us, but this discretion must serve as a way for us to enact
our choices about how to carry out these duties, rather than as a way to make
excuses for ourselves. We must take the responsibility of carrying out these duties very seriously.

Related to the issue of how to balance conflicting obligations, I want to address specifically an objection to duties toward the poor that seems to become
more and more popular, namely the concern that duties toward the poor conflict
with obligations that one has toward the self. In contemporary Western culture,
"obligations of self-fulfillment" have become paramount moral duties. The consumer aspect of culture encourages individuals to pursue personal self-
fulfillment, especially through consumer activities like pampering oneself with
services such as massages, or buying gifts like fashionable clothes and expensive jewelry for oneself. Even when spending money is not involved, contemporary Western culture encourages individuals in a variety of ways to pay more
attention to themselves, with their personal desires and goals, than to others.

In response, I want to note that certainly an individual does have duties toward the self, such as duties of self-perfection to continue to learn and grow
throughout her life. The projects that a person chooses to pursue, that she may in
fact design her life around, can be important in constructing her identity and
providing her with a sense of meaning and purpose in life; for example, pursuing
a specific career or realizing dreams like traveling to another country can be
immensely fulfilling. But, like the other obligations one has, these projects must
be carried out in balance with other obligations.

Obligations to the poor must be carried out in balance with, and not in conflict with, other obligations—to self, to family, and to various other commitments. Of course some conflict is inevitable, and individuals must simply do the
best they can to negotiate that conflict through balance and compensation. But
an individual can also plan her life in such a way as to minimize that conflict, by
making obligations to others *part of*, rather than separate from, her personal projects. Taking duties to others seriously requires making our own projects and
goals cohere, not compete, with the demands of justice.

We must keep in mind that being able to pursue personal projects is itself a
condition of privilege. A precondition of the value of personal projects is relative affluence, for a person must have her basic needs met to be able to devote at
least part of her life to concerns other than survival. The poorest in the world,
those who need the affluent to respond to them, do not even have the ability to
create and pursue projects beyond basic survival needs.

The value of personal projects arises in a particular cultural context, one
that is highly individualistic and in which individuals have the means to plan

and pursue projects. Consumer-oriented societies encourage people to value choice and profit inordinately, even if the only choices they have significant power over are which products to buy, and even if profit is accumulated at the expense of all other potential values. With the value of choice comes the value of freedom—not only freedom to choose, but also freedom to do what one wishes, which sometimes becomes translated as freedom from responsibilities and commitments to others.

In a culture which over-values profit and choice, and which conflates choice with freedom, and freedom with lack of responsibilities, we lose something gravely important, namely our connections to other people. This individualized, privatized, consumer culture easily makes us callous, uncaring, and isolated. In this mindset we forget that humans are necessarily interdependent—not only in economic ways, but more importantly in social and cultural ways as well. The values of choice and freedom as articulated here assume a conception of the self that is atomistic and independently self-sufficient. But even Immanuel Kant, whose concept of the autonomous moral agent has inspired libertarians espousing choice, freedom, and independence, recognized the interdependent nature of humankind and the normative force of duties to help others. We could not will a world in which no one helped anyone else, because such ruggedly independent individualism is impossible to realize. It simply goes against human nature.

I am not claiming here that choice and freedom should not be valued, any more than I said above that we should not value economic profit. Rather, we need to re-conceptualize what we mean by choice and freedom, and reconsider what makes them valuable. The freedom to do whatever we want, to be free from responsibilities or commitments to others, is shallow and harmful. Just as we need to re-conceptualize capitalism to include ethical as well as economic value, we also need to re-conceptualize choice and freedom as necessarily linked to our responsibilities and commitments rather than in opposition to them. I have heard many philosophers quote or paraphrase, in the context of discussions about responsibility, the comic book superhero Spiderman: "With great power comes great responsibility." Affluent individuals have more power than they often realize, and their power connects them inextricably to the global poor in a variety of ways. They also have great freedom in being able to plan a life of meaning and fulfillment, and to be able to pursue a myriad of choices; these are freedoms that the poor are unable to enjoy. With their great power and great freedoms, and because of their great connection to the poor, the affluent should take up the great responsibility they have toward global poverty.

Because affluent individuals benefit from institutions that burden the poor unjustly, because they occupy roles in corporations and governments that give them some degree of power over how the group acts, because they are citizens and consumers who make choices that affect activity in the political and economic spheres, and because they are moral agents who have reason to care and respond to those in need—affluent individuals have various duties with respect to global poverty. Fulfilling these duties is not easy, especially since some of these duties are very demanding, and individuals frequently encounter conflicts between their different obligations. Nonetheless, a person must do the best she can. She should look at her actions on a holistic level and evaluate them as a whole, not just each action taken separately. If she generally tries to stay knowledgeable about what is going on in the world and what are the causal and structural factors leading to situations of global poverty, if she leaves a smaller ecological "footprint" and gets involved with politics, and if she tries to make a difference in the lives of others, then she is probably doing her part. What an affluent individual is responsible for, ultimately, is her portion of the work required for the shared responsibility that all agents have with respect to global poverty.

Notes

1. In arguing for the moral responsibilities of corporations, Andrew Kuper argues that, "with greater powers, opportunities, and freedoms come greater responsibilities—different not merely in degree [from those of individuals] but in kind." Andrew Kuper, "Redistributing Responsibilities—The UN Global Compact with Corporations," in *Real World Justice: Grounds, Principles, Human Rights, and Social Institutions*, ed. Andreas Follesdal and Thomas Pogge (Dordrecht: Springer, 2005), 373.

2. Ser-Min Shei, "World Poverty and Moral Responsibility," in *Real World Justice: Grounds, Principles, Human Rights, and Social Institutions*, ed. Andreas Follesdal and Thomas Pogge (Dordrecht: Springer, 2005), 147-48.

3. Note that there is not a one-to-one correlation between each model of responsibility and each way to group people collectively. Each collective grouping features predominantly in one of the models (random collectives in beneficence, conglomerates in redress, and congregations in institutional justice), because this is how individuals most significantly relate to the relevant form of responsibility. Yet each collective grouping may be relevant to other models of responsibility as well. For example, as I said above, conglomerates have all three kinds of duties, although they are discussed most in the context of redress as a result of having more power, more ability to harm, and more responsibility to prevent or rectify harm than individuals.

4. This view of choice is known as the Principle of Alternative Possibilities and is endorsed by free will advocates. Note that this "choice" to work for a particular corporation is not necessarily a choice in the compatibilist sense of a decision that one undertakes willfully or voluntarily. People frequently feel unsatisfied by the meager options available to them, such as job opportunities—and so a "choice" to pursue one of them is not necessarily one that a person does whole-heartedly and willfully, or that one "owns," no matter how unforced it is. A reluctant action undertaken in the face of much constraint and (at least a perceived) lack of comparable alternatives, but where no force or coercion is involved, is only a "choice" in the thinnest sense, and certainly not a meaningful choice at that.

5. For some discussion on this, see Hannah Arendt, *Eichmann in Jerusalem: A Report on the Banality of Evil* (New York: Penguin, 1964), 57 and 289.

6. Larry May, "Socialization and Institutional Evil," in *Hannah Arendt: Twenty Years Later*, ed. Larry May and Jerome Kohn (Cambridge, MA: MIT Press, 1996), 89. See also Arendt, *Eichmann in Jerusalem*, 232 and 289.

7. Lawrence E. Mitchell, *Corporate Irresponsibility: America's Newest Export* (New Haven, CT and London: Yale University Press, 2001), 148.

8. For more on the way that inevitability of causal consequences is used as a defense, see Arendt, *Eichmann in Jerusalem*, 295-96, and Haskell Fain, "Some Moral Infirmities of Justice," in *Individual and Collective Responsibility, Second Edition*, ed. Peter A. French (Rochester, VT: Schenkman Books, 1998, 87-90.

9. See Arendt, *Eichmann in Jerusalem*, 71-72 and 289; Andrew Brennan, "Poverty, Puritanism, and Environmental Conflict," *Environmental Values* 7, no. 3 (1998), 323.

10. See the discussion in Thomas Friedman, *The World is Flat: A Brief History of the Twenty-first Century* (New York: Farrar, Straus, and Giroux, 2005), 214-16.

11. This topic is widely discussed in the literature on soldier responsibility with respect to obeying their commanding officers. See the various articles in *Individual and Collective Responsibility, Second Edition*, ed. Peter A. French (Rochester, VT: Schenkman Books, 1998).

12. For more on this asymmetry of praise and blame, see Susan Wolf, *Freedom Within Reason* (New York: Oxford University Press, 1990), 79-81.

13. See Arendt, *Eichmann in Jerusalem*, 114 and 295-96.

14. Alasdair MacIntyre, "Social Structures and Their Threats to Moral Agency," in *Ethics and Politics: Selected Essays, Volume 2* (Cambridge and New York: Cambridge University Press, 2006), 197.

15. Arendt, *Eichmann in Jerusalem*, 252, 287-88.

16. John L. Mackie describes causes as necessary *post factum* or necessary in the circumstances. John L. Mackie, "Causes and Conditions," in *Causation*, ed. Ernest Sosa and Michael Tooley (Oxford: Oxford University Press, 1993), 38; John L. Mackie, *The Cement of the Universe: A Study of Causation* (Oxford: Clarendon Press, 1974), 31 and 37-43.

17. This example comes from Arendt, *Eichmann in Jerusalem*, 289.

18. Peter Unger, *Living High and Letting Die: Our Illusion of Innocence* (New York: Oxford University Press, 1996), 3-4.

19. Such practices may present other ethical problems, such as paternalism, that I will not address here.

20. See the discussions in Samuel Scheffler, "Individual Responsibility in a Global Age," in his book *Boundaries and Allegiances: Problems of Justice and Responsibility in Liberal Thought* (Oxford: Oxford University Press, 2001), 32-47; and Samuel Scheffler, "The Conflict between Justice and Responsibility," in *Global Justice (Nomos XLI)*, ed. Ian Shapiro and Lea Brilmayer (New York and London: New York University Press, 1999), 86-106.

21. See Larry May, *Sharing Responsibility* (Chicago: University of Chicago Press, 1992), especially chapters 1 and 8.

22. Larry May, *The Socially Responsible Self: Social Theory and Professional Ethics* (Chicago and London: University of Chicago Press, 1996), 122. See also his discussion on how role responsibility frequently reduces to individualism on pages 107-10.

23. Alasdair MacIntyre gives accounts of individuals that he observed making grave decisions like this in their occupational roles as profit-maximizers that they would never condone in their domestic roles as caretakers and community members. MacIntyre, "Social Structures and Their Threats to Moral Agency," 196-99.

24. MacIntyre, "Social Structures and Their Threats to Moral Agency," 200-202.

25. Robert Goodin, *Utilitarianism as Public Philosophy* (Cambridge: Cambridge University Press, 1995), 86.

26. Goodin, *Utilitarianism as Public Philosophy*, 33-34. For further discussion of task-responsibility, see Kurt Baier, "Guilt and Responsibility," in *Collective Responsibility: Five Decades of Debate in Theoretical and Applied Ethics*, ed. Larry May and Stacey Hoffman (Savage, MD: Rowman and Littlefield, 1991), especially 208-10; and Goodin, *Utilitarianism as Public Philosophy*, especially chapter 2.

27. Virginia Held, "Can a Random Collection of Individuals Be Morally Responsible?" in *Collective Responsibility: Five Decades of Debate in Theoretical and Applied Ethics*, ed. Larry May and Stacey Hoffman (Savage, MD: Rowman and Littlefield, 1991), 94-97.

28. This is one reason why political philosophers like Iris Marion Young and Robert Goodin argue that responsibility toward global poverty should be understood as *responsibility* (discretionary, only partially dischargable, open-ended obligation) instead of as *duty* (non-discretionary, fully dischargeable, specific obligation). Goodin, *Utilitarianism as Public Philosophy*, 81; Iris Marion Young, "Responsibility and Global Labor Justice," *Journal of Political Philosophy* 12, no. 4 (December 2004), 379-80. Of course, this assumes that only a single kind of obligation is primarily relevant toward poverty; this does not take into account the multiple kinds of obligations that my proposal for pluralistic duties does.

29. Evasion of responsibility is also a justificatory issue, in that agents often will not act if they do not have sufficiently justifying reasons to act. I explain this in more detail in the next section.

30. Utilitarians who argue against the moral correctness of common intuitions suggest this line of reasoning as they try to minimize the role that psychology plays in our thinking about and responding to moral problems.

31. See Friedman, *The World is Flat*.

32. Steve Sternberg, "Bono Makes Fighting AIDS a Win All Around," *USA Today*, October 12, 2006, 1(D).

33. Jessica Peck Corry, "Other Diseases Have Ribbons, Too," *Rocky Mountain News*, October 14, 2006, 12(D).

34. Samantha King, *Pink Ribbons Inc.: Breast Cancer and the Politics of Philanthropy* (Minneapolis, MN: University of Minnesota Press, 2006), chapter 3.

35. Some philosophers are very critical of middle-class individuals who feel poor, suggesting that they spend their money frivolously and underestimate how much they have to give. For some people, to some extent, this is true; I address frivolous spending in the section on duties of ethical consumption. But this criticism unfairly ignores the fact that for many middle-class individuals, a decent standard of living is simply more expensive. I am not referring to the expense of consumerist luxuries like restaurant meals, extensive cable television packages, or private lessons for children; I am referring to the increase in price of basic necessities like housing, groceries, fuel, and utilities, most of which are more expensive in urban areas, where people are more likely to be middle-class, and all of which are more expensive in affluent countries. In pointing this out, I am also not trying to excuse middle-class individuals' large failure to respond to poverty with beneficence; I merely want philosophers to acknowledge the complicated nature of individuals' resources and abilities to help.

36. Thomas W. Pogge, "Severe Poverty as a Violation of Negative Duties," *Ethics and International Affairs* 19, no. 1 (March, 2005), 69.

37. The idea of the remainder comes from Rosalind Hursthouse, *On Virtue Ethics* (Oxford and New York: Oxford University Press, 1999), 47. The point about response as excluding all the others to whom one is *not* responding comes from Jacques Derrida, *The*

Gift of Death, trans. David Wills (Chicago: University of Chicago Press, 1995), 70. I owe this understanding of Derrida, and its relevance to Hursthouse's argument about the remainder left over from responding to moral dilemmas, to Jamal Lyksett and Todd Trembley, who made this connection for me in an Ethical Theory seminar at Washington State University when we discussed virtue ethics and responsibility.

38. The appropriateness of regret in response to the remainder comes from Hursthouse, *On Virtue Ethics*, 76.

Bibliography

ABC News. "Women Forced to Work." *20/20 Special Investigation*. April 1, 2000. On the Global Exchange website: http://www.globalexchange.org/ campaigns/sweatshops/saipan/abc040100.html (accessed on October 9, 2006).

Alcoff, Linda Martin. "The Problem of Speaking for Others." *Cultural Critique* (Winter 1991/1992): 5-32.

Anwander, Norbert. "Contributing and Benefiting: Two Grounds for Duties to the Victims of Injustice." *Ethics and International Affairs* 19, no. 1 (March 2005): 39-45.

Arendt, Hannah. *Eichmann in Jerusalem: A Report on the Banality of Evil*. New York: Penguin, 1964.

Aristotle. "Nicomachean Ethics." Pp. 363-478 in *A New Aristotle Reader*, edited by J. L. Ackrill. Princeton, NJ: Princeton University Press, 1987.

Arneson, Richard J. "Moral Limits on the Demands of Beneficence?" Pp. 33-58 in *The Ethics of Assistance: Morality and the Distant Needy*, edited by Deen K. Chatterjee. Cambridge and New York: Cambridge University Press, 2004.

Arthur, John. "Equality, Entitlements, and the Distribution of Income." Pp. 705-19 in *Moral Philosophy: Selected Readings, Second Edition*, edited by George Sher. Belmont, CA: Wadsworth, 2001.

———. "Rights and the Duty to Bring Aid." Pp. 39-50 in *World Hunger and Morality: Second Edition*, edited by William Aiken and Hugh LaFollette. Upper Saddle River, NJ: Prentice Hall, 1996.

Baby Milk Action. "Baby Milk Action." http://www.babymilkaction.org/ (accessed on September 12, 2006).

Badhwar, Neera K. "International Aid: When Giving Becomes a Vice." *Social Philosophy and Policy* (2006): 69-101.

Baier, Annette C. "The Need for More than Justice." Pp. 47-58 in *Justice and Care: Essential Readings in Feminist Ethics*, edited by Virginia Held. Boulder, CO: Westview Press, 1995.

Baier, Kurt. "Guilt and Responsibility." Pp. 197-218 in *Collective Responsibility: Five Decades of Debate in Theoretical and Applied Ethics*, edited by Larry May and Stacey Hoffman. Savage, MD: Rowman and Littlefield, 1991.

Balakrishnan, Radhika and Uma Narayan. "Combining Justice with Development: Rethinking Rights and Responsibilities in the Context of World Hunger and Poverty." Pp. 230-247 in *World Hunger and Morality: Second Edition*, edited by William Aiken and Hugh LaFollette. Upper Saddle River, NJ: Prentice Hall, 1996.

Barry, Brian. "Justice as Reciprocity." Pp. 463-93 in *Democracy, Power and Justice: Essays in Political Theory*. Oxford: Clarendon Press, 1989.

Barry, Christian. "Understanding and Evaluating the Contribution Principle." Pp. 103-38 in *Real World Justice: Grounds, Principles, Human Rights, and Social Institutions*, edited by Andreas Follesdal and Thomas Pogge. Dordrecht: Springer, 2005.

Bar-Yam, Naomi Bromberg. "The Nestle Boycott: The Story of the WHO/UNICEF Code for Marketing Breastmilk Substitutes." *Mothering*. Winter 1995. http://www.findarticle.com/p/articles/mi_m0838/is_n77/ai_17623557 (accessed on September 12, 2006).

Bas, Nikki F., Medea Benjamin, and Joannie C. Chang. "Saipan Sweatshop Lawsuit Ends with Important Gains for Workers and Lessons for Activists." January 8, 2004. http://cleanclothes.org/legal/04-01-08.htm (accessed December 4, 2006).

Bentham, Jeremy. *An Introduction to the Principles of Morals and Legislation*. Oxford: Clarendon Press, 1879.

Bhagwati, Jagdish. *In Defense of Globalization*. Oxford and New York: Oxford University Press, 2004.

Bittner, Rudiger. "Morality and World Hunger." Pp. 24-31 in *Global Justice*, edited by Thomas W. Pogge. Oxford: Blackwell Publishers, 2001.

Brandt, Richard B. *Ethical Theory: The Problems of Normative and Critical Ethics*. Englewood Cliffs, NJ: Prentice-Hall, 1959.

———. *Morality, Utilitarianism, and Rights*. Cambridge: Cambridge University Press, 1992.

———. *A Theory of the Good and the Right*. Oxford: Clarendon Press, 1979.

Brennan, Andrew. "Poverty, Puritanism, and Environmental Conflict." *Environmental Values* 7, no. 3 (1998): 305-31.

Campbell, Greg. "Blood Diamonds." *Amnesty Magazine*. 2002. http://www.amnestyusa.org/amnestynow/diamonds.html (accessed October 10, 2006).

Cappelen, Alexander. "Responsibility and International Distributive Justice." Pp. 215-28 in *Real World Justice: Grounds, Principles, Human Rights, and Social Institutions*, edited by Andreas Follesdal and Thomas Pogge. Dordrecht: Springer, 2005.

Casey, John. "Actions and Consequences." Pp. 155-205 in *Morality and Moral Reasoning: Five Essays in Ethics*, edited by John Casey. London: Methuen, 1971.

Cohen, L. Jonathan. "Who is Starving Whom?" *Theoria* 47 (1981): 65-81.

Coleman, Jules. *Risks and Wrongs*. Cambridge: Cambridge University Press, 1992.

Corlett, J. Angelo. *Responsibility and Punishment*. Dordrecht: Kluwer Academic Publishers, 2001.

Corry, Jessica Peck. "Other Diseases Have Ribbons, Too," *Rocky Mountain News*, October 14, 2006, 12(D).

Cottingham, John. "Partiality, Favouritism, and Morality." *The Philosophical Quarterly* 36, no. 144 (July 1986): 357-73.

Cruft, Rowan. "Human Rights and Positive Duties." *Ethics and International Affairs* 19, no. 1 (March 2005): 29-37.

Davis, Lawrence H. "Wayward Causal Chains." Pp. 55-65 in *Action and Responsibility: Bowling Green Studies in Applied Philosophy, Volume II-1980*, edited by Michael Bradie and Myles Brand. Bowling Green, OH: Applied Philosophy Program. Bowling Green State University, 1980.

Davis, N. Ann. "The Priority of Avoiding Harm." Pp. 298-354 in *Killing and Letting Die: Second Edition*, edited by Bonnie Steinbock and Alastair Norcross. New York: Fordham University Press, 1994.

Derrida, Jacques. *The Gift of Death*, translated by David Wills. Chicago: University of Chicago Press, 1995.

Donnelly, Jack. *Universal Human Rights in Theory and Practice, Second Edition*. Ithaca, NY and London: Cornell University Press, 2003.

Dreier, Peter and Richard Appelbaum. "Campus Breakthrough on Sweatshop Labor." *The Nation*. June 1, 2006. On the Global Exchange website: http://www.globalexchange.org/campaigns/sweatshops/3959.pf (accessed on September 20, 2006).

Dreze, Jean and Amartya Sen. *Hunger and Public Action*. Oxford and Clarendon Press, 1989.

Dworkin, Ronald. "Rights as Trumps." Pp. 153-67 in *Theories of Rights*, edited by Jeremy Waldron, Oxford: Oxford University Press, 1984.

———. *Taking Rights Seriously*. Cambridge, MA: Harvard University Press, 1977.

Easterly, William. *The White Man's Burden: Why the West's Efforts to Aid the Rest Have Done So Much Ill and So Little Good*. New York: Penguin Press, 2006.

Elgin, Duane. *Voluntary Simplicity: Toward a Way of Life that is Outwardly Simple, Inwardly Rich: Revised Edition*. New York: Quill, 1993.

Fain, Haskell. "Some Moral Infirmities of Justice." Pp. 77-92 in *Individual and Collective Responsibility, Second Edition*, edited by Peter A. French. Rochester, VT: Schenkman Books, 1998.

Feinberg, Joel. "Causing Voluntary Actions." Pp. 152-86 in *Doing and Deserving: Essays in the Theory of Responsibility*. Princeton, NJ: Princeton University Press, 1970.

———. "Collective Responsibility." Pp. 53-76 in *Collective Responsibility:
Five Decades of Debate in Theoretical and Applied Ethics*, edited by Larry
May and Stacey Hoffman. Savage, MD: Rowman and Littlefield, 1991.

———. "Duties, Rights, and Claims." Pp. 130-42 in *Rights, Justice, and the
Bounds of Liberty: Essays in Social Philosophy*. Princeton, NJ: Princeton
University Press, 1980.

———. *Harm to Others: The Moral Limits of the Criminal Law, Volume One*.
New York: Oxford University Press, 1984.

———. *Harmless Wrongdoing: The Moral Limits of the Criminal Law, Volume
Four*. New York: Oxford University Press, 1988.

———. "Problematic Responsibility in Law and Morals." Pp. 25-37 in *Doing
and Deserving: Essays in the Theory of Responsibility*. Princeton, NJ:
Princeton University Press, 1970.

———. "Sua Culpa." Pp. 187-221 in *Doing and Deserving: Essays in the Theory of Responsibility*. Princeton, NJ: Princeton University Press, 1970.

———. "Supererogation and Rules." Pp. 3-24 in *Doing and Deserving*. Princeton, NJ: Princeton University Press, 1970.

Fischer, John Martin and Mark Ravizza, S. J. *Responsibility and Control: A
Theory of Moral Responsibility*. Cambridge: Cambridge University Press,
1998.

———, eds. *Perspectives on Moral Responsibility*. Ithaca, NY: Cornell University Press, 1993.

Food First. "Lessons from the Green Revolution." *Food First*. 2000.
http://www.foodfirst.org/media/opeds/2000/4.greenrev.html   (accessed
January 15, 2004).

"FoodWatch: Setback in the War Against Hunger." *United Nations Chronicle
Online Edition*. http://www.un.org/Pubs/chronicle/2003/issue4/0403p66.asp
(accessed October 25, 2004).

Foot, Philippa. "Killing and Letting Die." Pp. 280-89 in *Killing and Letting Die,
Second Edition*, edited by Bonnie Steinbock and Alastair Norcross. New
York: Fordham University Press, 1994.

French, Peter A. *Collective and Corporate Responsibility*. New York: Columbia
University Press, 1984.

———. *Responsibility Matters*. Lawrence, KA: University Press of Kansas,
1992.

———. "The Responsibility of Monsters and Their Makers." Pp. 1-12 in *Individual and Collective Responsibility, Second Edition*, edited by Peter A.
French. Rochester, VT: Schenkman Books, 1998.

———. "Types of Collectivities." Pp. 33-50 in *Individual and Collective Responsibility, Second Edition*, edited by Peter A. French. Rochester, VT: Schenkman Books, 1998.

French, Peter A., ed. *Individual and Collective Responsibility, Second Edition*. Rochester ,VT: Schenkman Books, 1998.

Friedman, Marilyn. "The Practice of Partiality." *Ethics* 101, no. 4 (July 1991): 818-35.

Friedman, Thomas. *The World is Flat: A Brief History of the Twenty-first Century*. New York: Farrar, Straus, and Giroux, 2005.

Gauthier, David. *Morals by Agreement*. Oxford: Clarendon Press, 1986.

Gewirth, Alan. "Are There Any Absolute Rights?" Pp. 91-109 in *Theories of Rights*, edited by Jeremy Waldron. Oxford: Oxford University Press, 1984.

———. *The Community of Rights*. Chicago: University of Chicago Press, 1996.

———. *Human Rights: Essays on Justification and Applications*. Chicago and London: University of Chicago Press, 1982.

———. *Reason and Morality*, Chicago and London: University of Chicago Press, 1978.

———. "Starvation and Human Rights." Pp. 139-58 in *Ethics and Problems of the 21st Century*, edited by K.E. Goodpaster and K.M. Sayre. London: University of Notre Dame Press, 1979.

Gilligan, Carol. *In a Different Voice: Psychological Theory and Women's Development*. Cambridge, MA: Harvard University Press, 1982.

Global Envision, "The End of Gap Sweatshops?" *Global Envision.* July 8, 2004. www.globalenvision.org/library/8/639 (accessed on September 20, 2006).

Global Exchange, "Sweatfree Bay Area." *Global Exchange.* 2006. http://www.globalexchange.org/ campaigns/sweatshops/sfbayarea.html (accessed October 18, 2006).

Global Fund, "The Global Fund." *Product RED.* 2008. http://www.joinred.com/globalfund/ (accessed on May 13, 2008).

Glover, Jonathan. *Responsibility*. New York: Humanities Press, 1970.

Goodin, Robert. *Protecting the Vulnerable: A Reanalysis of Our Social Responsibilities*. Chicago and London: University of Chicago Press, 1985.

———. *Utilitarianism as Public Philosophy*. Cambridge: Cambridge University Press, 1995.

Gosepath, Stefan. "The Global Scope of Justice." Pp. 145-68 in *Global Justice*, edited by Thomas W. Pogge. Oxford: Blackwell, 2001.

Green, Michael J. "Institutional Responsibility for Global Problems." *Philosophical Topics* 30, no. 2 (Fall 2002): 79-95.

Griffin, James. *Well-Being: Its Meaning, Measurement, and Moral Importance*. Oxford: Clarendon Press, 1986.

Hardin, Garrett. "Lifeboat Ethics: The Case Against Helping the Poor." Pp. 5-15 in *World Hunger and Morality, Second Edition*, edited by William Aiken and Hugh LaFollette. Upper Saddle River, NJ: Prentice Hall, 1996.

Hardin, Russell. *Morality within the Limits of Reason*. Chicago and London: University of Chicago Press, 1998.

Hare, R.M. *Freedom and Reason*. Oxford: Clarendon Press, 1963.

Harris, George W. *Agent-Centered Morality: An Aristotelian Alternative to Kantian Internalism*. Berkeley, CA: University of California Press, 1999.

Harris, John. "The Marxist Conception of Violence." *Philosophy and Public Affairs* 3, no. 2 (Winter 1974): 192-220.

Harsanyi, John C. *Essays on Ethics, Social Behavior, and Scientific Explanation*. Dordrecht and Boston: D. Reidel, 1976.

————. "Rule Utilitarianism and Decision Theory." Pp. 3-31 in *Decision Theory and Social Ethics: Issues in Social Choice*, edited by Hans W. Gottinger and Werner Leinfellner. Dordrecht, Boston, and London: D. Reidel, 1978.

Hart, H.L.A. and Tony Honore. *Causation in the Law, Second Edition*. Oxford: Clarendon Press, 1985.

Hart, H.L.A. "Are There Any Absolute Rights?" Pp. 77-90 in *Theories of Rights*, edited by Jeremy Waldron. Oxford: Oxford University Press, 1984.

Held, Virginia. "Can a Random Collection of Individuals Be Morally Responsible?" Pp. 89-100 in *Collective Responsibility: Five Decades of Debate in Theoretical and Applied Ethics*, edited by Larry May and Stacey Hoffman. Savage, MD: Rowman and Littlefield, 1991.

————. *The Ethics of Care: Personal, Political, and Global*. Oxford and New York: Oxford University Press, 2006.

Hiatt, Fred. "Massachusetts Takes on Burma." *Washington Post*. January 31, 1999. http://www.burmalibrary.org/reg.burma/archives/199902/msg00071. html (accessed October 10, 2006).

Hinsch, Wilfried and Markus Stepanians. "Severe Poverty as a Human Rights Violation—Weak and Strong." Pp. 295-315 in *Real World Justice: Grounds, Principles, Human Rights, and Social Institutions*, edited by Andreas Follesdal and Thomas Pogge. Dordrecht: Springer, 2005.

Honore, Tony. "Are Omissions Less Culpable?" Pp. 41-93 in *Responsibility and Fault*. Oxford and Portland, OR: Hart Publishing, 1999.

————. *Responsibility and Fault*. Oxford and Portland, OR: Hart Publishing, 1999.

————."Responsibility and Luck: The Moral Basis of Strict Liability." Pp. 14-40 in *Responsibility and Fault*. Oxford and Portland, OR: Hart Publishing, 1999.

Hurrell, Andrew. "Global Inequality and International Institutions." Pp. 32-54 in *Global Justice*, edited by Thomas W. Pogge. Oxford: Blackwell, 2001.

Hursthouse, Rosalind. *On Virtue Ethics*. Oxford and New York: Oxford University Press, 1999.

International Baby Food Action Network (IBFAN). "History of the Campaign." *IBFAN*. http://www.ibfan.org/english/issue/history01.html (accessed September 12, 2006).

————. "Overview: The International Code" *IBFAN.* http://www.ibfan.org/
english/issue/overview01.html#2 (accessed September 12, 2006).

Jaggar, Alison M. "Challenging Women's Global Inequalities: Some Priorities
for Western Philosophers." *Philosophical Topics* 30, no. 2 (Fall 2002): 229-
52.

————. "Is Globalization Good for Women?" *Comparative Literature* 53, no. 4
(Fall 2001): 298-314.

————. "Reasoning about Well-Being: Nussbaum's Methods of Justifying the
Capabilities." *The Journal of Political Philosophy* 14, no. 3 (2006): 301-22.

————. "'Saving Amina': Global Justice for Women and Intercultural Dialogue." *Ethics and International Affairs* 19, no. 3 (2005): 55-75.

————. "Western Feminism and Global Responsibility." Pp. 185-200 in *Feminist Interventions in Ethics and Politics,* edited by Barbara S. Andrew, Jean
Keller, and Lisa H. Schwartzman. Lanham, MD: Rowman and Littlefield,
2004.

Jaspers, Karl. *The Question of German Guilt,* translated by E. B. Ashton. New
York: Capricorn Books, 1961.

Kagan, Shelly. *The Limits of Morality.* Oxford: Clarendon Press, 1989.

Kamm, F. M. "Fa minine Ethics: The Problem of Distance in Morality and
Singer's Ethical Theory." Pp. 162-208 in *Singer and His Critics,* edited by
Dale Jamieson. Malden, MA: Blackwell Publishers, 1999.

————. "The New Problem of Distance in Morality." Pp. 59-74 in *The Ethics of
Assistance: Morality and the Distant Needy,* edited by Deen K. Chatterjee.
Cambridge and New York: Cambridge University Press, 2004.

Kant, Immanuel. *Grounding for the Metaphysics of Morals, with On a Supposed
Right to Lie Because of Philanthropic Concerns, Third Edition,* translated
by James W. Ellington. Indianapolis: Hackett, 1993.

Kekes, John. "Morality and Impartiality." *American Philosophical Quarterly* 18,
no. 4 (October 1981): 295-303.

King, Samantha. *Pink Ribbons Inc.: Breast Cancer and the Politics of Philanthropy.* Minneapolis, MN: University of Minnesota Press, 2006.

Kittay, Eva Feder and Diana T. Meyers, eds. *Women and Moral Theory.* Savage,
MD: Rowman and Littlefield, 1987.

Klein, Naomi. *No Logo: Taking Aim at the Brand Bullies.* New York: Picador,
1999.

Korsgaard, Christine M. *Creating the Kingdom of Ends.* Cambridge: Cambridge
University Press, 1996.

Kuper, Andrew. "Global Poverty Relief: More than Charity." Pp. 155-72 in
Global Responsibilities: Who Must Deliver on Human Rights? edited by
Andrew Kuper. New York and London: Routledge, 2005.

————. "Redistributing Responsibilities—The UN Global Compact with Corporations." Pp. 359-80 in *Real World Justice: Grounds, Principles, Human*

Rights, and Social Institutions, edited by Andreas Follesdal and Thomas Pogge. Dordrecht: Springer, 2005.

Lalander, Philip. *Hooked on Heroin: Drugs and Drifters in a Globalized World.* Oxford and New York: Berg, 2003.

Lane, Melissa. "The Moral Dimension of Corporate Accountability." Pp. 229-50 in *Global Responsibilities: Who Must Deliver on Human Rights?* edited by Andrew Kuper. New York and London: Routledge, 2005.

Lappe, Francis Moore, Joseph Collins, and Peter Rosset with Luis Esparza (Food First). *World Hunger: Twelve Myths, Second Edition.* New York: Grove Press, 1998.

Lewis, H. D. "Collective Responsibility." Pp. 17-33 in *Collective Responsibility: Five Decades of Debate in Theoretical and Applied Ethics*, edited by Larry May and Stacey Hoffman. Savage, MD: Rowman and Littlefield, 1991.

Lichtenberg, Judith. "The Moral Equivalence of Action and Omission." Pp. 210-29 in *Killing and Letting Die, Second Edition*, edited by Bonnie Steinbock and Alastair Norcross. New York: Fordham University Press, 1994.

Locke, John. "An Essay Concerning the True Original, Extent, and End of Civil Government." Pp. 265-428 in *John Locke: Two Treatises of Government*, edited by Peter Laslett. Cambridge: Cambridge University Press, 1988.

MacIntyre, Alasdair. *After Virtue: A Study in Moral Theory, Second Edition.* Notre Dame, IN: Notre Dame Press, 1984.

———. "Social Structures and Their Threats to Moral Agency." Pp.186-204 in *Ethics and Politics: Selected Essays, Volume 2.* Cambridge and New York: Cambridge University Press, 2006.

Mackie, J.L. "Can There Be a Right-Based Moral Theory?" Pp. 168-81 in *Theories of Rights*, edited by Jeremy Waldron. Oxford: Oxford University Press, 1984.

———. "Causes and Conditions." Pp. 33-55 in *Causation*, edited by Ernest Sosa and Michael Tooley. Oxford: Oxford University Press, 1993.

———. *The Cement of the Universe: A Study of Causation.* Oxford: Clarendon Press, 1974.

———. *Ethics: Inventing Right and Wrong.* New York: Penguin Books, 1977.

Marshall, Sandra. "Noncompensatable Wrongs, or Having to Say You're Sorry." Pp. 209-24 in *Rights, Wrongs and Responsibilities*, edited by Matthew H. Kramer. Basingstoke and New York: Palgrave, 2001.

May, Larry. "Metaphysical Guilt and Moral Taint." Pp. 239-54 in *Collective Responsibility: Five Decades of Debate in Theoretical and Applied Ethics*, edited by Larry May and Stacey Hoffman. Savage, MD: Rowman and Littlefield, 1991.

———. *Sharing Responsibility.* Chicago: University of Chicago Press, 1992.

———. "Socialization and Institutional Evil." Pp. 83-106 in *Hannah Arendt: Twenty Years Later*, edited by Larry May and Jerome Kohn. Cambridge MA: MIT Press, 1996.

————. *The Socially Responsible Self: Social Theory and Professional Ethics.* Chicago and London: University of Chicago Press, 1996.

Mayerfeld, Jamie. *Suffering and Moral Responsibility.* Oxford: Oxford University Press, 1999.

McGary, Howard. "Morality and Collective Liability." Pp. 81-92 in *Race and Social Justice.* Malden, MA: Blackwell, 1999.

Milgram, Stanley. "Obedience to Authority." Pp. 26-34 in *Delight in Thinking: An Introduction to Philosophy Reader,* edited by Steven D. Hales and Scott C. Lowe. Boston: McGraw-Hill, 2007.

Mill, John Stuart. *On Liberty,* edited by Currin V. Shields. New York: Liberal Arts Press, 1956.

————. *Utilitarianism,* edited by George Sher. Indianapolis: Hackett, 1979.

Miller, David. "Distributing Responsibilities." Pp. 95-115 in *Global Responsibilities: Who Must Deliver on Human Rights?* edited by Andrew Kuper. New York and London: Routledge, 2005.

————. "National Responsibility and International Justice." Pp. 123-46 in *The Ethics of Assistance: Morality and the Distant Needy,* edited by Deen K. Chatterjee. Cambridge and New York: Cambridge University Press, 2004.

————. *On Nationality.* Oxford: Clarendon Press, 1995.

Miller, Richard W. "Moral Closeness and World Community." Pp. 101-22 in *The Ethics of Assistance: Morality and the Distant Needy,* edited by Deen K. Chatterjee. Cambridge and New York: Cambridge University Press, 2004.

Mitchell, Lawrence E. *Corporate Irresponsibility: America's Newest Export.* New Haven, CT and London: Yale University Press, 2001.

Moore, Michael. *Placing Blame: A General Theory of the Criminal Law.* Oxford: Clarendon Press, 1997.

Mulgan, Tim. "Rule Consequentialism and Famine." *Analysis* 54, no. 3 (1994): 187-92.

Murphy, Liam. *Moral Demands in Nonideal Theory.* Oxford: Oxford University Press, 2000.

Nagel, Thomas. *The View from Nowhere.* New York and Oxford: Oxford University Press, 1986.

————. "War and Massacre." Pp. 749-65 in *Moral Philosophy: Selected Readings, Second Edition,* edited by George Sher. Belmont, CA: Wadsworth, 2001.

Narayan, Deepa, et al. *Voices of the Poor: Can Anyone Hear Us?* New York and Oxford: Oxford University Press, 2000.

————. *Voices of the Poor: Crying Out for Change.* New York and Oxford: Oxford University Press, 2000.

Narveson, Jan. *The Libertarian Idea.* Philadelphia: Temple University Press, 1988.

Nickel, James W. "A Human Rights Approach to World Hunger." Pp. 171-85 in *World Hunger and Morality: Second Edition*, edited by William Aiken and Hugh LaFollette. Upper Saddle River, NJ: Prentice Hall, 1996.

————. *Making Sense of Human Rights: Philosophical Reflections on the Universal Declaration of Human Rights*. Berkeley, CA: University of California Press, 1987.

Noddings, Nel. "Caring." Pp. 7-30 in *Justice and Care: Essential Readings in Feminist Ethics*, edited by Virginia Held. Boulder, CO: Westview Press, 1995.

Nossiter, Bernard D. "U.N. Dispute Looms on Infant Formula." *New York Times*. 1981. http://query.nytimes.com/gst/fullpage.html?sec=health&res= 9a04eed71738f937a25756c0a967948260 (accessed September 12, 2006).

Nothing But Nets. "Nets Save Lives." *Nothing But Nets Campaign*. 2007. http://www/nothingbutnets.net/nets-save-lives/ (accessed on May 12, 2008).

Nozick, Robert. *Anarchy, State, and Utopia*. New York: Basic Books, 1974.

Nussbaum, Martha. *Women and Human Development: The Capabilities Approach*. Cambridge: Cambridge University Press, 2000.

O'Connor, Peg. *Oppression and Responsibility: A Wittgensteinian Approach to Social Practices and Moral Theory*. University Park, PA: Pennsylvania State University Press, 2002.

Okin, Susan Moller. "Poverty, Well-Being, and Gender: What Counts, Who's Heard?" *Philosophy and Public Affairs* 31, no. 3 (2003): 280-316.

O'Neill, Onora. "Agents of Justice." Pp. 188-203 in *Global Justice*, edited by Thomas W. Pogge. Oxford: Blackwell, 2001.

————. *Faces of Hunger: An Essay on Poverty, Justice, and Development*. London: Allen and Unwin, 1986.

————. "Global Justice: Whose Obligations?" Pp. 242-59 in *The Ethics of Assistance: Morality and the Distant Needy*, edited by Deen K. Chatterjee. Cambridge and New York: Cambridge University Press, 2004.

————. "Kantian Approaches to Some Famine Problems." Pp. 639-45 in *Reason and Responsibility: Readings in Some Basic Problems of Philosophy, Twelfth Edition*, edited by Joel Feinberg and Russ Shafer-Landau. Belmont, CA: Thomson Wadsworth, 2005.

————. *Towards Justice and Virtue: A Constructive Account of Practical Reasoning*. Cambridge: Cambridge University Press, 1996.

Parfit, Derek. *Reasons and Persons*. Oxford: Clarendon Press, 1984.

Peffer, Rodney. "World Hunger, Moral Theory, and Radical Rawlsianism." *International Journal of Politics and Ethics* 2, no. 4 (March 22, 2003). Pp. 1-39 archived by High Beam Research at http://www.highbeam.com/doc/1g1-115035534.html (accessed October 31, 2006).

Pinzani, Alessandro. "'It's the Power, Stupid!' On the Unmentioned Precondition of Social Justice." Pp. 171-97 in *Real World Justice: Grounds, Princi-

ples, *Human Rights, and Social Institutions,* edited by Andreas Follesdal
and Thomas Pogge. Dordrecht: Springer, 2005.
Pogge, Thomas W. "'Assisting' the Poor." Pp. 260-288 in *The Ethics of Assis-
tance: Morality and the Distant Needy,* edited by Deen K. Chatterjee. Cam-
bridge and New York: Cambridge University Press, 2004.
————. "Can the Capability Approach Be Justified?" *Philosophical Topics* 30,
no. 2 (Fall 2002): 167-228.
————. "The First UN Millenium Development Goal: A Cause for Celebra-
tion?" Pp. 317-38 in *Real World Justice: Grounds, Principles, Human
Rights, and Social Institutions,* edited by Andreas Follesdal and Thomas
Pogge. Dordrecht: Springer, 2005.
————. "A Global Resources Dividend." Pp. 501-36 in *Ethics of Consumption:
The Good Life, Justice, and Global Stewardship,* edited by David A.
Crocker and Toby Linden. Lanham, MD: Rowman and Littlefield, 1998.
————. "Human Flourishing and Universal Justice." *Social Philosophy and
Policy* 16, no. 1 (Winter 1999): 333-61.
————. "Human Rights and Human Responsibilities." Pp. 151-95 in *Global
Justice and Transnational Politics: Essays on the Moral and Political Chal-
lenges of Globalization,* edited by Pablo De Greiff and Ciaran Cronin. Cam-
bridge and London: MIT Press, 2002.
————. "Priorities of Global Justice." Pp. 6-23 in *Global Justice,* edited by
Thomas W. Pogge. Oxford: Blackwell Publishers, 2001.
————. "Severe Poverty as a Violation of Negative Duties." *Ethics and Interna-
tional Affairs* 19, no. 1 (March 2005): 55-83.
————. "Three Problems with Contractarian-Consequentialist Ways of Assess-
ing Social Institutions." *Social Philosophy and Policy* (Summer 1995): 241-
66.
————. *World Poverty and Human Rights: Cosmopolitan Responsibilities and
Reforms.* Cambridge: Polity and Malden, MA: Blackwell, 2002.
Popper, Karl. *The Open Society and Its Enemies, Vol. 1: The Spell of Plato.*
Princeton, NJ: Princeton University Press, 1966.
Public Citizen. "MA Burma Procurement Law Challenged at WTO." *Public
Citizen.* http://www.citizen.org/trade/issues/burma/articles.cfm?ID=11103
(accessed October 10, 2006).
Rachels, James. "Feeding the Hungry: Killing and Starving to Death." Pp. 154-
66 in *Moral Issues,* edited by Jan Narveson. Toronto: Oxford University
Press, 1983.
————. "Killing, Letting Die, and the Value of Life." Pp. 67-80 in *Can Ethics
Provide Answers? And Other Essays in Moral Philosophy.* Lanham, MD:
Rowman and Littlefield, 1997.
Rawls, John. *The Idea of Public Reason Revisited and the Law of Nations.* Cam-
bridge, MA: Harvard University Press, 1999.
————. *A Theory of Justice.* Cambridge, MA: Belknap Press, 1971.

Raz, Joseph. *The Morality of Freedom*. Oxford: Clarendon Press, 1986.

Robinson, Fiona. *Globalizing Care: Ethics, Feminist Theory, and International Relations*. Boulder, CO: Westview, 1999.

Ryberg, Jesper. "Population and Third World Assistance: A Comment on Hardin's Lifeboat Ethics." *Journal of Applied Philosophy* 14, no. 3 (1997): 207-19.

Sachs, Jeffrey D. *The End of Poverty: Economic Possibilities for Our Time*. New York: Penguin Press, 2005.

Sample, Ruth J. *Exploitation: What it Is and Why It's Wrong*. Lanham, MD: Rowman and Littlefield, 2003.

Sandel, Michael J. *Liberalism and the Limits of Justice, Second Edition*. Cambridge: Cambridge University Press, 1998.

Sartre, Jean-Paul. "The Humanism of Existentialism," translated by Bernard Frechtman. Pp. 31-62 in *Essays in Existentialism*. Secaucus, NJ: Citadel Press Book, 1993.

Satz, Debra. "What Do We Owe the Global Poor?" *Ethics and International Affairs* 19, no. 1 (March 2005): 47-54.

Scanlon, T.M. "Rights, Goals, and Fairness." Pp. 137-52 in *Theories of Rights*, edited by Jeremy Waldron. Oxford: Oxford University Press, 1984.

———. *What We Owe to Each Other*. Cambridge, MA and London: Belknap Press, 1998.

Scheffler, Samuel. "The Conflict between Justice and Responsibility." Pp. 86-106 in *Global Justice (Nomos XLI)*, edited by Ian Shapiro and Lea Brilmayer. New York and London: New York University Press, 1999.

———. "Doing and Allowing." *Ethics* 114 (January 2004): 215-39.

———. "Individual Responsibility in a Global Age." Pp. 32-47 in *Boundaries and Allegiances: Problems of Justice and Responsibility in Liberal Thought*. Oxford: Oxford University Press, 2001.

———. *The Rejection of Consequentialism: A Philosophical Investigation of the Considerations Underlying Rival Moral Conceptions*. Oxford: Clarendon Press, 1982.

Schor, Juliet B. and Douglas B. Holt, eds. *The Consumer Society Reader*. New York: New Press, 2000.

Scriven, Michael. "Defects of the Necessary Condition Analysis of Causation." Pp. 56-59 in *Causation*, edited by Ernest Sosa and Michael Tooley. Oxford: Oxford University Press, 1993.

"Secrets, Lies, and Sweatshops." *BusinessWeek*. November 27, 2006. http://www.businessweek.com/magazine/content/06_48/b4011001.htm (accessed April 21, 2008).

Segal, Jerome M. *Graceful Simplicity: The Philosophy and Politics of the Alternative American Dream*. Berkeley, CA: University of California Press, 2003.

————. "Living at a High Economic Standard: A Functionings Analysis." Pp. 342-65 in *Ethics of Consumption: The Good Life, Justice, and Global Stewardship*, edited by David A. Crocker and Toby Linden. Lanham, MD: Rowman and Littlefield, 1998.

Sen, Amartya. *Commodities and Capabilities*. Amsterdam and New York: Elsevier Science Publishers, 1985.

————. *Development as Freedom*. New York: Alfred A. Knopf, 1999.

————. *Inequality Reexamined*. New York: Russell Sage Foundation and Cambridge, MA: Harvard University Press, 1992.

————. *Poverty and Famines: An Essay on Entitlement and Deprivation*. Oxford and New York: Oxford University Press, 1981.

Sengupta, Somini. "Global Hunger Increases: U.N. Report Blames 'Lack of Political Will' Amid Ample Food," *New York Times*, reprinted in *Denver Post*, November 26, 2003, 14(A).

Sethi, S. Prakesh. "Corporate Codes of Conduct and the Success of Globalization." Pp. 205-227 in *Global Responsibilities: Who Must Deliver on Human Rights?* edited by Andrew Kuper. New York and London: Routledge, 2005.

Shei, Ser-Min. "World Poverty and Moral Responsibility." Pp. 139-55 in *Real World Justice: Grounds, Principles, Human Rights, and Social Institutions*, edited by Andreas Follesdal and Thomas Pogge. Dordrecht: Springer, 2005.

Shiva, Vandana. *Stolen Harvest: The Hijacking of the Global Food Supply*. Cambridge, MA: South End Press, 2000.

————. *The Violence of the Green Revolution: Third World Agriculture, Ecology and Politics*. London and New Jersey: Zed Books, 1991.

Shklar, Judith N. *The Faces of Injustice*. New Haven, CT and London: Yale University Press, 1990.

Shue, Henry. *Basic Rights: Subsistence, Affluence, and U.S. Foreign Policy, Second Edition*. Princeton, NJ: Princeton University Press, 1996.

Sidgwick, Henry. *The Methods of Ethics*. Chicago: University of Chicago Press, 1962.

Singer, Peter. "Famine, Affluence, and Morality." *Philosophy and Public Affairs* 1 (1972): 229-43.

————. *One World: The Ethics of Globalization, Second Edition*. New Haven, CT and London: Yale University Press, 2002.

————. *Practical Ethics, Second Edition*. Cambridge: Cambridge University Press, 1993.

————. "Reconsidering the Famine Relief Argument." Pp. 36-53 in *Food Policy: The Responsibility of the United States in the Life and Death Choices*, edited by Peter G. Brown and Henry Shue. New York: The Free Press, 1977.

Slote, Michael. *Beyond Optimizing: A Study of Rational Choice*. Cambridge, MA: Harvard University Press, 1989.

————. *Common-Sense Morality and Consequentialism*. London and Boston: Routledge and Kegan Paul, 1985.

————. *From Morality to Virtue*. Oxford and New York: Oxford University Press, 1992.

————. *Morals from Motives*. Oxford and New York: Oxford University Press, 2001.

Smart, J.J.C. "An Outline of a System of Utilitarian Ethics." Pp. 3-64 in *Utilitarianism: For and Against*, by J.J.C. Smart and Bernard Williams. Cambridge: Cambridge University Press, 1973.

Smiley, Marion. *Moral Responsibility and the Boundaries of Community: Power and Accountability from a Pragmatic Point of View*. Chicago and London: University of Chicago Press, 1992.

Sontag, Susan. *Regarding the Pain of Others*. New York: Farrar, Straus, and Giroux, 2003.

Steinbock, Bonnie and Alastair Norcross, eds. *Killing and Letting Die: Second Edition*. New York: Fordham University Press, 1994.

Steiner, Hillel. "Choice and Circumstance." Pp. 225-41 in *Rights, Wrongs and Responsibilities*, edited by Matthew H. Kramer. Basingstoke and New York: Palgrave, 2001.

Sternberg, Steve. "Bono Makes Fighting AIDS a Win All Around," *USA Today*, October 12, 2006, 1(D).

Strawson, Peter. "Freedom and Resentment." *Proceedings of the British Academy* 48 (1962): 1-25.

Sumner, L.W. *The Moral Foundation of Rights*. Oxford: Clarendon Press, 1987.

Taylor, Charles. *Sources of the Self: The Making of the Modern Identity*. Cambridge, MA: Harvard University Press, 1989.

Unger, Peter. *Living High and Letting Die: Our Illusion of Innocence*. New York: Oxford University Press, 1996.

"UNICEF Ethiopia Malaria." *UNICEF*. 2008. http://www.unicef.org/ethiopia/malaria.html (accessed on May 12, 2008).

United Nations Development Programme. *Human Development Report 2007-2008: Fighting Global Climate Change: Human Solidarity in a Divided World*. Basingstoke and New York: Palgrave Macmillan, 2007. http://hdr.undp.org/en/reports/global/hdr2007-2008/ (accessed June 30, 2008).

United Nations Development Programme (UNDP). *Human Development Report 1998*. New York: Oxford University Press, 1998. www.undp.org/hdr1998/

"United Nations International Covenant on Civil and Political Rights (1966)." Pp. 424-32 in *The Human Rights Reader: Major Political Writings, Essays, Speeches, and Documents from the Bible to the Present*, edited by Micheline R. Ishay. New York: Routledge, 1997.

"United Nations International Covenant on Economic, Social and Cultural Rights (1966)." Pp. 433-40 in *The Human Rights Reader: Major Political*

Writings, Essays, Speeches, and Documents from the Bible to the Present, edited by Micheline R. Ishay. New York: Routledge, 1997.

Velasquez, Manuel G. "Why Corporations Are Not Morally Responsible for Anything They Do." Pp. 111-31 in *Collective Responsibility: Five Decades of Debate in Theoretical and Applied Ethics*, eds. Larry May and Stacey Hoffman. Savage, MD: Rowman and Littlefield, 1991.

Vogel, David. *The Market for Virtue: The Potential and Limits of Corporate Social Responsibility*. Washington, DC: Brookings Institute Press, 2005.

Wachtel, Paul L. "Alternatives to the Consumer Society." Pp. 198-217 in *Ethics of Consumption: The Good Life, Justice, and Global Stewardship*, edited by David A. Crocker and Toby Linden. Lanham, MD: Rowman and Littlefield, 1998.

Wallace, R. Jay. *Responsibility and the Moral Sentiments*. Cambridge, MA: Harvard University Press, 1994.

Walzer, Michael. *Thick and Thin: Moral Argument at Home and Abroad*. Notre Dame: University of Notre Dame Press, 1994.

Watson, Gary. "Excusing Addiction." *Law and Philosophy* 18 (1999): 589-619.

Wellman, Carl. *A Theory of Rights: Persons Under Laws, Institutions, and Morals*. Totowa, NJ: Rowman and Allanheld, 1985.

Wertheimer, Alan. *Exploitation*. Princeton, NJ: Princeton University Press, 1996.

Williams, Bernard. "A Critique of Utilitarianism." Pp. 77-150 in *Utilitarianism: For and Against*, by J.J.C. Smart and Bernard Williams. Cambridge: Cambridge University Press, 1973.

———. "Persons, Character, and Morality." Pp. 1-19 in *Moral Luck: Philosophical Papers 1973-1980*. Cambridge: Cambridge University Press, 1980.

Wolf, Susan. *Freedom Within Reason*. New York: Oxford University Press, 1990.

———. "Moral Saints." *The Journal of Philosophy* 79, no. 8 (August 1982): 419-39.

World Bank. *World Development Bank Report 2003*. New York: The World Bank and Oxford University Press, 2003.

Young, Iris Marion. "Equality of Whom? Social Groups and Judgments of Injustice." *The Journal of Political Philosophy* 9, no. 1 (2001): 1-18.

———. *Inclusion and Democracy*. Oxford: Oxford University Press, 2000.

———. "Responsibility and Global Justice: A Social Connection Model." *Social Philosophy and Policy* 23, no. 1 (January 2006): 102-30.

———. "Responsibility and Global Labor Justice." *Journal of Political Philosophy* 12, no. 4 (December 2004): 365-88.

Zimmerman, Michael J. *The Concept of Moral Obligation*. Cambridge and New York: Cambridge University Press, 1996.

Index

213

About the Author

Abigail Gosselin is assistant professor of philosophy at Regis University in Denver, Colorado. She graduated with her Ph.D. in philosophy from the University of Colorado at Boulder in 2005, having worked under the advisement of Dr. Alison M. Jaggar. Her first professional position was assistant professor of philosophy at Washington State University.

Dr. Gosselin specializes in ethics, social and political philosophy, and philosophy of law, with focuses on global justice, responsibility and free will, narrative ethics, and feminist philosophy. Her other research interests include exploring issues of agency and identity in mental illness and addiction. She has published articles in *International Studies in Philosophy*, *Human Rights Review*, and *Discourse*.

Dr. Gosselin is married to her college sweetheart, Derrick Belanger, who is a middle-school language arts teacher and comic book writer. They have a young daughter, Rhea.